Performance, Power and the Art of the Aegean Bronze Age

Senta C. German

BAR International Series 1347
2005

Published in 2016 by
BAR Publishing, Oxford

BAR International Series 1347

Performance, Power and the Art of the Aegean Bronze Age

ISBN 978 1 84171 693 0

© S C German and the Publisher 2005

The author's moral rights under the 1988 UK Copyright,
Designs and Patents Act are hereby expressly asserted.

All rights reserved. No part of this work may be copied, reproduced, stored,
sold, distributed, scanned, saved in any form of digital format or transmitted
in any form digitally, without the written permission of the Publisher.

BAR Publishing is the trading name of British Archaeological Reports (Oxford) Ltd.
British Archaeological Reports was first incorporated in 1974 to publish the BAR
Series, International and British. In 1992 Hadrian Books Ltd became part of the BAR
group. This volume was originally published by Archaeopress in conjunction with
British Archaeological Reports (Oxford) Ltd / Hadrian Books Ltd, the Series principal
publisher, in 2005. This present volume is published by BAR Publishing, 2016.

Printed in England

PUBLISHING

BAR titles are available from:

        BAR Publishing
        122 Banbury Rd, Oxford, OX2 7BP, UK
EMAIL   info@barpublishing.com
PHONE +44 (0)1865 310431
  FAX   +44 (0)1865 316916
        www.barpublishing.com

Contents

List of Illustrations	2
Preface	5
Introduction: Why Performance?	7
Chapter 1: Performance and Social Categories	18
Chapter 2: Bull Leaping	33
Chapter 3: Measured Movement: Dance and Procession	50
Chapter 4: Issues of Archaeological Context and Interpretation	72
Chapter 5: Meanings of Performance: Interpreting the Images	85
Conclusions	94
Bibliography	97
APPENDICES	
Appendix 1.	106
Appendix 2.	115

SENTA C. GERMAN

List of Illustrations

Figure 1: Steatite lentoid seal from Knossos; after CMS II3.8. Catalogue # 22. 8

Figure 2: Agate amygdaloid seal from Mycenae; after CMS I.68. Catalogue # 4. 8

Figure 3: Onyx amygdaloid seal from Vaphio; after CMS I.225. Catalogue # 16. 8

Figure 4: Knossos Procession Fresco, reconstruction; after Immerwahr (1990), plate 40. Catalgue # 91. 14

Figure 5: Cup bearer from Procession Fresco at Knossos; after PofM II2, pl. XII. Catalogue # 91. 15

Figure 6: Gold ring from Knossos; after CMS II3.51. Catalogue # 24. 20

Figure 7: Gold ring from Anthia; after CMS V.Sup.1B.135. Catalogue # 59. 20

Figure 8: Knossos Grandstand fresco; after PofM III, pl. XVI. Catalogue # 71. 20

Figure 9: Knossos Toreador fresco; after PofM III, fig. 144. Catalogue # 89. 21

Figure 10: Amethyst amygdaloid from Mycenae, after CMS I.5. Catalogue # 1. 21

Figure 11: Gold ring from Aidonia; after CMS V.Sup.IB.114. Catalogue # 57. 22

Figure 12: Carnelian amygdaloid from Mycenae; after CMS I.152. Catalogue # 11. 22

Figure 13: Agate lentoid from Mycenae; after CMS V2.597. Catalogue # 61. 22

Figure 14: Sardonyx amygdaloid from Vaphio; after CMS I.226. Catalogue # 17. 22

Figure 15: Seal impression from Aghia Triada; after CMS II6.36. Catalogue # 34. 23

Figure 16: Miniature fresco, West House, Thera; after Doumas (1992) pl. 38. Catalogue # 79. 24

Figure 17: Three "adorants", Xeste 3, Thera; after Doumas (1992) pl. 100. Catalogue # 98. 24

Figure 18: Gold ring from Mycenae; after CMS I.17. Catalogue # 3. 25

Figure 19: Gold ring from Mycenae; after CMS I.16. Catalogue # 2. 26

Figure 20: Sacred Grove and Dance fresco from Knossos; after PofM III, pl. XVIII. Catalogue # 95. 29

Figure 21: Knossos miniature bull leaping fresco; after PofM III, fig. 443. Catalogue # 85. 30

Figure 22: Knossos miniature bull leaping fresco; after PofM III, fig. 446. Catalogue # 85. 30

Figure 23: Knossos miniature bull leaping fresco; after PofM I, fig. 385. Catalogue # 85. 30

Figure 24: Knossos miniature bull leaping fresco; after PofM III, fig. 15B. Catalogue # 85. 30

Figure 25: Koumasa rhyton; after Xanthoudides (1924) pl. XXVIII. Catalogue # 78. 34

Figure 26: Porti figurine; after Xanthoudides (1924) pl. XXVII. Catalogue # 90. 34

Figure 27: Ivory leaper from Knossos; after Hood (1978), pl. 105. Catalogue # 74. 35

Figure 28: Katsambas pyxis; after Hood (1978) fig. 111. Catalogue # 75. 35

Figure 29: Boxer rhyton; after Hood (1978), fig. 139. Catalogue # 102. 35

Figure 30: Knossos 3D arm and horn wall painting; after PofM III, fig. 350A. Catalogue # 65. 35

Figure 31: Seal impression from Zakros; after CMS II7.34. Catalogu # 47. 36

Figure 32: Seal impression from Aghia Triada; after CMS II6.41. Catalogue # 36. 36

Figure 33: Seal impression from Aghia Triada; after CMS II6.42. Catalogue # 37. 36

Figure 34: Seal impression from Chania; after CMS V.Sup. 1A. 171. Catalogue # 53. 36

Figure 35: Seal impression from Aghia Triada; after CMS II6.43. Catalogue # 38. 36

Figure 36: Seal impression from Zakros; after CMS II7.36. Catalogue # 48. 37

Figure 37: Seal impression from Aghia Triada; after CMS II6.44. Catalogue # 39. 37

Figure 38: Seal impression from Aghia Triada; after CMS II6.39. Catalogue # 35. 37

Figure 39: Ivory plaque from Mycenae; after Poursat (1977) fig. 245. Catalogue # 72. 37

Figure 40: Knossos Toreador panel; after PofM III, plate XXI. Catalogue # 87. 38

Figure 41: Knossos Toreador panel; after PofM III, fig. 148. Catalogue # 87. 39

Figure 42: Knossos Toreador panel; after PofM III, fig. 146. Catalogue # 87. 39

Figure 43: Knossos bull and tree grappling scene; after PofM II2, fig. 389. Catalogue # 86. 40

Figure 44: Knossos miniature bull leaping scene, Queen's megaron; after PofM III, fig. 143. Catalogue # 88. 40

Figure 45: Agate lentoid seal from Praisos; after CMS II3.271. Catalogue # 27. 40

Figure 46: Lapis lentoid seal from Gournes; after CMS II4.157. Catalogue # 28. 41

Figure 47: Seal impression from Knossos; after CMS II8.222. Catalogue # 49. 41

Figure 48: Bull leaping fresco from Tiryns; after Schliemann (1976), plate XIII. Catalogue # 99 41

Figure 49: Bull leaping fresco from Pylos; after Lang (1966), plate 24. Catalogue # 93 42

Figure 50: Mycenae miniature bull leaping fresco; after Shaw (1996), plate 1. Catalogue # 80. 42

Figure 51: Stone vase fragment from Acropolis; after Sakellarakis (1976), plate XII-32. Catalogue # 66. 42

Figure 52: Larnax from Tanagra; after Immerwahr (1990) plate XXII. Catalogue # 96 42

Figure 53: Agate lentoid from Dimini; after CMS I.408. Catalogue # 21 43

Figure 54: Agate half cylinder from Thebes; after CMS V2.674. Catalogue # 63 43

Figure 55: Chalcedony lentoid form Koukounara; after CMS V2.638. Catalogue # 62. 43

Figure 56: Carnelian amygdaloid from Mycenae; after CMS I.137. Catalogue # 10 43

Figure 57: Carnelian amygdaloid from Mycenae; after CMS I.79. Catalogue # 5 43

Figure 58: Gold and bronze ring from Asine; after CMS I.200. Catalogue # 14. 43

Figure 59: Seal impression from Pylos; after CMS I.305. Catalogue # 18. 44

Figure 60: Bull fresco from Catal Huyuk; after Mellaart (1967), fig. 48. 47

Figure 61: Cylinder seal impressions from Tel Lelan and Allalak; after Colon (1994), plate 2. 47

Figure 62: Plan of Knossos. 51

Figure 63: Plan of Phaistos. 51

Figure 64: Plan of Mallia. 52

Figure 65: Plan of Gournia. 52

Figure 66: Figurines of dancing women from Palaikastro; after Warren (1984), plate 35. Catalogue # 84 53

Figure 67: Poussin, Dance to the Music of Time; The Wallace Collection, London. 54

Figure 68: Screen painted with Kabuki dancers; Victoria and Albert Museum, London. 55

Figure 69: Diagram of dance steps. 56

Figure 70: Seal impression from Knossos; after CMS II8.266. Catalogue # 50. 56

Figure 71: Seal impression from Zakros; after CMS II7.17. Catalogue # 46. 56

Figure 72: Gold ring from Aidonia; after CMS V.Sup.IB.115. Catalogue # 58 57

Figure 73: Seal impression from Mycenae; after CMS I.162. Catalogue # 12. 57

Figure 74: Seal impression from Chania; after CMS V.Sup.IA.178. Catalogue # 54. 57

Figure 75: Quartz lentoid from Mycenae; after CMS I.132. Catalogue # 9. 57

Figure 76: Pylos women fresco; after Immerwahr (1990), plate 57. Catalogue # 92. 58

Figure 77: Bowl with dancing women from Phaistos; after Levi (1976), plate LXVII. Catalogue # 82 58

Figure 78: Fruitstand with dancing women from Phaistos; after Levi (1976), plate LXVI. Catalogue # 83. .. 59

Figure 79: Serpentine cushion seal from Knossos; after CMS II3.17. Catalogue # 23. 59

Figure 80: Serpentine lentoid from Gournia; after CMS II3.236. Catalogue # 26. 59

Figure 81: Seal impression from Aghia Triada; after CMS II6.13. Catalogue # 33. 60

Figure 82: Seal impression from Pylos; after CMS I.313. Catalogue # 19. 60

Figure 83: Seal impression from Aghia Triada; after CMS II6.1. Catalogue # 29. 60

Figure 84: Seal impression from Zakros; after CMS II7.7. Catalogue # 40. 61

Figure 85: Seal impression from Aghia Triada; after CMS II6.10. Catalogue # 31. 61

Figure 86: Seal impression from Aghia Triada; after CMS II6.9. Catalogue # 30. 61

Figure 87: Seal impression from Zakros; after CMS II7.8. Catalogue # 41. 62

Figure 88: Seal impression from Zakros; after CMS II7.15. Catalogue # 44. 62

Figure 89: Seal impression from Zakros; after CMS II7.13. Catalogue # 42. 62

Figure 90: Seal impression from Zakros; after CMS II7.14. Catalogue # 43. 62

Figure 91: Serpentine lentoid from Nerokourou; after CMS V.Sup.1A.186. Catalogue # 45 63

Figure 92: Seal impression from Zakros; after CMA II7.16. Catalogue # 55. 63

Figure 93: Seal impression from Aghia Triada; after CMS II6.11. Catalogue # 32. 64

Figure 94: Dancing woman fresco from Knossos; after Immerwahr (1990) plate 43. Catalogue # 76. 64

Figure 95: Electrum ring from Knossos; after CMS II3.56. Catalogue # 25. 64

Figure 96: Aghia Triada sarcophagus; after Long (1977), plate 13. Catalogue # 73. 64

Figure 97: Gold ring from Mega Monasiri; after CMS V2.728. Catalogue # 64. 65

Figure 98: Gold and silver ring from Mycenae; after CMS I.108. Catalogue # 8. 65

Figure 99: Procession fresco from Thebes; after Reusch (1948-9), fig. 11. Catalogue # 68. 65

Figure 100: Procession fresco from Tiryns; after Immerwahr (1990), plate 56. Catalogue # 100. 66

Figure 101: Miniature procession fresco from Pylos; after Lang (1966), plate 4-6. Catalogue # 94. 66

Figure 102: Palaquin fresco from Mycenae; after Wace (1956), plate 9. Catalogue # 81 66

Figure 103: Gold ring from Aidonia; after CMS V.Sup.1B.113. Catalogue # 56. 67

Figure 104: Gold ring from Midea; after CMS I.191. Catalogue # 13. 67

Figure 105: Gold ring from Mycenae; after CMS I.86. Catalogue # 7. 67

Figure 106: Steatite lentoid from Eleusis; after V2.422. Catalogue # 60. 67

Figure 107: Chalcedony lentoid from Vaphio; after CMS I.220. Catalogue # 15. 67

Figure 108: Seal impression from Pylos; after CMS I.361. Catalogue # 20. 68

Figure 109: Seal impression from Knossos; after CMS II8.267. Catalogue # 51. 76

Figure 110: Crystal plaque from Knossos; after PofM III, pl. XIX. Catalogue # 69. 76

Figure 111: Onyx lentoid from Mycenae; after CMS I.82. Catalogue # 52. 82

Figure 112: Fresco of dancing woman from Aghia Triada; after Immerwahr (1990), plate 18. Catalogue # 67. 83

Preface

The origin of this book is my PhD dissertation, completed in 1999 at Columbia University, in the department of Art History and Archaeology. My approach in this project has been a marriage of archaeological and art historical methods, research and deduction. This seems,to be a necessary approach when dealing with visual materials from the Aegean Bronze Age as the materials themselves are embedded parts of archaeological sites but more than typical social-science approachs are required in their examination. It is, however, the case that such a combined humanities and social science approach is rare in the field. This no doubt has to do with the historiography of the field of Aegean Prehistory as well as the circumstance of the training of scholars in either departments of art history or among archaeologists in classics or archaeology departments. This is regrettable as a combined approach has the potential of greatly expanding the amount of information we can extract from visual materials discovered at archaeological sites as well as offering a wider range of theoretical and methodological paradigms to consult.

As the following chapters will explicate in greater detail, most basically, I am interested in the sudden appearance of the human form in the visual remains of the Aegean Bronze Age at the beginning of the historical period referred to as Late Minoan. Found in a range of media, the beauty of the images of men and women, as well as the great skill of their execution emerging so suddenly, to my mind, begged exploration. Reviewing the range of formal images which do emerge, it immediately becomes clear that a number of image types existed, representations of people doing various things which were repeated again and again. Remarkably, the medium which most frequently exhibited the formal images is glyptic, the seal stone and seal impressions which remain from the sphragistic action of Minoan and Mycenaean public and private administration. The one theme or element which unites nearly all of these images is performance, regularized action with specific social meanings. Gathering these repeated representations of performance allowed me to take a quantitative approach (although only modestly so) when analyzing the seals and seal impressions; this also afforded the knowledge of which performances were the most popular: bull leaping and dancing. Next I concentrated on these two performances, examining their full range of representation as well as archaeological evidence for their practice. Most importantly, I attempt to get at the specific social meanings of these performances as they would be understood to the people who enacted them. Having comprised a workable set of meanings for images of bull leaping and dancing, I turn to the larger historical framework of the period, and again ask why these images of performance emerged at this specific time during the Aegean Bronze Age. The conclusions I come to locate a specifically political function for the emergence of these images, connected with the consolidation of power around palatial centers in the last periods of the Minoan period and the employment, with modifications, of this visual power by the succeeding Mycenaeans.

Preparing the original dissertation and this monograph, I turned to many people for help and support and I would like to acknowledge these people here. First, I would like to thank the department of Art History and Archaeology at Columbia University for its generous support of not only my graduate study but also this project. I would also like to thank those at the Corpus der minoischen und mykenishen Siegel in Marburg, specifically Ingo Pini and Walter Muller, for giving me generous access to the excellent collection of seal impressions there. I also thank them for their kind permission to reproduce the photographs of so many of these impressions here. I thank the American School of Classical Studies and the British School of Archaeology at Athens for hosting me while I conducted research. I am grateful to various people at the Greek Archaeological Service, specifically Kate Demakopoulou, for their kindness in allowing me to examine various objects at the National Archaeological, Napflion, and Chania museums. I thank my dissertation committee, Ellen Davis, Natalie Kampen, Robert Koehl, Sandy MacGillivray, and Steven Murray, who were always full of help, encouragement and good will. The vast majority of the illustrations in this monograph were completed by MaryAnna Roberts, to whom I am very grateful.

No less integral to the completion of this project is a group people comprised not of academics but friends. First, I must thank Renate Kierey, upon whom I could always count to share every triumph and failure regardless of how small; without her, I would have been lost. I thank my sister, Alexandra German and her beloved, John Whele, who were an unfailing source of support of various kinds (especially the high-tech variety). Others I must thank for their encouragement and affection throughout my work are Jennifer and John Truitt, Danielle Kolker, Johanna Werbach and Frank Karel. More recently on the scene, I must thank my husband Clive Belfield. I could not hope for a more reliable and complete support of my life and work.

Lastly, I dedicate this book to my father, who passed on to me his great passion for history and to my mother, who taught me strength and discipline without which this project could have never been completed.

Introduction: Why Performance?

"What performances, it may be asked, are likely to have been given...bull leaping...shows of pugilists...dances, possibly of a ceremonial kind...."

        Sir Arthur Evans: *The Palace of Minos*. vol. 11.1
                (London: Macmillan 1921-35) 82.

During the 1903 season of excavation at the palace of Knossos, Sir Arthur Evans made a discovery which would later be referred to as "the culminating point of interest in the [first] four years' excavation."[1] On the west side of the central court, in a room behind the tripartite columnar shrine, Evans discovered two rectangular cists sunk into the floor which he named the Temple Repositories because of their apparent cultic contents. Inside the cists were several faience objects (including the famous snake goddesses), ivory, gold foil, inscribed tablets, high quality painted pottery and some 160 seal impressions.[2] The extraordinary contents of the Temple Repositories has thrust them into the center of numerous controversies since their discovery; among Aegean prehistorians the most contentious debate has concerned the date of the deposit. It is now generally believed that the material resulted from a cleaning after a major destruction at the site near the end of the first palace period.[3] If this dating is correct, the materials in the deposit can be viewed as characteristic of this first and somewhat obscure period during which the first palaces were constructed on Crete.

Taken as a group, the 160 sealings are eclectic, including examples of MMII first palace flat faced seals, at least one example of the MMIII hieroglyphic class and a number of precocious LM style seals.[4] What this stylistically diverse group of seals reveals is a "snapshot" of seal use at the end of the first palace period which reflects an expansion of seal styles developing from geometric and hieroglyphic compositions into naturalistic representations of people, animals and nature. Thus, the deposit of sealings from the Temple Repositories offers a unique view into the fascinating but seldom discussed issue of stylistic transition in Minoan art which was apparent not only in seals but also in other media such as pottery and wall painting. Simply put, this transition was from the abstracted to the naturalistic, from the aniconic to the figural. Even more interesting is the uniformity with which the new naturalistic style would soon be practiced.

As Sarah Immerwahr has pointed out in her study of Aegean painting, the human figures painted on the walls of the reconstructed second palace at Knossos have no recognizable precedent or experimental stage.[5] During the previous first palace period abstract lines[6] or sponge patterns[7] had decorated walls. In the following second palace period, large scale and, in some cases, three-dimensional, representations of men and women are found. Famous among these are the "Priest-King" stucco relief fresco fragments which illustrate (likely) two men, one who strides with muscular legs, skirt and cod-piece and another who stands with his closed hand upon his full chest over which long locks delicately hang.[8] In short, during the second palace period, human representation arrives in the palaces fully formed and in sensual detail. Similarly, in vase painting, there is a marked difference in naturalism between the first and second palace periods. Floral motives which had often been stiff in the first palace period become fluid and more natural in the second, implying a sense of movement.[9] Later, in the mature second palace period the marine style, the most famous style of Minoan vase painting, is created, its name derived from the delicate and organic painted representations of marine life.

Naturalistic figural representation occurs in glyptic art during the second palace period similarly without precedent. With the exception of the precocious LMI style seals found in the Temple Repositories, there is no prior instance of the representations of men and women which quickly become commonplace in LMI glyptic. Women's bodies (fig. 1) are elegantly long, yet fleshy, curvaceous with large thighs and arms, swelling hips and breasts, and long hair.

The torso is held in a pose to suggest swinging of the hips and shoulders. These female bodies are clothed almost invariably in identical attire: a full flounced skirt and short jacket, open to leave breasts fully exposed.[10] Men's bodies come in two forms. The first, (fig. 2) and by far the most common, appears youthful, tall and slim with a narrow waist and broad muscular chest. This body is clothed with either a belt and breechcloth or a kilt[11] and sometimes protected by armor.

---

[1] Duncan Mackenzie, "The Pottery of Knossos," *Journal of Hellenic Studies* 23 (1903) 199.

[2] Arthur Evans, *The Palace of Minos at Knossos*, vol. I: 496. [hereafter *PofM*]; Arthur Evans, "Knossos 1901,"*Annual of the British School of Athens* 9 (1902/3) 38-94. The number of impressions first reported was 150; another ten were included in the group discussed in *PofM*, bringing the total to 160.

[3] Evidence of this destruction is found at sites all over the island and is likely connected to the eruption of the volcano on the island of Santorini. For the most current discussion of this see Jan Driessen and Colin MacDonald, *The Troubled Isle: Minoan Crete Before and After the Santorini Eruption*, Aegaeum 17 (1995), especially chapter 6.

[4] Ingo Pini, "The Hieroglyphic Deposit and the Temple Repositories at Knossos," *Aegean Seals, Sealings and Administration*, Aegaeum 5 (1990) 52-53.

[5] Sara Immerwahr, *Aegean Painting in the Bronze Age* (College Park: Pennsylvania State University Press, 1990) 52.

[6] For example, *PofM*, vo. I, fig. 188, a-b.

[7] For example, *PofM*, vol. IV, fig 75.

[8] Arthur Evans, "Knossos 1900"BSA 1900-01, 15-16; *PofM*, figs, 504, 508, 510-11, pl. XIV. Also see Wolf-Dietrich Niemeier, "The 'Priest King' Fresco from Knossos. A New Reconstruction." in *Problems in Greek Prehistory*, ed. E.B. French and K. Wardle (Bristol: Bristol Classical Press, 1988). Here Niemeier argues that the reconstructed fresco contains fragments from at least two separate frescoes.

[9] Philip. P. Betancourt, *The History of Minoan Pottery* (Princeton: Princeton University Press, 1985) 123.

[10] Bernice Jones, "Women's Costume in the Aegean Bronze Age" (Ph.D. Dissertation., New York University, 1998) for a discussion.

[11] Paul Rehak, "Aegean Breechcloths, Kilts, and the Keftiu Paintings," *American Journal of Archaeology* 100 (1996) 35-51, for a full description of male clothes of this type.

Figure 1: Steatite lentoid seal from Knossos; after CMS II3.8. Catalogue # 22.

The other male body type (fig. 3) is obscured completely by a large robe, and the face often has a full beard. As is the case with wall and vase painting, these figures are naturalistic and at times quite delicate and elegant.

Among art historians, the seals which feature the human form are considered some of the great masterpieces of prehistoric art: dancing women, tumbling acrobats, boxing boys, and devotees engaged in solemn ritual carved in exquisite detail and with astonishing realism on semi-precious stones often no larger than thirty centimeters in diameter.

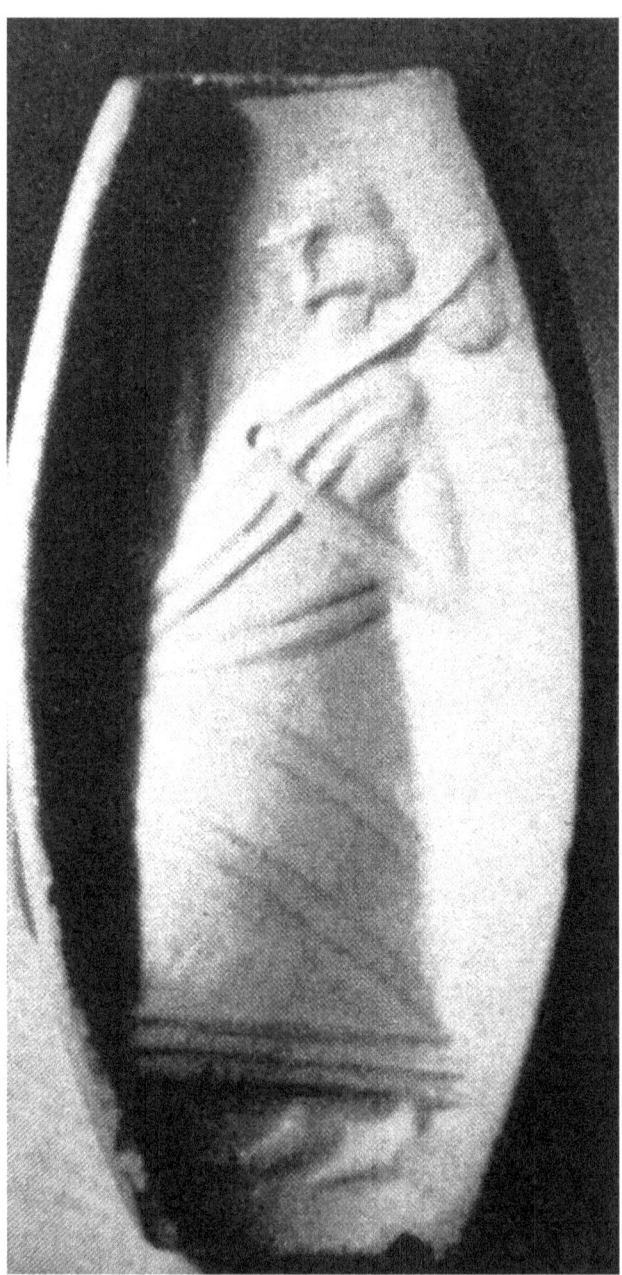

Figure 3: Onyx amygdaloid seal from Vaphio; after CMS I.225. Catalogue # 16.

Figure 2: Agate amygdaloid seal from Mycenae; after CMS I.68. Catalogue # 4.

In an age before the invention of locks, seals or engraved gems offered a way of identifying property and control access to it. A lump of clay over the lid of a jar or covering the string which secured a box or a door could not be removed or replaced without detection if it was stamped with a seal. The resulting stamped clay impression is called a sealing, the positive impression of the negative carving on the stone seal. Critical to this stamp system is the uniqueness of the pattern carved on the seal and, presumably, an understanding of the image itself. It is believed that a combination of the image on the seal and the way in which it was used not only identified the origin of the stamper but functioned as a signal of the status and/or occupation of the owner. Stamp seals were used in a system of elite administration during the late Bronze Age in Greece which connected palatial sites to periphery areas and even foreign peoples in the more remote areas of the Aegean.

Because of the beauty and highly collectable nature of the stones, their study has existed largely within the realm of connoisseurship, regarding seals as "objet d'art," concentrating on issues such as style and the identification of individual artists' hands.[12] However, in the past fifteen years the study of the use of seals within sealing systems, mostly executed by Judith Weingarten and Erik Hallager, has provided a better understanding of their function in the administration of late Bronze Age palatial society. This more integrated kind of study of seals and sealings, explicitly in connection with the social history of the Aegean Bronze Age, I believe, can also be made in the examination of the *images* carved onto these objects as well. This is the broader aim of this work.

Along these lines, Jan Driessen and Colin MacDonald recently have discussed the production of palatial centers on Crete, artistic and otherwise, within the context of the social history of the period.[13] In their thesis, they argue that much of the art made during the first half of the second palace period was propaganda, religious and social, the aim of which was to influence the population whose confidence had been weakened by the recent Theran eruption and ensuing seismic, environmental and likely social aftereffects.[14] Driessen and MacDonald's study, primarily of pottery and architecture, is the essential background for my work which looks at a specific instance of this propaganda and how it worked: the representations of performance.

The book examines representations of bull leaping and dancing (with a subset of procession) as examples of performance with the aim of better understanding both the larger social significance of these images and their individual performative power. I propose that images of bull leaping and dancing worked on the island of Crete during the second palace period (MMIIa/LHI to LMIIIb/LHIIIb2 or the second and third palace periods, absolute dates c. 1750-1720 to 1700-1680 to c. 1360-1325 to 1200/1190)[15] as identifiers of palatial authority through their indexical relationship to larger representations and performance of social drama found at the palaces. These social dramas emerged at the palaces in the second palace period at first to mitigate the social pressure of a change from kinship-based to social identity-based systems and later to address the social pressures created by the aftermath of the Santorini explosion. The Mycenaeans, when they controlled Knossos in the third palace period, adopted this means of visual identification as their own, even practicing it in palatial centers back on the Greek mainland.

* * *

In the following chapters, performance is not traditionally theatrical in the sense of a staged production with a written script. More akin to the idea of body language than formal choreographed movement, I see performance as comportment and/or activities which conform to social expectations or are in reaction to them. Because this meaning of non-theatrical performance is so broad, I have sub-divided this category into separate components. These three categories are performativity, the performance of an act, and social drama.

Most subtle of the three varieties of performance listed above, but potentially the most powerful, is performativity. Performativity has been most extensively explored by Judith Butler who is particularly intersted in its power in the construction of gender and sexual identity.[16] Butler see performativity as "styles of the flesh," repeated positions, moves, activities, and noises the body performs in order to conform to various social categories. For instance,

> ...gender is an identity tenuously constituted in time, instituted in an exterior space through a *stylized repetition of acts*. The effect of gender is produced through the stylization of the body and, hence, must be understood as the mundane way in which bodily gestures, movements, and styles of various kinds constitute the

---

[12] For instance, V. E. G. Kenna, Cretan Seals. With a Catalogue of the Minoan Gems in the Ashmolean Museum (Oxford: The Ashmolean Museum, 1960) and especially John Younger "Aegean Seals of the Late Bronze Age: Masters and Workshops I-VII" Kadmos 21-28 (1982-89).
[13] Supra note 3.
[14] Ibid., 61ff.
[15] Stuart Manning, *The Absolute Chronology of the Aegean Bronze Age: Archaeology, Radiocarbon and History*. Monographs in Mediterranean Archaeology 1.(1995) 217.
[16] Judith Butler, *Gender Trouble: Feminist and the Subversion of Identity* (New York: Routledge 1990), especially chapter three; "Performative Acts and Gender Constitution: An Essay in Phenomenology and Feminist Theory," in *Performing Feminisms: Feminist Critical Theory and Theatre*, Sue-Ellen Case, ed. (Baltimore: Johns Hopkins University Press, 1990; *Bodies That Matter: On the Discursive Limits of "Sex"* (New York: Routledge 1993) especially chapters one, three and seven.

illusion of an abiding gendered self (original emphasis).[17]

Fundamental to Butler's concept of performativity is its ability to actively construct meaning: physical, corporeal, visible guidelines and boundaries for gender and the process by which this meaning is created.[18] This is what we think of as conventional masculine or feminine behavior, including speech, eye contact, dress, voice, gesture, gait, etc. However, this behavior, performativity, which people affect every day, is historically specific and thus is ever changing over time. The way in which a man dressed and spoke 200 years ago in, for example, rural Turkey, is dramatically different from the kind of masculinity performed on the streets of Manhattan today. Yet, both are correct performances which work to define and perpetuate masculine ideals. Thus, performativity, through its repeated action, always creates *contemporary* and *geographically specific* social categories.

Indeed, it is this issue of historical specificity which lends perhaps the greatest weight to Butler's argument for the "illusion of an abiding gendered self." By illusion, she refers to the lack of concrete basis, biological or otherwise, within the self for gender realities.[19] Therefore, by definition, all gender is an illusion. But this illusion, within social practice, is solid reality, backed up by the not only the powerful momentum of repeat performance, but the danger of transgressing this illusion. Within Butler's configuration, correct gender performance reiterates perceived natural and original identity and is rewarded by social acceptance; incorrect performance, or purposeful subversive performance, is at diametric odds with the original and natural and is punished by social ostracism or more dire action.[20]

Although Butler is primarily concerned with gender and sex, the notion of performativity is useful to the present study in examining the construction and maintenance of other important social identities.[21] Because performativity takes the body, the ultimate personal signifier, as its primary prop, we must acknowledge that more than just gender identity is communicated. Performativity contributes to the construction of age, ethnic, racial, class, national, political and local identities. Just as a particular gesture or comportment can identify someone as a heterosexual woman or a lesbian; that same gesture could provide information about geography, age or ethnic identity. Thus, to observe the variety of the "styles of the flesh" is to gain access to rich social information. Thus, performativity has the potential to be tremendously useful in an examination of images of Bronze Age Aegean performance because it can reveal information about social categories and identity in Minoan and Mycenaean culture. I believe that the performative bodies, the wasp waisted sinewy men and voluptuous, gently swaying, elaborately dressed women, reveal rich information about contemporary social identity vis-a-vis specific social categories, specifically, gender, age, and class.

A social category is a grouping by which people are identified and identify with one another in simultaneous and conjunctive categories such as race, class, gender, ethnicity or age. Moreover, within each social category stirs a mixture of rules, values and meanings which overlap with other social categories and complexes. For instance, different genders within one social group may exist and maintain rigid boundaries between each other yet these groups might work together under another shared identity, for example, nationality. Or, relative value within one social category may help define another, such as the way some people are fixed within a certain class grouping largely by virtue of their race. Lastly, these categories, like the performativity which expresses them, are not static or universal but change over time and are expressed differently in various cultures simultaneously. Thus, insofar as social categories help to group people, they serve to identify them. However, it is important to appreciate that this identity is a rich web of relative and changeable values within various social categories. Each person, then, identifies with several social categories and functions within their complexes simultaneously; one is not merely a woman, but one of a certain age, race, ethnicity, nationality and class. These categories work together and change throughout life but at any one time serve as fundamental markers of identity. And, it is inevitable that these categories are the ones which we use today to explore, identify and understand people from past cultures.[22]

But, why use gender, class and age as social categories to examine bull leaping and dancing? I use three modern categories as points for analysis because they may produce a new insight into representations of bull leaping and dancing. These social categories can't be known to have been central to Minoans and Mycenaeans, but clearly their culture practiced some type of social differentiation which was dependent upon gender, class and age values. Thus, these categories, which we know in our own culture to reveal social hierarchy, may help us to understand the basis of their assessments of social differences and similarities.

---

[17] Ibid., *Gender Trouble*, 140.
[18] Ibid., 66ff. Butler see this as a critical component of gender differentiation, not biology.
[19] There is no biological reality to gender because, despite the presence or absence of sexual organs, one can "be" a man or a woman by virtue of performativity. Obviously, most people perform the gender associated with their sexual organs however, some do not and thus it is these exceptions which create the rule.
[20] Ibid., 139.
[21] Ibid. *Bodies that Matter*, 116. Butler writes that her study privileged gender over race, sexuality, class or "geopolitical positioning/displacement."

[22] I do not wish here to imply that social categories constitute the whole of identity. As post-processual archaeologists often point out, there were individuals in the past, as there are in the present, and we must endeavor to study them on that level as well. This is, sadly, very difficult.

The concept of gender as a social category is now widely recognized as a critical organizational structure in culture. Beneath the bold and now famous principles of Joan Scott[23] which pose gender, a social construction, as one of the fundamental tenets upon which a society is built, stands much work and decades of writing by anthropologists and historians which highlighted the significance of the construction of gender within various cultures and time periods.[24] It seems reasonable, then, to pose distinctions, briefly described above, between representations of men and women as an important element in the art of Bronze Age Greece. It is based upon these distinctions in the representation of gender, I propose that gender as a social category is invoked on Minoan and Mycenaean representation of the human form.

Age is a social category widely recognized in anthropology as a fundamental organizational structure. The first major study of age systems and their articulation to social structure was completed by Eisenstadt some forty years ago[25] and made the important observation that as a person matures, he or she acquires "citizenship" in social groups whose single definitional principle is the mark of maturation. This mark of maturation can be many different things. In our own society, this involves, for the most part, reaching a certain chronological age, such as eighteen. In cultures where chronological ages are not kept or are less important, this marker may be an achievement of some sort or simply the recognition by those in the age grouping. Different age groups play different roles in society, and passage between them is often marked by some ceremony.[26] As no human is immune from the phenomenon of aging and its effects, good and bad, we might conclude that the social negotiation of this is universal. In the field of Aegean prehistory there has been sparse effort to study age groupings, primarily due to a lack of data about them. Examination of visual evidence, however, has produced guidelines for the identification of age categories.[27] The currency of these guidelines is considerable in Aegean Bronze Age art and therefore I believe that age was an important component of social identification.

The third and last social category which I discuss is class or social status. Social status, by definition, implies relative position, often ascribed at birth, and thus a part of social life from the start. Put broadly, distinctions of social status indicate differential access to wealth, power and association. Class, in the sense that is implied by the usage of the word today, is historically specific and therefore its application in antiquity is necessarily by analogy. Despite this, the concept of class *per se* has been applied with some success to the various groups of people with relatively more or less wealth, status or power in the ancient world, and it is in this manner that I wish to use class here.[28] Evidence for different social status in the late Bronze Age Aegean is reasonably solid. Based upon evidence from the excavation of houses and tombs, clearly some people had access to and enjoyed more luxury items and amenities than others in the forms of painted pottery, jewelry, weapons, ashlar masonry and painted walls. Further evidence of differential access to commodities, not necessarily luxury items, comes from both Linear A and B evidence. The meager amount of Linear A (the written language of the second palace period) which can be translated reveals the usage of two different types of documents: the notation of rationing of agricultural produce to named individuals[29] and religious inscriptions.[30] Both kinds of Linear A evidence indicate the existence of relative status and perhaps then, class distinction. Beginning with the agricultural documents, we can safely assume that the people who owned and/or controlled the agricultural produce which was doled out in rations were of a higher status than those receiving it. From the Linear A examples of religious inscriptions there is perhaps more evidence of relative rank. All religious inscriptions in Linear A come from libation vessels and tables and other ritual objects of value found at cave or sanctuary sites. Not only do these objects have an intrinsic value, often made of attractive or semi-precious materials and carefully worked, but also their provenience in ritual areas elevate them in status. Additionally, an inscription on an object might well have elevated its value as it was associated with a literate class; given the paucity of Linear A materials, it seems likely that literacy was rare. A group of specially trained scribes might very well have been regarded as a higher class, differentiated not necessarily by wealth but by education and access to those who controlled wealth.

This evidence which suggests the existence of a class

---

[23] Joan Scott, "Gender: A Useful Category of Historical Analysis," *American Historical Review* 91 (1986) 1053-1075.
[24] See Sherry Ortner and Harriet Whitehead eds. *Sexual Meanings: The Cultural Construction of Gender* (New York: Cambridge University Press, 1981).; Micaela de Leonardo, "Gender, Culture and Political Economy: Feminist Anthropology in Historical Perspective," in Micaela di Leonardo ed., *Gender at the Crossroads of Knowledge: Feminist Anthropology in the Postmodern Era* (Berkeley: University of California Press, 1991) for a good literature review of the feminist underpinnings of gender investigation in anthropology and history.
[25] S.N. Eisenstadt, *From Generation to Generation: Age Groups and Social Structure* (Glencoe, Free Press, 1956).
[26] This concept was first put forward by E. van Gennep, *The Rites of Passage*, trans. Monika B. Vizedom and Gabrielle Caffee (Chicago: University of Chicago Press, 1960).
[27] See discussion of these visual clues in chapter one.

[28] In ancient Greece, Rome and Mesopotamia written records greatly aid in the archaeological identification of remains associated with different social classes. In prehistory, however, things are more difficult and a sliding scale applies; when digging a grave, the wealthier the contents the higher the status of the occupant and vice versa. Relative value, however, must be regarded with care in archaeological interpretation so that contemporary scales are not given to past cultures and interpretations be left open to include among valuable objects those which do not seem intrinsically so to us today.
[29] These sorts of documents and, indeed, most Linear A inscriptions, come primarily from Aghia Triada and Zakros.
[30] These are found most commonly in caves and at peak sanctuaries.

system found in Linear A documents is also found in Linear B (the written language of the third palace period) documents. Linear B documents record different groups of workers at Knossos, Mycenae and Pylos, and some workers are given more rations for their work than others. If this does not indicate a higher class, it at least suggests a higher income.[31] Also, in the archives various individuals are listed as owning land privately and even land leases. People named in association with religious activity, most them women[32] bearing direct relationships to deities through their service, also seem to have enjoyed a higher status in the tablets. Although it would probably be impossible to reveal the exact nature or specific limitations of class in the Linear B documents, evidence for some sort of social differentiation does exist. In the following, I shall discuss how relative values within these three social categories are embedded within, for one, representations of performative bodies.

From a discussion of performativity and social categories, we move to the second kind of performance used in this work, performance of an act. More than just performative behavior, the performance of an act is a discrete regularized activity, simple or complex, executed with deliberate action such as walking, throwing a ball or brushing hair. As described above, a performed act can bear social meaning by virtue of the social complexes with which it is identified. An example from contemporary culture helps make this clear. The act of smoking a cigar is gendered male because traditionally only western men participated in this brash and untidy act. Smoking and its befouling conditions (smoke, ash, stench) became gendered male in a binary framework where men do brash and untidy things and women are modest and clean. Significantly, it is not the cigar itself which makes the connection to the social complex of gender but the act of smoking it, creating sooty ash and thick smoke, and sucking flagrantly. A consideration of the occasion and social circumstances of smoking a cigar, in all male clubs, "out with the boys," reveals even more information about the social category of gender. Masculinity is in part defined by the performance of the act of smoking a cigar together with other men, in an environment which is often exclusive of women. On the other hand, a woman performing the act of smoking a cigar often performs precisely to challenge or destabilize the binary "males smoke cigars/female's don't" framework. Interestingly, at the same time, the act of cigar smoking communicates information about class by virtue of its association with this complex. In contemporary American culture, cigar smoking is associated primarily with the "upper" class because cigars are often expensive, hand made, and imported from exotic lands. This was, however, not always the case; one need recall only twenty years ago when most cigar smoking was performed by poor immigrant men. Just like performativity, correct performance of an act is historically specific.

What then is the difference between performativity and the performance of an act, and why is this distinction important for the present work? Most importantly, the sense of obligation in performativity to the creation of identity and the risk of punishment if the performance is not executed correctly is missing from the performance of an act. For, indeed, as I have explained, performative aspects of gender are very basic, often unconscious in the creation of this and other social categories. There is no one performed act which is obligatory to the creation or maintenance of a social category although they do function in this regard. One is not necessarily not a man if one does not smoke a cigar; there are alternative performed acts which could be performed which would contribute just as effectively to gender identification and construction such as, within the same contemporary framework, spitting on the street. However, if that same person does not execute the performative aspects of masculinity such as gait, gesture and facial expression, questions as to his/her gender identity are raised.

The performance of an act is, necessarily, something which occurs over a period of time and when it is illustrated, save by means of cartoon-like serial representation, only a glimpse of it is seen. A consideration of the representation of movement in the performance of an act is necessary here given the static visual nature of the evidence I examine. In order for the representation of the performance of an act to be understandable and potent, the *action* of the act must be captured. That is, in keeping with our example of cigar smoking, an image which shows someone in the process of smoking a cigar would perhaps be the richest representation of the performed act. Although a picture of a cigar might signify the performed act of smoking a cigar, it is ambiguous; it might also allude to Cuban nationalism. Using an example closer to the Aegean Bronze Age, every representation of a bull does not represent bull leaping. But, images found so often on seals and elsewhere which show bull leapers around the bull likely represent the performed act.

Some acts are simple in their physical execution, such as carrying an object. Other acts, such as chariot driving, are more complex. Although more complex in form, the performance of an act works in the same way as performativity in so far as it builds and maintain social complexes and identity. That is, returning again to the contemporary example above, the performance of the act of cigar smoking creates part of the topography of modern American "upper" class masculinity. The man smoking a cigar simultaneously references, makes real, "upper" class and masculine identities and associates himself with those identities. Therefore, by approaching

---

[31] It is interesting to note here that by and large, male and female workers earned the same income. See Jon-Christian Billigmeier and Judy Turner, "The Socio-Economic Roles of Women in Mycenaean Greece: A Brief Survey from evidence of the Linear B Tablets," in Helene Foley ed., *Reflections of Women in Antiquity* (New York: Gordon and Breach Science Publisher, 1981).
[32] Ibid., 3ff.

certain representations in the art of the Aegean Bronze Age as performed acts, not only can a richer context for these images be discovered, but also a view to the social complexes which they are engaged in creating and maintaining can be revealed.

The third type of performance I discuss here is social drama. Simply, social drama is a series of structured social events which address crisis in a culture. Again, some definitions are in order. Social events are occasions in which groups within a culture get together to participate in or watch an activity. Structured social events are those which bear a relationship to one another either by succession or by hierarchy, such as baptism prior to confirmation in the Christian church or the swearing in of a president before his or her first official duty. By crisis, I mean stress, conflict or disharmony which effects a cultural group such as rites of passage, leadership transitions, political power struggles, war, or even famine. Social drama is a concept from anthropology and grew out of ritual studies as anthropologists tried to explain the social function of regularized action within cultures they observed. Ritual is practical action, something which is acted out in order to attain a desired result.[33] Although some performances of social drama are staged to serve a specific purpose, such as a rain dances among native Americans, and others are more concerned with masculine definition, such as the running of the bulls in Spain. No performance is exclusively either efficacy or entertainment. Rain dances were exciting and diversionary events during difficult times of drought, and the running of the bulls in Spain was the activity which marked the passage of a young man into adulthood.

The form and characteristics of social drama and its relationship to performance was the lifetime work of Victor Turner. Using a broad range of ethnographic material, Turner developed a multi-step model of social drama describing dramatic performances which, he argued, take place in all societies to address disharmonious, or crisis or transgressive situations. These situations, arguments, combats, are "dramatic" because participants not only perform but do so before a group. As Turner has described:

> A social drama is initiated when the peaceful tenor of regular, norm-governed social life is interrupted by the breach of a rule controlling one of its salient relationships. This shifts swiftly or slowly to a state of crisis, which if not soon sealed off may split the community into contending factions and coalitions. To prevent this, redressive means are taken by those who consider themselves or are considered the most legitimate or authoritative representatives of the relevant community. Redress usually involves ritualized action, whether legal, religious, or military. If the situation does not regress to crisis, the next phase of social drama comes into play, which involves alternative solutions to the problem. The first is reconciliation of the conflicting parties followed by judicial, ritual, or military processes; the second, consensual recognition of irremediable breach, usually followed by the spatial separation of the parties. Since social dramas suspend normal everyday life and thus social life, they force a group to take cognizance of its own behavior in relation to its own values, even to question at times the value of those values. In other words, dramas induce and contain reflexive processes and generate cultural frames in which reflexivity can find a legitimate place.[34]

Therefore, the salient features of social dramas are the following: they address some event in society which is constituted by a transgression of a "rule" which polices social boundaries, they are performed by or under the auspices of those in authority through some legal, religious or military action, and they suspend normal social behavior to address a crisis whose resolution may result in a change of that norm.

The forms of social drama are many; there is no one specific venue, performance, time or duration; they can occur regularly within cultural cycles tied to the seasons or human maturity such as harvest celebrations or rites of passage. They do, however, always address dilemmas within social complexes. An example is helpful here to fully appreciate how social drama works. Among the Igbo of contemporary Nigeria, O.A.C. Anigbo has argued that the seemingly informal affair of community meals is in fact, during certain times of year, a social drama which addresses a struggle for leadership within the village.[35] For the Igbo, a communal meal during the seventh month of the year, called the *Onwa Asaa,* marks the first eating of the new yams, and it is an occasion when the yams are presented as gifts to those in authority in the village. The date of this festival and those in authority are determined at a prior community meal. This prior meal is hosted by the senior family members with the maximal lineage (those who had married-off the most people into other

---

[33] The configuration of ritual and social drama was first made by Victor Turner, *Dramas, Fields, and Metaphores: Symbolic Action in Human Society* (Ithaca: Cornell University Press, 1974).

[34] Victor Turner, *From Ritual to Theatre: the Human Seriousness of Play* (New York: Performing Arts Journal Publication, 1982) 92.

[35] O.A.C. Anigbo, "Commensality as Cultural Performance: the Struggle for Leadership in an Igbo Village,: in D. Parkin, L. Caplan and H. Fisher eds, *The Politics of Cultural Performance* (London: Berghahn Books, 1996).

families and therefore had the greatest amount of inter-family connections) in the village. At this feast, their relative authority among those at the feast is determined by age, social relationships and the extent of one's family which throughout the year changes with marriage, death and birth. In other words, here authority is determined through relative status in a number of different social complexes, namely age, class and kinship. Status within these social complexes, as discussed above, is in part established through performativity and the performance of acts. Once authority is determined, it is exercised for the first time by determining the date of the eating of the first yams.[36]

Thus, the feast of the *Onwa Asaa* can be understood as a social drama which regularly arises by virtue of the need to harvest a subsistence crop and is sanctioned by a similar social drama of feasting which arises out of the need to determine authority within the community to make decisions. Authority is determined within certain social complexes, based upon the success of the participants' performativity and performance of acts during the feast. Following these two feasts, normal social activity continues but those in authority have changed. As Turner's model indicates, the social drama presents the opportunity for the community to think about the nature of social complexes, in the case of the Igbo, structures of authority or social class, and to make changes as necessary.

What, then, is the relationship between performativity, the performance of an act and social drama? Most importantly, all three kinds of performance work to define and maintain social complexes and identities. Further, these three performances work together. Just as performative bodies take part in performed acts, so performed acts make up social drama. The person who walks, talks and moves his body to conform to masculine performative rules, strengthens and makes richer their identification with masculinity and gender complexes with the performance of male gendered performed acts. In the Igbo example above, eating and the presentation of yams are two discrete performed acts, however, within the context of social drama, they are an integrated part of a larger rite. Just as the performative body and certain acts which it executes create and maintain social complexes and identities, their regulatory roles in social drama help to bring to resolution the crisis of the transgression of these complexes and identities.

Issues of the representation of social drama are again important to touch upon here. There are two important criteria for the representation of a social drama. First, it is important that a large enough number of people, either participants or spectators, is included in a representation of a social drama in order to capture the sense that it is a significant event witnessd by a portion of society and therefore the scene would include a public space venue.

Second, a sense of time-lapse needs to be represented. Yet, like the performance of an act, the representation of an activity which takes place over time can be problematic. This is further complicated by the fact that, as I have described above, important components of social drama are discrete performed acts and therefore discrete parts of a social drama can look different. An example from the Bronze Age may be helpful in describing what I mean. The Procession Fresco (fig.4), painted in the Corridor of the Procession at Knossos can be seen as an example of the illustration of a social drama, a procession ceremony of some kind.[37]

Figure 4: Knossos Procession Fresco, reconstruction; after Immerwahr (1990), plate 40. Catalgue # 91.

In this fragmentary fresco the feet and full torso of several people remain, mostly male, who proceed to the right, with a few characters facing the opposite direction. The size of the painting and its many figures communicates the sense of an event which was attended by many people. Its location, in a major public entrance to the palace during the second palace period, where processions could have taken place, contributes to the supposition that the paintings represent a social drama which would have takn place in that local. One figure in the fresco who is largely preserved, a youthful slender male with long curly locks who carries a large conical rhyton, is referred to as the Cup Bearer (fig. 5).

He, taken alone, is the illustration of the performance of an act, carrying a ceremonial object. However, together with the other characters in the fresco he is merely a component of the larger social drama of procession. Further, as a part of this illustration of the social event of procession, a part of the performed act of carrying an object is the performing masculine body. The man, wasp-waisted and slender with muscular legs, performs the conventional Minoan masculine performance. Thus, the example of the Procession Fresco, illustrates together the three kinds of representations of performance I employ in my analysis: performativity, performance of an act and social drama. The representation of social drama is the greatest in extent, includes a public space with spectators. Contained within this representation are discrete representations of performed acts which constitute the social drama. These discrete acts are each executed by bodies which exhibit performative aspects.

---

[36] Ibid., 105-108.

[37] Arthur Evans, "Knossos 1899," *Annual of the British School at Athens* (1899-1900) 12-16, *PofM* II, 704ff, 719ff, figs 428 and 450. See drawing of Gilliéron's reconstruction in S. Immerwahr, *Aegean Painting in the Bronze Age* (College Park: Pennsylvania State University Press, 1990) pl. 40.

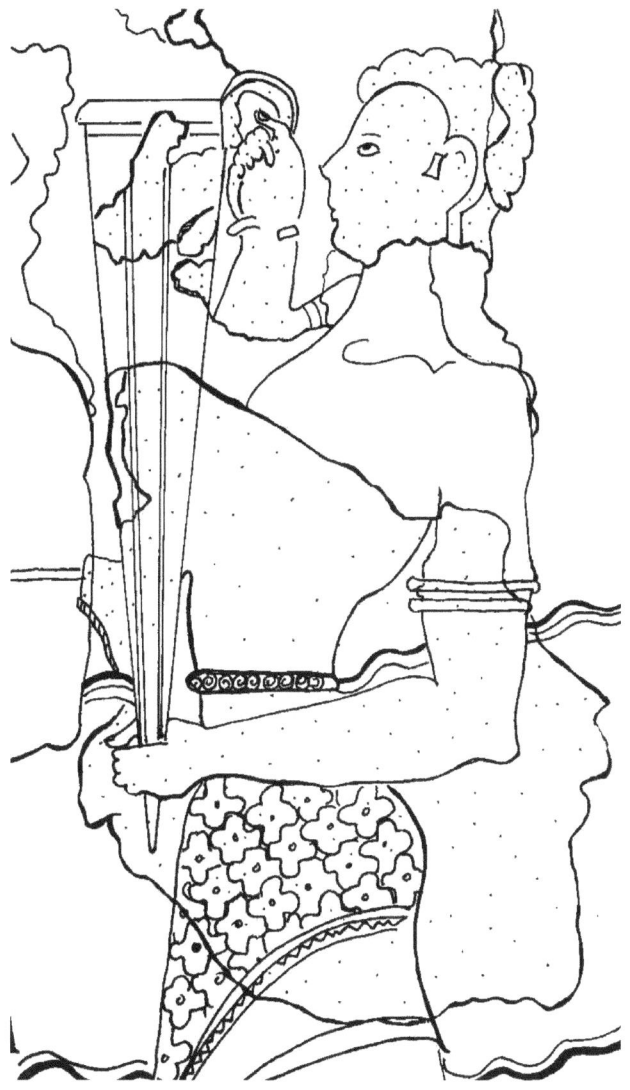

Figure 5: Cup bearer from Procession Fresco at Knossos; after PofM II2, pl. XII. Catalogue # 91.

Yet, the above explanation and example of the conjunctive and cooperative relationship between the representation of performativity, the performance of an act and social drama is not to imply that this is the only means of imaging these performances. In other words, not all representations of crowds illustrate a social drama nor does every representation of a performed act necessarily exist as a component of such. By the same token, with regard to the location of these events, I do not argue that every open space in the Bronze Age was used for social dramas. I shall argue, however, that representations of bull leaping and dancing, both shown performed in a public space with a crowd watching are components of social dramas important to Minoan and Mycenaean culture.

* * *

This book, in as much as it emphasizes an active rather than a passive role for archaeological materials, stands among a small number of works on the Aegean Bronze Age which examine how images might have worked in ancient culture. As, for instance, Robert Laffineur has pointed out, Aegean prehistorians generally agree that certain iconographic motifs express the status of their owners, but there have been no systematic studies of this phenomenon.[38] Laffineur himself has conducted two important studies which attempt to identify images which connote status in Mycenaean art in general and in glyptic iconography in particular.[39] His first study, on seal iconography, concludes that the most potent symbols of ruler status are man-to-man combat scenes, man-animal combat scenes and chariot scenes.[40] In his later study of social and political status as indicated by iconography, Laffineur traces a general shift in ruler iconography from exclusively combat and chariot scenes during the shaft-grave period to one including griffins and antithetical lions in the later LHIIIb period. In both of these articles, however, Laffineur neglects to address two important issues. First, he does not explain explicitly how these images of combat and fantastic animals were symbolic of a ruler's power and therefore suited to function as a indicator of that status. Second, he doesn't discuss how this political/power message was communicated.

Similarly, two recent studies on bull iconography propose that the image of a bull in palatial Crete, either engaged in bull sports or merely charging alone, was used to signify the high political status of its wearer.[41] The first, by Erik and Brigitte Hallager, surveys representations of bulls from wall painting at Knossos and the use of the same images on seals and sealings. They concluded that the bull was a symbol of Knossian power. However the Hallagers, like Laffineur, don't describe by what means images of bulls were symbolic (except to say they were big and powerful[42]) and don't discuss the way in which these symbolic images functioned. The second study, by Nanno Marinatos suggests that images of bull hunting and leaping were symbols of the Minoan elite. Interestingly, Marinatos indicates that the skill needed to master feats of bull hunting and leaping was what the Minoan elite associated with in these images, and therefore it was this aspect of physical prowess that made the images potent. This explanation goes a long way in explaining why images of bull hunting and leaping were symbolic, but Marinatos does not discuss how exactly this message was communicated. Marinatos' and the Hallgers' studies make a positivist leap from what we today believe about images that look like those from

---

[38] Robert Laffineur, "Iconography as Evidence of Social and Political Status in Mycenaean Greece." *IKON: Aegean Bronze Age Iconography; Shaping a Methodology*, Aegaeum 8 (1992) 105.
[39] Ibid; Robert Laffineur, "The Iconography of Mycenaean Seals and their Status of Their Owners." *Aegaeum* 6, (1990) 117-160.
[40] Ibid., 154f.
[41] Nanno Marinatos, "The 'Export' Significance of Minoan Bull Hunting and Bull Leaping Scenes," *Egypten und Levante* 4. (1994); Birgitta and Erik Hallager, "The Knossian Bull – Political Propaganda in Neo-Palatial Crete?" *Politea: Society and State in the Aegean Bronze Age*. Aegaeum 12 (1995) 547-556.
[42] Ibid Hallager & Hallager, 554.

antiquity and project this meaning on the past.

A recent dissertation, however, takes an important step forward.[43] Alexandra Alexandri examines gender-related patterns in Minoan and Mycenaean glyptic art and discovers that gender differentiated representations not only play a role in the legitimization of certain forms of authority (religious, military, political), but she also sees these representations as actively reinforcing these types of authority.[44] This study moves well beyond those described above because it explicitly poses imagery as an active element in social hierarchies, not merely reflective of abstract ideas such as power but engaged in constructing cultural sub-systems such as religion, the military and politics.

My work builds upon the work of Alexandri's in as far as it takes for granted that images of the human form in the late Bronze Age, in the glyptic and other media, are active elements in the construction of social hierarchies. By using performance as the context in which I examine the images of bull leaping and dancing, an active role for them is implicit. They do not merely reflect a status but contribute to the construction and maintenance of that social value. By recognizing the larger framework of performance in Aegean Bronze Age society, the mechanisms by which these social values were communicated are revealed.

* * *

The first chapter, Performanc and Social Catgories, examines various representations of performance found in Minoan and Mycenaean art.[45] These performances are classed within the typologies discussed above: performativity, performative acts, and social drama. Here I make a leap from the theories discussed above which are concerned with "real-life" performance to the representations of these performances in art. By doing this, I propose that images of performance had powers to construct and maintain social complexes and identity comparable to performances themselves. In other words, I argue that representations of performance were not simply reflective of social categories and identities but actively worked to create and maintain them. Beginning with the most basic performance, performativity, images of men and women are examined. Concentrating on the performative body, I isolate various consistent components of male and female representation such as details of secondary sexual characteristics, represented as large breasts and wide hips for women and broad chest and narrow waist for men, details of physical youth, such as strong musculature and age-related hair styles, and details of status such as elaborate dress and jewelry.

Next, I determine three modern social categories which are represented in these details, namely, gender, age and social status. The nature and limitations of each social category is explored with specific attention to the evidence for the social categories on the performative bodies in Bronze Age Aegean art.

Turning next to the performance of an act, again, using evidence from seals and sealings, images are identified and listed. Among these performances are animal combat, bull leaping, bull wrestling, chariot driving, dancing, and carrying an object. The occurrence and frequency of these performed acts as illustrated on seals and sealings is examined with the goal in mind of identifying the most popular and potentially important performed acts. Dancing and bull leaping emerge as the two most frequent performed acts in glyptic art throughout the late Bronze Age. Assuming that this frequency and endurance among glyptic images is proof of some cultural significance, I focus on these two performed acts, the performative bodies which execute them and ultimately the social dramas they reference for the duration of the book.

Next, evidence for social drama is explored. This evidence comes exclusively from the medium of wall painting, chiefly, three frescoes from palatial contexts, all of which include large groups of people who gather to witness an event. Significantly, the events in two of the wall paintings correspond to the two most popular performed acts found illustrated on seals and sealings: dancing and bull leaping. Presenting these frescoes as representations of social drama, I argue that the many seals and sealings which featured the performed acts of dancing and bull leaping bore an indexical relationship to these larger scale representations of social drama. This indexical relationship, based upon the visual application of semiotic theory, specifically the second trichotomy of Charles Sanders Peirce, poses the index as that which bears a causal and dependent relationship with the object that it represents. Applied to the present example of the representation of performance, I argue that the representations of the performed acts of bull leaping and dancing found on seals and sealings bear an indexical relationship to the more complete representations of social drama. By virtue of this connection I argue that the performed acts of bull leaping and dancing carved on seals and sealings, already active in the construction and maintenance of social complexes and identities, are enhanced with the contestive and redressive action of social drama.

Having identified images of bull leaping and dancing as focal points in the investigation of performance, the second and third chapters discuss them each respectively as a formal type. The discussion of each begins with an analysis of the performative body that executes the performed act, male, in the case of bull leapers and female in the case of dancers. This is followed by an analysis of the way in which these bodies construct and

---
[43] Alexandra Alexandri. *Gender Symbolism in Late Bronze Age Aegean Glyptic Art.* PhD Dissertation, Cambridge University, 1994.
[44] Ibid., 169-178.
[45] Given the sort of social information I aim to extract, I only use provenienced materials in my analysis. By provenienced, I means objects which have secure archaeological contexts, good enough for stratigraphic dating.

maintain the social categories of gender, age and social status. Then, each act itself is examined as it developed diachronically both on the mainland and Crete, determining the range of variety within each type. Focal points of discussion include the swooping movement, accentuation of breasts and hips and relationship to plants and architecture for dancing and crisp pointed leaping, a built environment, and fast action for bull leaping. Next, in each chapter I discuss how these details enhance a reading of these performed acts in relation to the three social categories of age, social status and gender. Following this, I discuss the historiography of the performed acts of bull leaping and dancing and their representations. This serves not only to explore contemporary associations with these acts, which no doubt color our interpretation of them, but also to illustrate their potential to bear meaning. In sum, the second and third chapters provide a formal mapping of the two performed acts, an historiographic overview of them and their articulation to the social categories of gender, class and age which they work to construct and maintain.

The topic of the fourth chapter, the archaeological provenience, has the ultimate aim of providing specific contextual information for the materials which bear representations of performance. In order to ease comparison, the find spots of the objects discussed are gathered together into four general categories: palatial, tomb, villa, and storage/administrative. Each of these general provenience categories is significant because they have been identified by Aegean prehistorians as important interpretive loci of Late Bronze Age culture, namely within the realms of political power, cult and economic activity. The importance of each general provenience category is discussed individually and in relation to the others. Next, the specific provenience of the objects which illustrate bull leaping and dancing is described and divided among the four broad provenience types. Relative distribution among these provenience types is presented, and the conclusion is drawn that representations of the performed acts of bull leaping and dancing were popular on Crete in the second palace period in administrative contexts and on the Mainland during the third in palatial and burial contexts.

The fifth chapter combines the work of the three preceding chapters and asks what the creation and maintenance of social categories and identities through the representation of bull leaping and dancing might mean in light of their archaeological provenience. In other words, meanings derived from the formal data of the representation of performances which speak to social categories and identity are combined with the archaeological data which indicate function and historical place. What is revealed is a chain of associations and meanings of performance begun in second palace period Crete and then adopted by the Mycenaeans in their own palaces on the mainland and continued at Knossos in the third palace period. Specifically, I propose that the owner of a seal or ring with a representation of bull leaping or dancing, by using it in personal and business transactions, by using that image to stand for him or herself, identifies with the social complexes and identities of gender, age and class created and maintained in these performances. I further argue that the representations of the performed acts of bull leaping and dancing bear an indexical relationship to the larger, more complete representations of performance, the illustrations of social drama found at palatial centers in wall painting and other media. The use of a ring or seal also invokes the contestive and redressive action of social drama and thus identifies the user with this elite authority. Therefore, seals fulfilled a special function, as the vehicles of the value-laden message of performance at the palaces, not only contributing to the status of the owner and materials which it stamped but performce itself.

Testing this hypothesis, I compare the periods when images of bull leaping and dancing gained currency to the known social history of Crete and the Mainland. The assumption here is that signs of identification with palatial authority would have been important and necessary during certain periods and not others. It is determined that bull leaping and dancing are found on seals from Crete in contexts primarily associated with the palaces during the second palace period when trade networking and activity with the mainland reach a new height and, further, that these images emerge as dominant motifs on the mainland in the following period, primarily in elite burial contexts, at exactly the times of political consolidation under chiefs around palatial centers such as Mycenae and Tiryns. This implies that representations of performed acts such as dancing and bull leaping which work at creating social complexes and identities were popular at exactly the times when such identifiers, or, badges of identity, would have been needed, during times of expansion and political consolidation.

Chapter One:
Performance and Social Categories

"...girls had to first undergo a kind of sexual transformation, by divesting themselves of all articles of feminine dress... and by adopting the sporting costume of the male performers, including the universal exterior sign of the masculine sex, the Minoan version of the 'Libyan sheath.'"

A. Evans, Palace of Minos, vol. IV2, (London: Macmillan 1921-35) 22.

"The smooth prepared field is an invention of a later stage of humanity. It accompanies the development of polished tools in the Neolithic and Bronze Ages and the creation of pottery and an architecture with regular courses of jointed masonry. It might have come about through the use of these artifacts as sign-bearing objects."
Meyer Schapiro, "On Some Problems in the Semiotics of Visual Art: Field and Vehicle in Image-Signs," *Semiotica* 1:3 (1969) 224.

This chapter has two aims: first to explore three types of representation of performance in the art of the Minoans and Mycenaeans: performativity, the performance of an act, and social drama. Second, this chapter aims to establish the relationship of these representations to social categories. I begin with the first of the three performances, performativity, and describe how the bodies of men and women in Late Bronze Age art were performative and of what. For this analysis, and the remainder of the chapter, I use seals and sealings as my primary source of visual data as the glyptic medium in Aegean Bronze Age art exhibits the most examples of the human form. Concentrating on the performative body, I isolate various consistent aspects of male and female representation such as details of secondary sexual characteristics like breasts, and wide hips for women and broad chest and narrow waist for men, details of physical youth, such as strong musculature and age-related hair styles, and details of status such as elaborate dress and jewelry. Based upon this visual evidence, I discuss three social categories, gender, age and social status, as potential foci for performativity in these images. Turning next to the performance of an act, images on seals are examined. Among these performances are animal combat, bull leaping, bull wrestling, acrobatics, chariot racing, dancing, and carrying an object. The occurrence and frequency of these images on seals and sealings is examined with the goal of identifying the most popular and potentially important performed acts. Dancing and bull leaping are revealed as the two most frequent performed acts in glyptic art throughout the late Bronze Age. Concluding that this frequency and endurance among glyptic images is significant, I center upon these two performed acts and the performative bodies which execute them for the duration of the work.

Next, evidence for the practice of social drama in the Aegean Bronze Age is explored. This evidence comes exclusively from the medium of wall painting, chiefly, three frescoes from palatial contexts all of which include large groups of people who gather to watch an event. Significantly, the events in two of the wall paintings correspond to the two most popular performed acts found illustrated on seals and sealings, dancing and bull leaping. Presenting these frescoes as representations of social drama, I argue that the many seals and sealings which featured the performed acts of dancing and bull leaping bear an indexical relationship to these larger scale representations of social drama. This indexical relationship, based upon the visual application of semiotic theory, poses the index as that which bears a causal and dependent relationship with the object that it represents. Applied to the present example of the representation of performance, I argue that the representations of the performed acts of bull leaping and dancing found on seals and sealings bear an indexical relationship to the more complete wall painting representations of social drama at the palaces.

* * *

The appearance of the human form in Minoan art at the start of the second palace period on Crete is extraordinary, not only for its suddenness but also because of its full-formed style. The first student of Aegean Bronze Age art to discuss this swift emergence was Groenewegen-Frankfort, almost fifty years ago.[46] Seeking to understand the phenomenon as part of an organic development of Minoan art, Gronewegen-Frankfort likened the emergence of figural art, and its relatively short floruit, to the "genius of a child prodigy,"[47] a brilliant invention abandoned quickly. As part of an evolutionary description of the art of the Minoans, this sort of metaphor works nicely. However, within the present performative framework of our investigation, such an explanation for this dramatic shift in representation must be sought elsewhere. Did these new representations of men and women bear some relationship to new ideas about and/or a coding shift of social identity in Minoan and later Mycenaean culture? The idea of coding social information in art or artifacts is not unique and has been most engagingly discussed in relation to archaeological materials by Martin Wobst.[48] Focusing on the issues of stylistic "behavior," Wobst proposes that this aspect of an artifact can convey varying degrees of information depending on a number of variables such as the message content, visibility, and social contexts in which artifacts are used as well as the cultural matrix in which the stylistic communication takes place. Wobst brings out the dynamic and active element

---

[46] H. A. Groenewegen-Frankfort. *Arrest and Movement: An Essay on Space and Time in the Representational Art of the Ancient Near East* (New York: Hackert Art Books, 1978) 195.
[47] Ibid. Interestingly, Arnold Hauser, *The Social History of Art*, vol.I (New York, Vintage, 1985) 51-3 interprets this floruit as the result of the subordinate role of oppressive social systems such as religion which produced more rigid forms elsewhere in the ancient world.
[48] H. Martin Wobst, "Stylistic Behavior and Information Exchange," in E. Cleland ed. *For the Director: Research Essays in Honor of James B. Groffin* (Ann Arbor, University of Michigan Press, 1977)

of style, posing it as a larger constituent part of cultural process as evidence through artifactual remains.[49] Key to this hypothesis is the idea of "target groups" which would create and receive stylistic "behavior." In other words, specific styles come about because they are targeted to communicate between specific groups; the extent of stylistic behavior should positively correlate with the size of the social networks that individuals participate in. In fact, within this model, Wobst predicts that,

> given a category of material culture, stylistic messaging is either absent altogether or it is all-pervasive. This set of considerations has some interesting implications for the evolution of signaling in the artifact mode. For example, it argues for the sudden appearance of stylistic form in material culture, instead of the gradual incremental evolution often anticipated....[50]

Thus Wobst proposes that it is the dynamic communication and relationship between social networks or categories that cause revolutions in stylistic behavior to occur. Is this the case with the sudden creation of naturalistic representations of men and women in Minoan and later Mycenaean art? In order to know this with any certainty, one would need to understand more about changes in social categories or networks which would have led to changes in representation. The question then becomes, what social categories were evoked in the highly standardized representation of men and women in Aegean Bronze Age art? What clues to social networks can be found in these representations?

The first step in beginning to answer these questions is an examination of the visual evidence. The visual evidence I use is the representations from seals and sealings, the media in which the largest number of human representations can be found.[51] As discussed in the introduction, I choose to begin with an examination of the way in which bodies perform. I employ here Judith Butler's theory of performativity which states that critical social categories are created and maintained in part through the movement and appearance of the body. The social categories which I propose were created and maintained through performativity are gender, age and social status. Organized by these social categories, I examine several representations and demonstrate how bodies performed social information.

* * *

Age:
Two Aegean Bronze Age scholars have studied the manifestation of age in the representations of Minoan men and women, both using hair styles as primary indicators. The consistency of these age distinctions leads us to believe that the representation of specific age classes was an important detail in the human depiction. Interestingly, many of these age-specific hair styles are also gender specific, a topic which I shall discuss below. Let us start with women's hair styles. Ellen Davis, in an article on the representation of age in the frescoes found at the site of Akrotiri on Santorini, identifies six distinct stages of female maturity.[52] The first and youngest stage consists of a shaved head with a couple of locks growing out. The second stage is indicated by longer locks growing from a still shaved head but with new locks are shown growing in. The third state is indicated by the removal of the new locks of stage two and now with the shaved hair of the rest of the head growing in around them. The fourth stage is indicated by a full head of long hair which is wound around with a long cloth and tied in a loop at the forehead.[53] The fifth stage is illustrated by a full head of hair completely bound up in a cloth. The sixth and last stage of maturity is indicated not only by free flowing long hair but also by signs of stress, red veins, visible in the whites of the eyes.[54]

In an article of the same year,[55] Robert Koehl identifies age classes of males also based on hair styles. He proposes that the most youthful children in Minoan art are represented with completely shaved or hairless heads. The next stage of maturity is illustrated by a shaved head with only a couple of locks growing out. This is the same as Davis' first stage for girls. The next stage is a collection of the locks tied together in a top knot and the remaining hair, now growing in, combed forward like bangs. The hair style that indicated the next, fourth, stage of male maturity is long waist-length individual tresses of hair and almost without exception, a single lock combed in front of the ear. Sometimes this hair style is accompanied by a back lock. The hair style that would appear to indicate the final age stage among male representations is hair cut short and hanging freely over the back of the neck. Some examples of this hair style include one or more locks of hair growing over the forehead. Some mature men who wear this hair style also have generous facial hair.[56]

Davis' and Koehl's analysis of hair styles and age are an important tool in the present analysis. How, then, are ages distributed throughout the images of performance we are concerned with here? Women of Davis' third

---

[49] Ibid., 318 ff.
[50] Ibid., 326. This observation is an interesting parallel to that of Meyer Schapiro's quoted at the start of the chapter.
[51] A number of the seals I use in the following analysis have traditionally identified as goddesses. See Martin P. Nilsson, *The Minoan-Mycenaean Religion and its Survival in Greek Religion* (Lund: Gleerup, 1968) passim, for such discussions. I, do not wish here to engage in a discussion of the religious identity of these women. Suffice it to say, goddess or not, they are surely women.
[52] Ellen Davis, Youth and Age in the Thera Frescoes," *American Journal of Archaeology* 90 (1986) 399-406.
[53] Ibid., 399-401.
[54] Ibid., 403-4.
[55] Robert Koehl, "The Chieftain Cup and a Minoan Rite of Passage," *Journal of Hellenic Studies* 106 (1986) 99-110.
[56] Ibid., 100-103.

Figure 6: Gold ring from Knossos; after CMS II3.51. Catalogue # 24.

Figure 7: Gold ring from Anthia; after CMS V.Sup.1B.135. Catalogue # 59.

stage and men of Koehl's fourth stage are the most common and men of the fourth stage are rather common as well. In fact, details of hair style which indicate membership in age groups seem to be a consistent element in the representation of men and women who are depicted on seals, and therefore one can conclude that these details are important to performative representation. For example, a gold ring from grave one at the Isopata cemetery at Knossos (fig. 6) dating to the third palace period illustrates four dancing women whose hair style indicates that they are at Davis' third stage of maturity, a uniform short length with one or two long locks trailing behind their heads. Another gold ring from a chamber tomb at Anthia (fig. 7) dating to the third palace period illustrates two men leaping over the back of a charging bull, one of whom who, like the dancing women, has uniformly short hair and a long lock growing from it. An example of Koehl's fourth stage of maturity can be found among the young men assembled for the Grandstand Fresco at Knossos (fig. 8). Among wall paintings, this hair style can also be found on the male and female participants in the Toreador fresco also at Knossos (fig. 9) and, in relief, on the boxer rhyton from Aghia Triada. An example of Koehl's last stage of maturity can be found on an unusual seal, an amethyst amygdaloid from Grave Circle B at Mycenae (fig. 10) dating to the second palace period which illustrates the head of a middle aged man with a goatee.

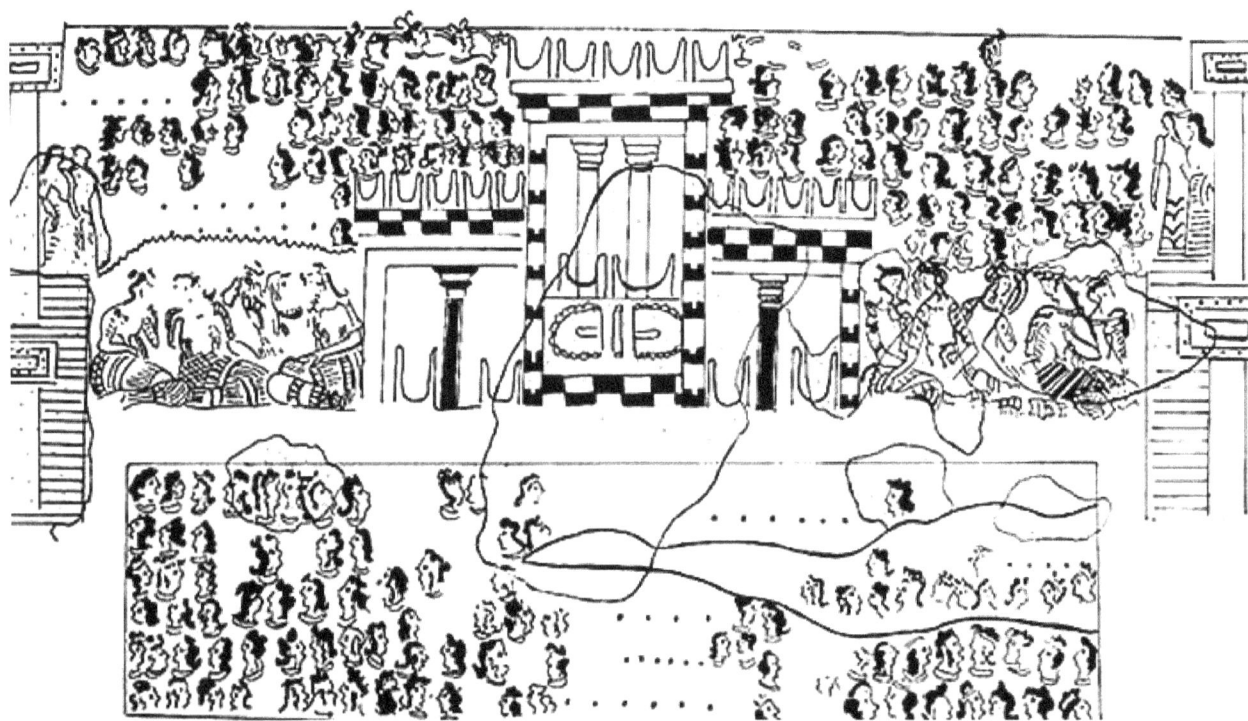

Figure 8: Knossos Grandstand fresco; after PofM III, pl. XVI. Catalogue # 71.

Figure 9: Knossos Toreador fresco; after PofM III, fig. 144. Catalogue # 89.

Gender:
As we have seen above in a discussion of various hair styles, in representations of men and women the physical attributes of gender are differentiated. We might see here a connection between social constructions of age and gender. For example, on seals which feature women, the key physical attributes of the feminine gender are large breasts and full hips, and these aspects to feminine representation are paramount, even to the exclusion of other detail, such as facial features. Two examples which illustrate groups of women dancing, a gold ring from a chamber tomb at Aidonia (fig. 11) dating to the third palace period and another gold ring, from a grave at the Isopata cemetery at Knossos (fig. 6; cat) dating to the third palace period, illustrate women with little more than stumps for heads, yet with great detail dedicated to the representation of their breasts, including even nipples on the ring from Knossos.

Representations of men, particularly in glyptic art, feature a cod piece, thus drawing attention to the penis and/or a broad muscular chest, again to the exclusion of other features. Again, two examples illustrate this point, both scenes of bull leaping. The first, a carnelian amygdaloid from a chamber tomb at Mycenae (fig. 12) dating to the third palace period, shows a man leaping over the back of a charging bull with elegant detail given to the man and bull's musculature (here, interestingly, even the penis of the bull is quite prominent) yet the face of the leaper is obscure. Similarly, an agate lentoid from the House of the Idols at Mycenae (fig. 13) dating to the third palace period illustrates the elegantly slim yet strong body of the leaper but shows nothing of his head and face. These male and female bodies seem to be full and youthful, at the peak of physical development.

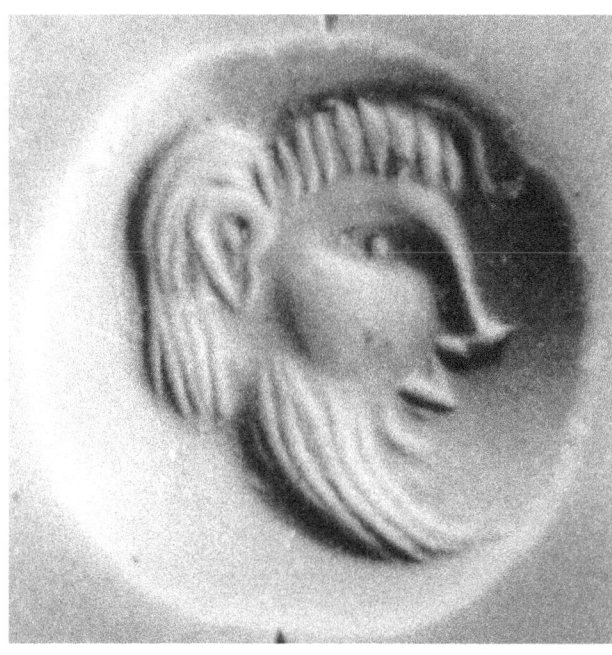

Figure 10: Amethyst amygdaloid from Mycenae, after CMS I.5. Catalogue # 1.

Figure 11: Gold ring from Aidonia; after CMS V.Sup.IB.114. Catalogue # 57.

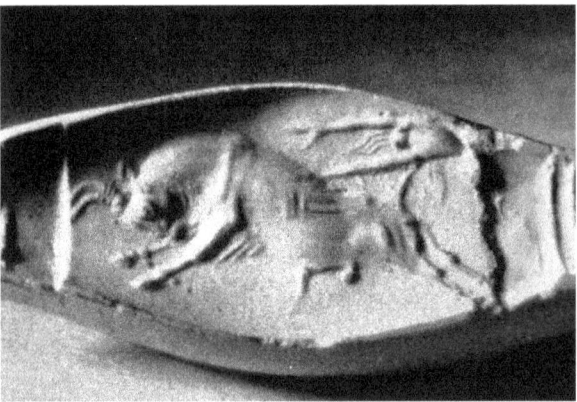

Figure 12: Carnelian amygdaloid from Mycenae; after CMS I.152. Catalogue # 11.

Figure 13: Agate lentoid from Mycenae; after CMS V2.597. Catalogue # 61.

Aside from these physical elements I argue that there are aspects to the comportment of men's and women's bodies which are also highly gendered. They are chiefly a swaying comportment for females and a rigid stance for males. By a swaying of the female body I mean an 'S' curve in profile created by the outward thrust of breasts and hips. Two seals illustrate this well. First, a sardonyx amygdaloid from a beehive tomb at Vaphio (fig. 14) dating to the second palace period illustrates a woman alone in an exaggerating swaying stance, seemingly holding a rod above her head. Another famous stone, a steatite lentoid from the Court of the Stone Spout at Knossos (fig. 1), illustrates a lone female in the 'S' curve stance, holding a portion of textile and a double axe. The rigid stance of men, legs locked and strong, hands at the waist and head up, is illustrated perfectly in on an agate lentoid from a chamber tomb at the Panagia cemetery at Mycenae (fig. 2) dating to the third palace period. A variation of this stance (fig. 15) is found on an impression from Aghia Triada dating to the second palace period. Here the man stands rigidly behind a lion with his head thrown back, one arm behind and one in front, his lean muscular torso turned toward the viewer.

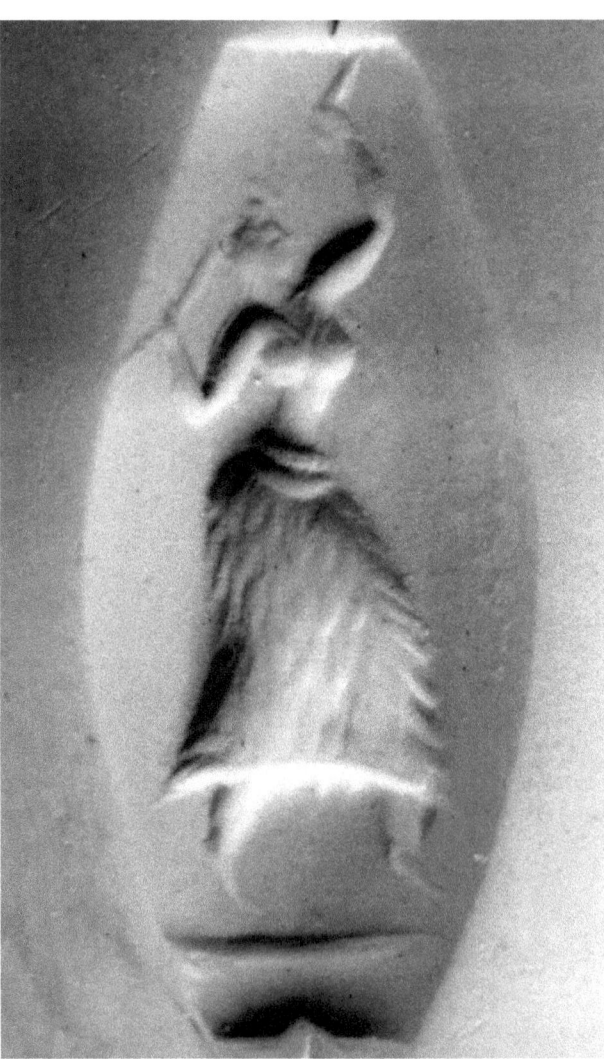

Figure 14: Sardonyx amygdaloid from Vaphio; after CMS I.226. Catalogue # 17.

Indeed, it is almost impossible to mistake a male for a female gendered body in Aegean Bronze Age art because of the very rigid means by which gender is performed. I believe that the images discussed above cannot help but bring to mind Butler's concept of performative gender. In the second palace period artists now illustrate not stick figure people but those whose bodies perform their gender in the subtle sense of the performative, through comportment, stance and gesture. A critical component of this performance is the presentation of voluptuous young bodies. Because of this, connotations of sex, the sexual nature of these performances, are implicit. We must then ask, what is the relationship between the representation of gender and sexuality in these images?

Figure 15: Seal impression from Aghia Triada; after CMS II6.36. Catalogue # 34.

Indeed, it is compelling to note that the way in which the body is posed in many different performances serves to emphasize secondary sexual characteristics. Secondary sexual characteristics are the many external characteristics that are not directly involved in human sexual reproduction (genitalia) but serve to distinguish males and females. These secondary characteristics develop along with primary, at the time of puberty when estrogen production in women and testosterone production in males increases. In females, estrogen induces the growth of adipose tissue under the skin in the region of the mammary glands, thighs and buttocks which help to create the classic "curvy" feminine silhouette. In males, testosterone induces the growth of facial hair and the broadening of the chest cavity. Interestingly, the lack of estrogen in males slows the triggering of epiphyseal (bone) plate closure which allows males to grow into larger people than women.[57]

The emphasis on secondary sexual characteristics in both feminine and masculine bodies is, in fact, as erotic as human representation gets in the Bronze Age Aegean; Minoan and Mycenaean culture is unique in its lack of sexually explicit representation of any sort. We can only speculate as to why this is the case. What does seem clear, however, is that these particular details of human representation go the greatest distance in implying sexual activity and, in turn, sexuality. Turning to our images, note that men's bodies are held erect, emphasizing the broadness of the chest and narrow waist. Women's arms are held back to thrust the breasts forward. Women often stand in a swaying posture which accentuates the hips and breasts. Men, for instance, lunge forward in battle with one muscular leg fully extended back and one arm raised behind the head, opening the whole body for view. I argue that the poses that males and females so consistently strike, in some subtle way, imply sexuality in as far as it is concerned with sexual activity. As these poses and the secondary sexual characteristics which they emphasize serve to differentiate gender, thus male and female sexuality helps to construct gender identity.[58]

Social Status:

As Ortner and Whitehead have pointed out, gender systems and prestige systems go hand in hand.[59] In other words, in a society where there is gender differentiation or hierarchy, so there is social differentiation or hierarchy. Indeed, among the representations of men and women in the Late Bronze Age glyptic, I have determined that social differentiation or a class system is in part illustrated through the representation of costume and other accoutrements.[60] Specifically, in Late Bronze Age art, men and women are found wearing highly elaborate costumes which are in stark contrast to the entirely unclothed, stick-like representations of humans

---

[57] Ann Stalheim-Smith and Greg Fitch, *Understanding Human Anatomy and Physiology* (Mineapolis/St. Paul: West Publishing, 1993) 973-4. Lauralee Sherwood, *Human Physiology: From Cells to Systems*. (Belmont: Wadsworth Publishing Company, 1997) 702.
[58] Michelle Marcus "Sex and the Politics of Female Adornment in Pre-Achaemenid Iran (1000-800 BCE)," and Gay Robins, "Dress, Undress, and the Representation of Fertility and Potency in New Kingdom Egyptian Art both in N. Kampen ed. *Sexuality in Ancient Art* (New York: Cambridge University Press, 1996) discuss how the representations of sexualized bodies help to construct ideas about sexual identification and behavior in culture. See discussion in chapter five for a proposal of the "target" audience or these sexualized performances.
[59] Sherry B. Ortner and Harriet Whitehead, "Accounting for Sexual Meanings." In S. Ortner and H. Whitehead eds., *Sexual Meanings: The Cultural Construction of Gender and Sexuality*. (New York: Cambridge University Press, 1981) 16-17.
[60] Scholars have used different kinds of evidence to determine social differentiation. For instance, Robert Laffineur, "Iconography as Evidence of Social and Political Status in Mycenaean Greece" *Ikion, Aegeaeum* 8, (1992) 105-112. Or I. Kilian-Dirlmeier, "Beobachtungen zu den Schachtgräbern von Mykenai und zu den Schmuchbeigaben mykenischer Männergräber. Untersuchungen zur Sozialstruktur in spätthelladischer Zeit," *Jahrbuch des R misch-germanischen Zentralmuseums Mainz* 33 (1986) 159-168.

found in art at the end of the first palace period. The assumption I am making here is that the sorts of elaborate costumes which men and women wear on seals are luxury items which would be reserved for the wealthier individuals. Simpler costumes which are in great contrast to the elaborate ones of the seals and which might indicate class difference can be found in the miniature fresco in room 5 of the West House at Akrotiri on the island of Thera (fig 16).[61]

Figure 16: Miniature fresco, West House, Thera; after Doumas (1992) pl. 38. Catalogue # 79.

Above Town II, a group of shepherds tend to their flock wearing very simple dark shaggy, smock-like garments which hang loose around their bodies. These shepherds are in stark contrast to other groups of men in the painting who, for instance, wear short skirts and march together in military formation carrying shields and spears in the Arrival Town, or others who are assembled facing each other in the Assembly on the Hill scene where several men wear long white broad bordered garments or short skirts also white. Although the exact social position of all these men are unclear, dress in addition to their activities seems to differentiate them, and this is likely to have meaning with regard to social rank.

There seems to be less differentiation in women's garments as represented in Late Bronze Age art in general, and on the seals almost none at all. That is, women are almost always represented wearing an elaborate flounced skirt and short jacket. The fact that there is so little variation in women's costume makes using this kind of evidence for class distinction difficult. However, there is other evidence to support the premise that these costumes indicate a higher social rank.

---

[61] Christos Doumas, *The Wall-Paintings of Thera* (Athens: The Thera Foundation, 1992) plate 29.

Women's costumes, especially the skirt, include several different patterns, in bands, woven into the cloth and elaborate edging sewn into the short jackets. Details of this ensemble are again found among the paintings from Akrotiri on Thera.[62] In Xeste 3 (fig. 17), the three "adorants" are shown approaching a structure; all of whom are dressed in garments flounced in the same way as those found in glyptic representations.

Figure 17: Three "adorants", Xeste 3, Thera; after Doumas (1992) pl. 100. Catalogue # 98.

The costume of the last female, on the far right, is particularly elaborate; beneath the diaphanous robe which she holds wrapped around herself, the girl wears a flounced skirt consisting of over 15 different bands of patterns. Her short jacket is primarily white but is bordered with more bands of woven cloth. The labor cost of this sort of weaving was not appreciated until the recent study of Aegean textiles by Elisabeth Barber. In her groundbreaking book, *Prehistoric Textiles*[63] Barber, an accomplished weaver herself, explores the complexity of the textile patterning and weaving practiced during the Aegean Bronze Age, its artistic representation and evidence in Linear B tablets. This last examination is interesting here. Of the Linear B archives Barber points out,

> We clearly have reference to several kinds of cloth - even if we aren't sure what they are - and to various grades or degrees of costliness suitable for different estates: "kingly," "for followers"(?), "for guests"(?) (KN Lc525, LD571, LD573; Ventris and Chadwick 1973, 315-18; Compare Driessen 1984, 53-56), as well as for normal uses. Bands and/or edging play an important role in the textiles, since we have as many as four different words that seem to refer to them *onukh-*, *odak-*, *termi-*, and *ampuk-*.[64]

---

[62] The paintings of the women at Akrotiri are somewhat unique however they are the best source of visual information about the fabric of the flounced garments the vast majority of Aegean Bonze Age women wear.

[63] Elizabeth Barber, *Prehistoric Textiles: The Development of Cloth in the Neolithic and Bronze Ages with Special Reference to the Aegean* (Princeton University Press, 1991).

[64] Ibid, 312.

What Barber's research uncovers is that among Aegean garments there was a hierarchy of value, and she draws the conclusion in her study that the types of garments illustrated at Thera and elsewhere are the most elaborate and therefore higher status variety than, for instance, the people in the shaggy garments.

Last, the obvious impracticality of women's garments could be another piece of evidence which may indicate differentiation in social status. Although practicality is also an historically specific idea and thus difficult to apply to the past, the discomfort and likely partial immobility experienced when wearing such garments as women wear seems obvious. These could not have been clothing for women who were, for instance, manual laborers. Admittedly, the representations of these garments are just that, representations, and not photographically accurate visual facts. At the same time, it is difficult to believe that these representations are totally fictional but are likely based on some reality. That reality is one of elite dress. What appears to be an exception to this elite dress is worth noting. Found in the miniature fresco at Thera in the West House, north wall, above the shipwreck scene, at least one, possibly two women, both of whom wear a flounced skirt and open jacket, proceed carrying two handled jugs on their heads.[65] This would seem to be an "every day" or at least utilitarian activity and thus contrary to what I have concluded above. If this is indeed a utilitarian activity, then it is the only example featuring women so dressed. I believe, however, that the vignettes features on the north wall of room five are not of the every day variety. Among these vignettes are elaborately dressed men meeting on top of a hill, a group of soldiers with spears drawn marching in formation, and a ship at the moment of its destruction, possibly run aground on the shore, its crew spilling out into the sea. Of each of these moments, the topic is not the everyday but rather the extraordinary. In the midst of them we find the two women with the jars on their head. Within the context of the scene painted on the north wall of room five, I interpret these women as engaged in an activity as extraordinary as the others represented around them.

As mentioned above, flounced skirts and decorated jackets like the Theran examples are repeatedly found worn by women on seals and sealings. For instance, a particularly readable representation of these highly elaborate garments is found on a gold ring from the Treasury Acropolis at Mycenae (fig. 18) dating to the second palace period. This ring illustrates what appears to be a presentation scene involving two women approaching another seated beneath a tree. Here we see all three women dressed in elaborate skirts and jackets the representations of which are so detailed that differences in pattern are obvious between the three ensembles.

Figure 18: Gold ring from Mycenae; after CMS I.17. Catalogue # 3.

Similarly, where details survive we can observe that men's costumes are elaborately woven, albeit briefer than women's, and the intricacy of their armor is sometimes extensive. Likely the best example from glyptic art of the representation of men's costumes and armor is a gold ring from Grave Circle A at Mycenae (fig. 19), also dating to the second palace period, which illustrates four men in the melee of battle. The details of the men's short garments are visible, down to the tassel which falls from the legs of each garment. Details of their armor are exceptional as well, including the individual tusk of the two boar's tusk helmets which two of the men wear, and the embossed decoration on one man's shield. This armor, no doubt, given the intrinsic value of the metal and ivory, were high status items. These and the elaborate costumes of men and women are all differentiated and indicate a differentiation in social status.

* * *

By expanding Butler's concept of performativity, the identification of three social categories, gender, age and social status, as performed by the bodies of late Bronze Age men and women is possible. As we have seen, gender, age and social status constitute a subtle variety of performance, played out in stance, gesture, dress and corporal detail. Yet, it does not take a trained eye to see that these performative bodies are very often engaged in various types of action which is not so subtle, such as bull leaping, presentation scenes, dancing, acrobatics, etc., what I have described as performed acts in the previous chapter. In the following I gather these repeated performed acts found on seals and sealings and I divided them by chronological period, provenience and gender in order to begin to discuss their meanings.[66]

---

[65] Ibid., Doumas, *The Wall-Paintings of Thera*, pl. 27-9.

[66] See Appendix A for a listing of all performed acts found in seals and sealings.

Figure 19: Gold ring from Mycenae; after CMS I.16. Catalogue # 2.

Beginning in the 2nd palace period on Crete, performances in which exclusively women are represented I break down into the following groups: women in groups of two or three in identical poses dancing, women carrying an object or animal, women occupied with plants, scenes of a formal presentation where a women is seated receiving an object, other women or an animal, and women riding on boats. Performances in which men are typically found on Crete during this period are more numerous than those featuring females. These are bull leaping, hand-to-hand combat with either other men or animals, walking or running together in pairs, possibly in procession, standing heraldically with animals, mostly lions, interacting with other males, including the older bearded male, carrying objects such as textiles and double axes in a seemingly procession-like circumstance, and driving a chariot.

From the mainland sites during the second palace period we find fewer representations of men and women across the board. Beginning with female performances we find seated representations with an animal, a frontal woman with arms raised and out holding an animal at either side, referred to as the "mistress of the animals," and presentation style scenes. Mainland performances that feature males in this period are animal combat, yet hand-to-hand combat, chariot scenes and heraldic scenes with animals are also found and are quite similar to the Cretan repertoire.

In the following third palace period on Crete the types of performances in which only women are found are similar to those from the proceeding second palace period. We find women again dancing in pairs, presentation scenes, and women occupied with plants and other women. New to the Cretan repertoire is the "mistress of the animal" and entirely new to this type are examples in which a double horned crown sits atop the head of the "mistress" out from the middle of which stands a double axe. Somewhat expanded during this period are male performances. Animal combat scenes, bull leaping and heraldic depictions with animals, and hand-to-hand combat are all similar to the proceeding 2nd palace period, but added to this repertoire we find a male counter-part to the mistress of the animals scene, a man standing frontally with both arms out and holding an animal in each hand. There are also representations of men in line wearing battle armor and holding a shield, acrobatics and, quite striking, a frontal face either surrounded by animals or atop a frontal bull's head, between its horns.

Strikingly limited is the range of performances involving women from the third palace period on the mainland. Essentially, all representations of females can be broken down into two types, groups of either two or three dancing before architecture (some examples of which have foliage growing from it) and the "mistress of the animals." Two examples of this latter type feature the double horned crown with the double axe. Male performance in the third palace period on the mainland repeats the second palace period scenes: animal combat, hand-to-hand human combat, bull leaping, heraldic scenes with an animal and chariot scenes. But, new is a "master" of the animals as we saw among the Cretan seals, as well as acrobatics and a scene in which a man confronts architecture in a landscape with a goat.

The above listing serves not only to illustrate the range of performed acts which were represented on seals and sealings but also shows how they passed in and out of popularity between Crete and the Mainland during the second and third palace periods. The acts themselves are highly regularized and, judging by their frequency in the glyptic corpus, enjoyed a certain popularity.[67] Furthermore, they are rigidly divided down gender lines. That is, men and women do not trade roles in these performances, with the exception of bull leaping and the mistress/master of the animals. However, these are an unusual case, which I shall discuss in the next chapter. Nonetheless, among the performed acts listed above, bull leaping and dancing are the most enduring both on the Mainland and Crete and during both the first and second palace periods. One cannot help but wonder about the existence of grander, more complex performance, with an audience and staging. Interestingly, there is evidence for more elaborate performance of this type in the medium of wall painting, although its relationship to the representations on seals has yet to be fully examined. In the following, I look at evidence for performance which includes an audience and then turn back to the performance of acts to determine the relationship between the two.

* * *

The most persuasive evidence for performance in the Aegean Bronze Age comes from wall paintings, and thus it is with a brief discussion of these works that I begin. Most compelling are three examples: The Sacred Grove and Dance, Grandstand frescoes and bull leaping frescos, all from Knossos. In the following, I shall discuss in some detail these three frescoes in order to determine some of the more salient characteristics of the representation of performance.

---

[67] There are several more examples of each type of act among unprovenienced seals. I have omitted these as they lack contextual data.

The Sacred Grove and Dance fresco (fig. 20),[68] exists as one of most compelling pieces of evidence for performance in the Aegean Bronze Age. In the foreground at least fourteen women are pictured all wearing identical dress, the familiar flounced skirt and short open jacket, and gesturing in various directions. They are set against a neutral blue background and separated from the rest of the action of the painting by a thick border broken into individual cells, likely depicting paving or a low wall. On the opposite side of this border, in the background of the painting, are two large groups of people, men and women separated; in the middle of the field are three large trees, the "grove" from which the wall painting derives its name. The two discrete groups are differentiated by the predominant color of their skin, women white, men brown.[69] The group of women, which is irregularly shaped, is pictured within the group of men, each seated and wearing identical clothes, similar again to the women before them. The group of men consists also of identically represented individuals, each wearing a white belt and loin cloth and bright necklace around his neck. At the very top of the field is the horizon of the scene which is defined by the crowns of several men's heads and thrust above them, every so often, a brown arm and open hand, with a bright bracelet around the wrist.

Several details of this work lead one to believe it is a representation of a performance given by the women in the foreground and watched by two groups of spectators. The women in the foreground, the performers, are separated from the rest of the scene not only against the contrasting background but by the paving stones or low wall. They are each painted quite deliberately, as if the detail of their action is important. They hold their arms out from their bodies and at least one has her head thrown back. The two groups of men and women behind the paving stones are depicted in such a repetitive schematic fashion that they are automatically taken in visually as homogenous groups and not scrutinized in the same way the women in the foreground are. In both groups, almost all of the faces are turned to the left, as if their attention is focused together. Last as evidence of these images representing performance is some archaeological intrigue; two years after the discovery of these frescoes, Evans excavated a space, which he called the Theatral Area, which is nearly identical to the one depicted.[70] This space consisted of two sets of low wide steps in front of which are paving stones in the same configuration as those illustrated in the painting.

Discovered in the same context as the Sacred Grove and Dance fresco was the Grandstand fresco.[71] The Grandstand fresco is a long narrow scene, as it is preserved, set within an architectural framework and can be divided into four minor and one major components. Four pairs of columns are evenly spaced across the fresco dividing the space almost rhythmically; between each pair a handful of women stand. A large tripartite structure dominates the center of the fresco and functions as the focal point in the highly symmetrical composition. It consists of a large opening in the center, supported by two columns and flanked by two smaller openings each of which has a column in the center flanked by pairs of horns. This whole structure is topped by a row of horns and at the middle of its base is a Minoan triglyph. To either side of the structure moving out in both directions is a row of women, gathered in seated or standing groups, each wearing similar dress and turned toward one another, as if in conversation. Behind the row of women in a smaller scale is a great crowd of men which, like the Sacred Grove and Dance fresco, is differentiated from the white group of women by its brown color. There are many more men than women pictured and they too are all similarly clothed. In front of the row of women is pictured a series of steps which lead down to an open space, as it is preserved. In the middle of this space and directly in front of the tripartite structure another space is set apart with a wide rectangular white band in which there are two more smaller separate groups of men and women, again differentiated by their skin color. As with the group above them, the men far outnumber the women here and they seem to look at one another. Possibly, this group of people set apart is the focal point of the audience. Sadly, the performance is not preserved.

Although the performance in the Grandstand fresco is not clear, it is tempting to identify the wall painting as the illustration of a performance because the audience in the grandstand is so similar to the one found in the Sacred Grove and Dance fresco where a performance indeed seems to be taking place. Similarities include large homogenous groups of men and women, divided by gender and separated from an open space by architecture. Several scholars have argued, based on the similarity of architectural remains and the tripartite structure, that the Grandstand fresco depicts the west facade of the central court at Knossos.[72] If this is true, then both paintings maintain a special relationship to Knossos. Shared also by these two paintings is their important archaeological provenance. They both were found fallen on the late basement floor of a room at the north end of the great central court. Judging by similar stratigraphy at the palace, it is safe to assume that the paintings had fallen

---

[68] See Arthur Evans, "Knossos 1899" *Annual of the British School at Athens* 47-48 (1899-1900), 1-123.for description of the find and *PofM* vol. III 66ff for full discussion. This wall painting and the Grandstand fresco which I next discuss were heavily restored after their discovery. My descriptions and analysis of these wall paintings take into account these restorations as little as possible as they are little more than the educated guess of Evans and deJong, his primary artists/restorer.

[69] This convention of white for females and brown for males is identical to the Egyptian convention. See S. Immerwahr, Aegean Painting in the Bronze Age (College Park: Pennsylvania State University Press, 1990) 53 and E. Davis, "Youth and Age in the Thera Frescos", American Journal of Archaeology 90 (1986) 401 for discussion of the diffusion of this convention. See my discussion of this in chapter two.

[70] See Arthur Evans, "Knossos 1901" *Annual of the British School at Athens* 9-10 (1902-1903) 109-110 for the find of the "Stepped Area" later called the "Theatral Area."

[71] Ibid Evans, "Knossos 1899" 10, 46ff. for the description of the original find and *PofM* vol. III, 19f. for a full description.

[72] *PofM* II. 2, 796-810; J. Graham, *The Palaces of Crete* (Princeton: Princeton University Press,1987) 140-141.

from an upper floor, presumably the same level as the central court and thus the frescos may indeed be associated with vast public spaces in the palace, similar to those painted on them.

A third miniature style painting is important to include in the discussion here as it forms, compositionally, a bridge between the Sacred Grove and Dance and Grandstand frescoes discussed above. Found in the lower stratum of cists in the thirteenth magazine were several pieces of a wall painting which contained together three components, an architectural facade, bull leaping and groups of spectators.[73] The fragments which illustrate a facade (fig.21 and fig 22) include several palatial details such as columns, horns of consecration, pillars and ashlar masonry, a combination not unlike the facade found in the Grandstand fresco. The bull leaping portion of the remains is quite small (fig. 23), including only a portion of the back profile and neck of a dark bull, but including the tips of four long curly locks of a leaper suspended over it. Lastly, the portions of the painting which includes the audience (fig. 24) are also small but clearly shows a group of young men. Looking nearly identical to the illustrations of groups of men in the Sacred Grove and Dance and Grandstand frescoes, these are all dark skinned and curly haired men, facing one direction, all painted together in one dark patch, with only the details of their hair and one bright white eye differentiating one from another. Evans offers an interpretation of the fragments as the illustration of a bull leaping show, which it surely is. It exists as a partner with the Sacred Grove and Dance and Grandstand fresco in the illustration of more elaborate performances which included an audience and which were staged in an architectural setting.

* * *

In order to define more clearly what is meant by a representation of performance as opposed to a performance itself, let me outline the important constituent characteristics of scenes of performance drawn from the paintings discussed above. Obviously the most elementary detail of any representation of performance is the action or event for which the audience has gathered. Associated with the performance itself, and also a defining element to representations of performance, is the existence of the "action" as the focal point in the image. By a focus on the performance, I mean not only within the composition of the scene, with the audience watching, but as it has been constructed by the artist such that the viewer's eye is drawn to the performance. This effect is accomplished in at least two different ways in the frescoes described above. Aside from setting the performance apart with architectural elements, the painter(s) of the scenes has made more elaborate and detailed the visual description of the dancers in the Sacred Grove and Dance fresco. Furthermore, the placement of the performance in both the Sacred Grove and Dance and Grandstand frescoes at the central foreground of the scene focuses the viewers attention first and always leads back to it. It is likely that the bull leaping show was similarly composed.

Another element which defines these images as performance is the inclusion of an audience. As has been noted above, the audience is composed of both females and males, grouped by gender in discrete areas. Furthermore, they are separated from the "action" with space. Lastly, the limits of the audience are marked by an architectural delineation in two of these paintings, the Sacred Grove and Dance and Grandstand frescos. In the illustration of the bull leaping show, this is unfortunately unclear but it is not ruled out by any of the fragments of the fresco uncovered. In sum, the composition is important and helps define the representation of performance. A prominent architectural framework is included in the composition of all three frescoes, and thus is presumably an important element in the representation of performance. Interestingly, the architectural frameworks indicate a variety of different venues, outside among vegetation in the Sacred Grove and Dance, or near large architectural facades in the Grandstand and bull leaping show frescoes.

* * *

As the above has illustrated, visual evidence for some sort of performance and audience around architecture at Knossos is clear; less clear is the exact nature of the performances, beyond the act of dancing and bull leaping. Many anthropologists who study performance do so through the lens of ritual. Ritual is practical action, something which is acted out in order to attain a desired result. To anthropologists, the efficacy of ritual and the entertainment of performance are not opposed to each other but rather form the poles of a continuum. Although some performances are staged to serve a specific purpose, heal or transform, others are more concerned with amusement. That performance as ritual has social significance and holds the attention of the audience is not difficult to understand. That performance as theatre entertains yet also holds social significance is more subtle. To understand the social dimensions of performance, an appreciation of the phenomenon of acting or taking on an identity and the textual nature of performance itself is needed.

---

[73] Arthur Evans, "Knossos 1902" *Annual of the British School at Athens* 11-12 (1903-1904) 40f; *PofM* vol I, 422ff, figs, 319, 321, 343, 384, and 385. There is no reconstruction drawing for this fresco.

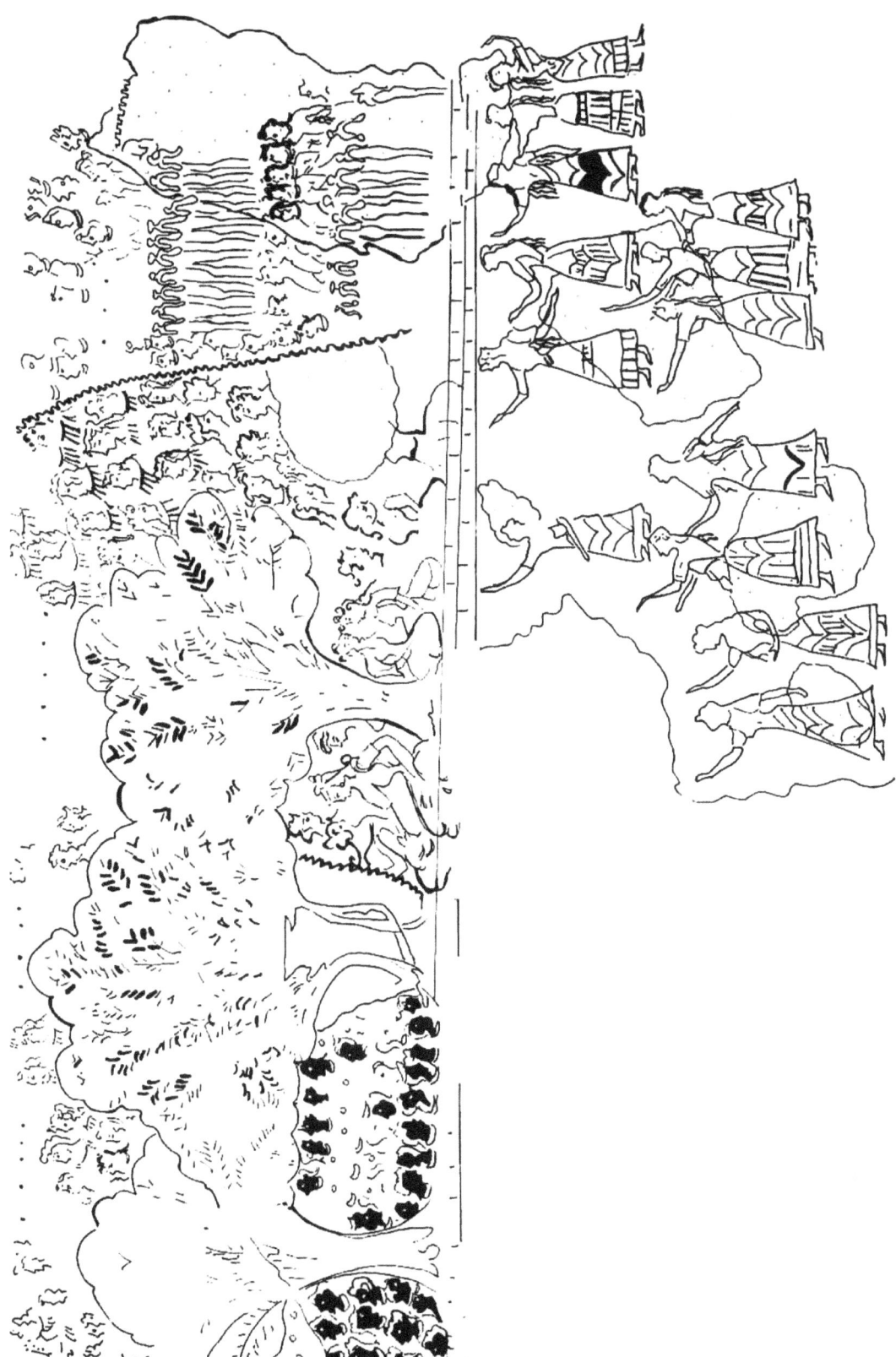

Figure 20: Sacred Grove and Dance fresco from Knossos; after PofM III, pl. XVIII. Catalogue # 95.

Figure 21: Knossos miniature bull leaping fresco; after PofM III, fig. 443. Catalogue # 85.

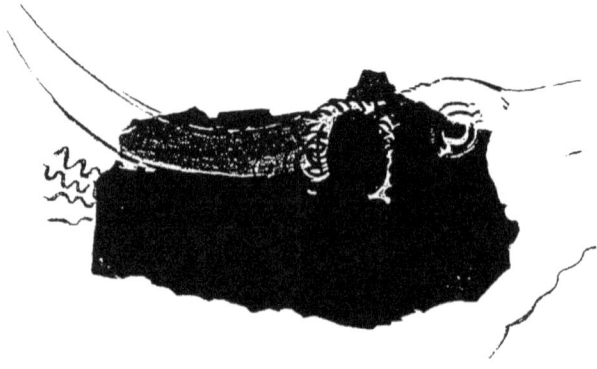

Figure 23: Knossos miniature bull leaping fresco; after PofM I, fig. 385. Catalogue # 85.

Figure 24: Knossos miniature bull leaping fresco; after PofM III, fig. 15B. Catalogue # 85.

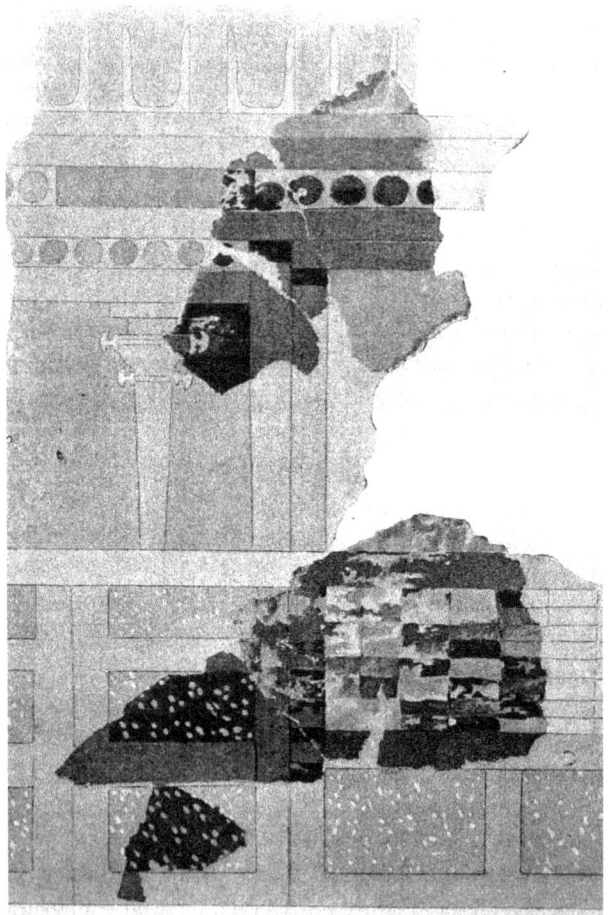

Figure 22: Knossos miniature bull leaping fresco; after PofM III, fig. 446. Catalogue # 85.

Fundamental to performance is the repeated play of the actor, putting aside one identity and taking on another. This conceit is understood by the audience and, in fact, is key to its social participation in the drama, as the audience imagines itself in the part of the characters.[74] As the members of the audience identify as characters, as the actors do, the drama seems real to their lives and allows an active reflection upon the text of the performance to take place. This reflection upon the text of the performance is the other key element to performance as theatre. Text in this circumstance can mean literally the spoken expression of the written text of a performance or simply the story of events performed. However, the performance is unstable as any literary text, something repeatedly and differently visited, translated and interpreted. The reflection by the audience, which takes place because of its identification with the actors, is not a simple mirror-like viewing but a phenomenon by which the audience sees itself in the text of play and reinterprets it in their own historically and socially specific image. Given this, no two performances, even when based upon the same script or sequence of events or movements, are exactly the same because audiences and their circumstances and thus their interpretations change.

---

[74] Richard Schechner, *Performance Theory* (New York, Routledge, 1988) 175-179; 193-206.

Therefore, the meanings of performances, again, despite the similarity of their form, are never static but ever shifting.

The concept of audience reflection on performance as a socially creative act is central to Victor Turner's theory of social drama. Turner's social drama recasts our understanding of theatrical performance into something more necessarily embedded in social practice and, thus, more significant. Far more than merely entertainment, it fulfills the necessary purpose of conscious constructive reflection and, in some cases, conflict resolution in society. Issues are presented, mitigated and resolved in performance, within the flow of social process; a socially sanctioned and approved program is determined and maintained. In this way Turner's view that the creation and maintenance of social values, precepts and rules are performed in theatre, I believe, brings much to Judith Butler's concept of the performative. Both social drama and performativity create and negotiate, by means of the active reflection of society, basic social principles.

If, then, we are to take the wall paintings of the Sacred Grove and Dance, the Grandstand fresco and the miniature bull leaping fresco from Knossos as evidence for social drama one issue remains to be discussed: that of representation. That is, to what extent are these wall paintings quasi-illustrations of an event that occurred at the palace and to what extent are they merely representations. Illustration, by definition, implies a higher level of realism and detail and, indeed, the existence of the thing being illustrated. Representation, however, is not held to this standard but instead had an almost symbolic quality and can take for its topic, for instance, myth or some other unobservable event. Which, then, is it in the case of these three wall paintings at Knossos? This, of course, cannot be known yet it is necessary to get closer to an answer to this question if these paintings are to be useful in better understanding performance in the Aegean Bronze Age. What can be said with some confidence is the activities represented in these wall paintings are performative and there is archaeological evidence to lead one to believe that these activities could have taken place at Knossos and palaces like it. Furthermore, it is no doubt the safest option to assume that these images are representations. To assume otherwise, that they are illustrations, could potentially lead to leaning too heavily on details of the images which might be no more than decorative or stylistic, the stuff of representation.

So, if indeed, they are social dramas which are represented in The Sacred Grove and Dance and Grandstand frescoes, what relationship do these images have to similar images in other media? In glyptic data, as mentioned above, there are a number of repeated scenes of performed acts such as bull leaping or dancing which may very well be illustrating performances the likes of which are illustrated in the two frescoes. If these images on seals are the same as the social dramas, they would also communicate some sort of social information and thus deserve special study. However, before this is begun, the specific relationship between these representations of performed acts and the larger illustrations of social drama and, indeed, the social drama themselves, needs to be explored. This is important for two reasons. First, the more explicit the connection between the relatively few full illustrations of social drama and the many illustrations of performed acts is, the more sure the connection can be between social action which is known to be at play in social drama and more simple performed acts. Second, the nature of this connection, which I shall argue is basically semiotic, offers a compelling paradigm for the way in which I think images of performed acts ultimately worked. Here I begin with Meyer Schapiro's ideas of semiotics as an entrée into the way in which I believe these images functioned in reference to each other.

At the beginning of Meyer Schapiro's important article "Some Problems in the Semiotics of Visual Art: Field and Vehicle in Image-Signs,"[75] he discusses the difference between art which is unbound by frames, such as found in stone-age caves, and art which is created to be bound by a frame. The frame, be it the constraints of 8.5x11 inch paper, gilt wood or the edges of a carnelian stone, he offers, "belongs to the space of the observer," and affects, through its properties, the sense of the image within it. These properties, akin to optical allusion, mostly have to do with the sense of space created by framing the subject so that it is at the top or bottom, broad or narrow area, etc. in the picture field. This is sometimes done also by intercepting objects in the field with the frame to give the sense that the images extend under and beyond the frame, like a picture out of a larger scene This phenomenon of cryptesthesia, as Schapiro calls it, is also at work when framing figures who are in motion. By putting figures in profile, capturing a moment of their moving in a certain direction, they are given not only a sense of directedness, but a sense of capturing a moment in motion in that direction. These aspects of framing a piece of art, Schapiro offers, stem from the desire to create image-signs, symbols which stand for larger images and concepts which, as the quote at the start of this chapter suggests, he guesses began in remote antiquity. What is important for us here is how Schapiro has identified the framing of a smaller scene from a larger image, imagined or real, as part of conscious image-sign making. Framing is used as a kind of an index, or means by which the viewer is helped to apprehend the point or focus of the work, the image-sign.

In a more recent treatment of semiotics and the visual, Mieke Bal and Norman Bryson also consider the index.[76] Their use of the sign relies most heavily upon Charles

---

[75] Meyer Schapiro, "On Some Problems in the Semiotics of Visual Art: Field and Vehicle in Image-Signs," *Semiotica* 1:3 (1969) 224.
[76] Mieke Bal and Norman Bryson, " Semiotics and Art History," *Art Bulletin* 75 (1991).174-208.

Sanders Peirce's interpretation of it, especially within his trichotomy of icon, index and symbol. It is worth pausing to discuss Peirce's trichotomy because of the centrality of this idea to Bal and Bryson's article. Named by Peirce the second trichotomy, the triad of icon, index and symbol can be described as the following. The sign represents its object because of its character or form, for example a diagram or map which stands for a physical space in the world. An index represents its object as it bears a causal relation to it; for example, mercury rises inside a thermometer when the temperature rises because it is dynamically connected with its object, heat, and serves as an index to it. Symbols represent objects by virtue of a rule or convention requiring that certain signs will always stand for certain things. Language is the classic example of Peirce's symbol, in this case; "dog" in English stands for the four legged beast who says bow-wow.[77] What distinguishes the index, of interest to us here, from the other parts of the semiotic process is that it is dependent upon the existence of the object.

What is furthermore of interest to us here, and what Bal and Bryson as art historians are interested in as well, are the different modes of the index. For, indeed, a greater understanding of semiotic phenomenon in the visual field ultimately leads to more complex interpretations of images. Bal and Bryson list several different categories of indexical signs such as the gaze, pointing elements and the stylistic "hand" of the artists and conclude that "the notion of the index suggests that we do not only account for images in terms of their provenance and making, but also of their functioning in relation to the viewer, their structure of address."[78] So, if Schapiro's frame is an indexical sign addressed to the viewer, its object can be seen as the remainder of the image which has escaped from the frame.

What I suggest here is that the representations of performed acts on seals functioned as an index to social drama and its illustration, the object of the semiotic system. More specifically, the way in which one element of the larger moment or illustration of social drama is taken as subject in these performed acts (typically the most dynamic), indeed, the manner in which the frame has been drawn, to indicate mid-movement and imply a scene stripped away, functions as an indexical sign. The object of this sign is social drama, which as we have discussed above, bears various social meanings.

* * *

As discussed in the introduction, the images which I take as the subject of in this book have previously been studied by iconographers. I propose to approach these images as performed acts, which is useful for two reasons. First, it moves interpretive frameworks for these objects away from iconography which has become an increasingly dead-end approach. By instead approaching these representations as bearing a relationship to performance, different questions, more associated with known social complexes, can be asked. Second, this approach is one which will address the question of the repetition of a number of scenes. Just as the theoretical paradigm of performativity was useful in looking at the consistent bodies of men and women, I suggest that theoretical paradigms of performance, which stress repetition, are useful in thinking about repeated scenes. The result, then, of looking at these scenes as performances takes them out of the realm of iconography and glyptic studies and puts them into the study of Aegean Bronze Age culture. They become sources of social information.

I have chosen dancing and bull leaping as two performances on which to concentrate for the duration of the work. I do this for a number of reasons. First, bull leaping and dancing, among the five performances which were especially popular, are the two which are perhaps the most understandable to us today as performances. Although popular repeated performances can certainly be classified as social drama, only bull leaping and dancing are activities which are not only intrinsically dramatic but also something which can be physically located in space. However, aside from the comfort of labeling dancing and bull leaping as performance because they seem similar to contemporary dramatic action, both representations include some of the important characteristics of performance which were derived from close examination of the Sacred Grove and Dance, Grandstand and bull leaping frescoes. These characteristics are the inclusion of architecture, a paved surface on which the performance takes place and the performance existing as the focal point of the scene by an audience. I do not center on these two acts to prove that they are part of a specific activity repeated in the Bronze Age Aegean (which, indeed, could hardly be done) but rather to explore their relationship to social drama, performativity and ultimately Minoan and Mycenaean culture.

To concentrate on these performed acts of bull leaping and dancing as expressions of Minoan and Mycenaean culture, it is necessary to examine their form, development and geographical distribution. This is the work of the following two chapters which discuss bull leaping and dancing, respectively.

---

[77] *Collected Papers of Charles Sanders Peirce*, vols. 1-6, C. Hartshorne and P. Weiss eds., (Cambridge: Harvard University Press, 1931-35) vol. 2, paragraphs 247-249.
[78] Ibid Bal and Bryson, "Semiotics and Art History" 190-191.

Chapter Two:
Bull Leaping

"Metaphor is, at its simplest, a way of proceeding from the known to the unknown."
Victor Turner, *Dramas, Fields, and Metaphors* (Ithaca: Cornell University Press, 1974) 46.

At the end of the previous chapter I indicated that the investigation of performance in the cultures of the Minoans and Mycenaeans would proceed through the examination of representations of performed acts which, I argue, bear a relationship to social drama. Victor Turner makes the observation above at the beginning of his stay with the Ndembu of Northwestern Zambia to study their ritual as a kind of social drama. The comment reveals the two-fold duties of an ethnographer, one to describe what is seen, and the second to interpret it. The work of this book is not unlike the work of the ethnographer, to observe foreign expressions (in this case, visual) and try to understand their meanings. The first step, as Turner implies, is careful looking and discovering what can be known.

Careful looking, however, is not as easy as it sounds. The ideal objectivity which all ethnographers desire and archaeologists attempt through their quasi-scientific practices is tricky. Quite basically, the process by which a member of one culture enters another with the desire to make the other understandable in his or her own terms (be that logical, symbolic or linguistic) is always essentially subjective. This point is perhaps most economically made by Pierre Bourdieu.

> The anthropologist's particular relation to the object of his study contains the makings of a theoretical distortion inasmuch as his situation as an observer, excluded from the real play of social activities by the fact that he has no place (except by choice or by way of a game) in the system observed and has no need to make a place for himself there, inclines him to a hermeneutic representation of practices, leading him to reduce all social relations to communicative relations and, more precisely, to decoding operations.[79]

The pitfalls, then, are great. As an observer who is trying to understand not just form but meaning, one runs the risk of finding within that meaning a reflection of the observer and the observer's culture. In other words, the meanings ascribed to observations may only be a transcription of the structures of the observer onto the observed. Bourdieu calls this the "objective limits of objectivism," and for this situation there is no clear remedy.

This circumstance of a lack of objectivity, however, cannot be the end of ethnography and archaeology. In response to such a crisis of objectivism, the only feasible strategy is one which takes the problems of objectivity seriously. Such a strategy must involve consciousness of one's own structures (Bourdieu's *habitus*), even to the extent that they are a clearly stated component of observation. In other words, one's own interpretive structures, symbolic systems and intentions of meaning must be set, not in opposition to, but next to observable phenomena in order for the reader to judge the observer's objectivism.

Although to be mindful of this is important in any investigation of past cultures, it is particularly so in the examination of representations of bull leaping because of the large amount of scholarship and "lay-myth" about it. These ideas which exist in our cultural context as well as our personal consciousness have the potential to make an impact on the way in which images of bull are interpreted. Thus, in order to "confront" these preconceptions about bulls, they must be discussed. Yet, at the same time, even with such a discussion, a full understanding of bull leaping is doubtful. Then, if indeed the exact practice of bull-games is unknowable from the archaeological evidence and the proposed hypothetical scenarios are unprovable, the question remains how one is to go about studying what is clearly an important aspect to Bronze Age Greek culture? I would propose that the attraction of constructing fantasy bull-games should be resisted, and instead these images should be looked at together as members of a large group representing the same event, eschewing divisions between leapers who are over the back of the bull versus those in front of the animal, versus those behind it, etc. but rather to take the scene in its totality. In the following chapter I have tried to apply this plan.

First, I examine the representations of bull leaping from the Bronze age in chronological order including representations from several different media such as seal stones, rings, impressions, wall painting, and small scale 3-D sculpture. Following this I discuss the various approaches Bronze Age scholars have taken to this activity and its representation as well as any archaeological evidence for its existence. Moving to classical antiquity, I then discuss ancient Greek recollections of bull sports vis-à-vis ancient Crete and mythology. Moving toward an interpretation for these images I next explore contemporary views of bull sports in order to "confront" preconceived notions about the meaning of bull leaping. Lastly, I discuss potential meanings for these representations based upon visual evidence of the three social categories I discussed in chapter one. This chapter, then, will not only provide the formal analysis of representations of bull leaping in Aegean Bronze Age art, but it will also provide an examination of the structures of meaning which are animate around them.

---

[79] Pierre Bourdieu, *Outline of a Theory of Practice*, trans; Richard Nice (New York: Cambridge University Press, 1977) 1.

* * *

Before I begin the analysis of representations of bull leaping in this chapter and before a similar examination of images of dancing and procession in the next chapter, I am compelled to comment on the way in which I determined which objects to include in these examinations. Several notorious images of bull leaping, dancing and procession I have not included in these two chapters because it is my intent to examine only objects that come from good archaeological contexts. By good archaeological contexts I mean from a controlled excavation environment. I have limited my study to objects from good contexts and excluded dubious pieces for two reasons. First, important information for my investigation of performance in the Aegean Bronze age is derived from archaeological evidence; pieces lack this information are useless to me. Second, I believe that these pieces are hazardous to include in synthetic and comparative analyses because the possibility exists that they are not genuine and their presence may skew results. Further, to use pieces that come from dubious sources alongside pieces that come from good archaeological contexts falsely raises the value of the questionable objects and ultimately encourages the market for illegal antiquities. This, then, encourages illicit excavation and forgery.[80]

* * *

The first examples of representations of bull leaping from the Aegean Bronze Age are found in the form of two ceramic rhyta discovered in the prepalatial cemeteries of Porti and Koumasa in the Mesara plane of Crete. The earlier one, from Koumasa (fig. 25) is a rhyton in the shape of a bull. The tail of this creature is modeled separately and loops around to form the handle of the vessel. Hanging on the large horns of the bull are two people, created in simple outline. A third leaper is spread across the forehead of the bull.[81] The later rhyton is of generally the same design, from the site of Porti (fig. 26) although this example of a bull shaped rhyton lacks the handle/tail. Nonetheless, two leapers cling to the horns of the creature.[82]

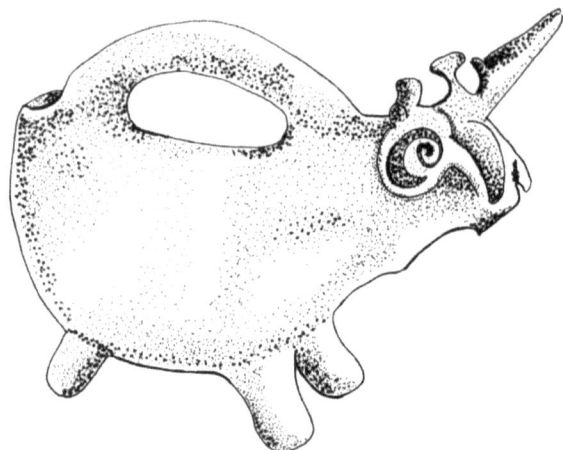

Figure 25: Koumasa rhyton; after Xanthoudides (1924) pl. XXVIII. Catalogue # 78.

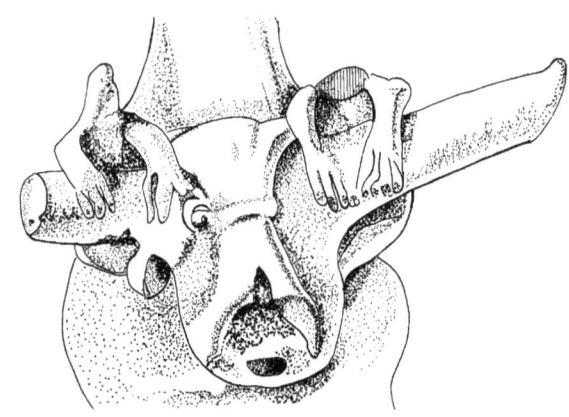

Figure 26: Porti figurine; after Xanthoudides (1924) pl. XXVII. Catalogue # 90.

Interestingly, no representations of bull leaping remain from the first palace period, yet in the second palace period there are several, almost all coming from Crete. I begin with examples of sculpture, perhaps along the tradition of the Mesara pieces. The first is an ivory figure of a male found in the Temple Treasure at Knossos, sculpted in mid leap (fig. 27), which, presumably, would have been placed in association with a figure of a bull, a fragment of which was found with the figure.[83] Also of ivory is a small pyxis (fig. 28), found in a tomb at Katsamba and dating to the second palace period, which illustrates a complex scene, part of which is bull leaping.[84] Wrapped around the body of the round box is a scene in which two men hunt and a third leaps around a charging bull.

---

[80] See Oscar White Muscarella "Unexcavated Objects and Ancient Near Eastern Art," in L. Levine and T. Cyler Young, Jr. eds., *Mountains and Lowlands*. (Malibu: University of Hawaii Press, 1977) 153-207 for a strong warning against the use of unexcavated objects and ancient art history. For perhaps a more evenly measured debate of the same topic see J. Elsner and R. Cardinal, eds. *The Cultures of Collecting* (New York, Cambridge University Press, 1994).

[81] S. Xanthoudides, *The Vaulted Tombs of the Mesara*, (Liverpool: Liverpool, University Press, 1921) 32-40, pl. XXVIII.

[82] Ibid., 52-59, pl. XXXVII.

[83] *PofM*. vol. III, 428-435. Evans reports that at least three figures were discovered but only one is in a well enough preserved state to be sure that it is a leaper of some sort. The head of a bull in the same scale found together (apparently in a box) makes the association between the two figures likely.

[84] S. Alexiou, *Isterominoikou Tafoi Limenos Knosou* (Katsama) (Athens: University of Athens, 1967) 55f, 71ff, pl.30-33.

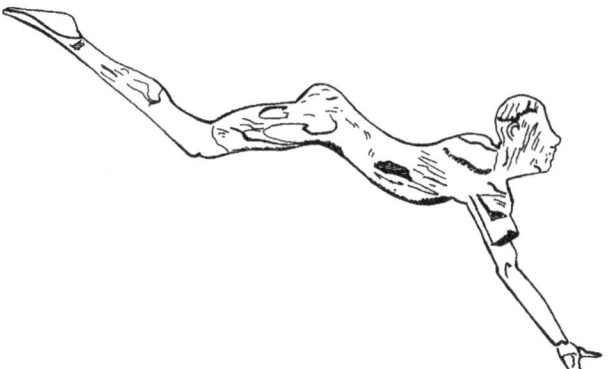

Figure 27: Ivory leaper from Knossos; after Hood (1978), pl. 105. Catalogue # 74.

Figure 28: Katsambas pyxis; after Hood (1978) fig. 111. Catalogue # 75.

Another relief example of bull leaping dating to the second palace period is the well-known boxer rhyton from Aghia Triada (fig. 29).[85] This steatite vessel is divided into four horizontal registers, the second one from the top of which illustrates two charging bulls, one of which has gored and tosses a man, presumably a less talented bull leaper. The rest of the decoration of the rhyton is of some interest as well. The other three registers of the rhyton illustrate men who wear helmets with cheek pieces and others who appear to wear gloves of some sort. In the background of the competitions stand columns with square protrusions. The potential significance of this unique object will be discussed in the concluding chapter.

Another unique piece is a crystal plaque from Knossos which has painted on it a bull leaping scene.[86] The bull is pictured in mid leap, front hooves off the ground and the leaper, angled toward the bull, holds his arms out and hair flying behind him. Also from Knossos comes a fragment of 3-D relief wall painting from this period (fig. 30)[87] which likely shows a fragment of a bull leaping scene. The fragment illustrates the strong forearm, presumably of a bull leaper, which holds a horn, presumably of a bull.

Figure 29: Boxer rhyton; after Hood (1978), fig. 139. Catalogue # 102.

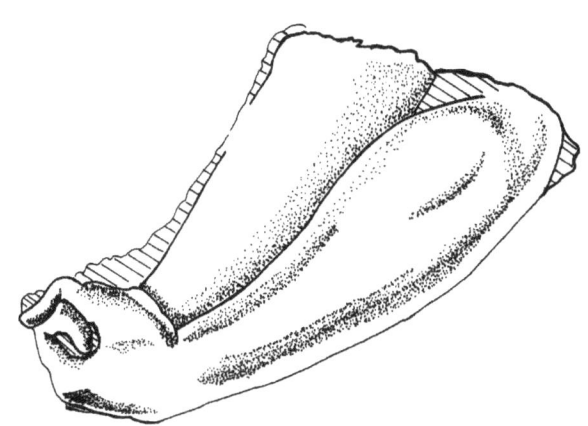

Figure 30: Knossos 3D arm and horn wall painting; after PofM III, fig. 350A. Catalogue # 65.

Several examples of glyptic art from this period on Crete illustrate bull leaping, all of which are sealings, eight to be exact. The first group, three sealings, two from Aghia Triada and one from Zakros (fig. 31, fig. 32 and fig. 33) all illustrate a bull in mid leap with a leaper "floating" over its back. The example from Zakros includes a ground line in the scene. The next group, two sealings,

---

[85] Federico Halbherr, Enrico Stefani and Luisa Banti, *Hagia Triada nel Perido Tardo Palaziale. Annualrio della Sculola Archaeologica di Atene e delle Missioni Italiane in Oriente* 55 (1977) 83ff., fig. 51.
[86] *PofM* vol. III. 108-111, pl. XIX.
[87] *PofM* vol. III, 504ff.

one from Chania (fig. 34) and one from Aghia Triada (fig. 35) illustrate a leaper arching elegantly over the hind quarters of the bull which is charging across the seal. The sealing from Aghia Triada includes a ground line. The next group, two sealings one from Zakros (fig. 36) and one from Aghia Triada (fig. 37) illustrate leapers who are flying directly over the bull's head which is thrown back as it charges. The example from Aghia Triada also includes a ground line underneath the feet of the bull. The last sealing, also from Aghia Triada (fig. 38) illustrates a leaper in front of the face of the charging bull.

The only example of second palace period representation of bull leaping from the mainland is a small fragment of an ivory plaque (fig. 39) which shows only the hoof of a charging bull and the leg of a leaping person.[88] This comes from Grave Circle B at Mycenae.

Figure 33: Seal impression from Aghia Triada; after CMS II6.42. Catalogue # 37.

Figure 31: Seal impression from Zakros; after CMS II7.34. Catalogu # 47.

Figure 34: Seal impression from Chania; after CMS V.Sup. 1A. 171. Catalogue # 53.

Figure 32: Seal impression from Aghia Triada; after CMS II6.41. Catalogue # 36.

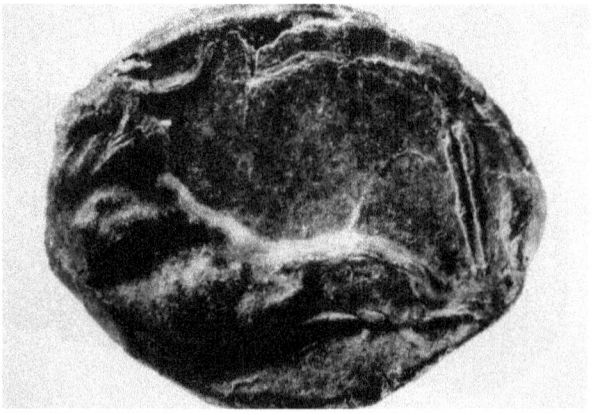

Figure 35: Seal impression from Aghia Triada; after CMS II6.43. Catalogue # 38.

---

[88] Jean-Claude Poursat, *Catalogue des Ivories Mycéniens du Musée National d'Athènes* (Athènes: Icole FranHaise d'Athènes, 1977) 68, pl. XIX.

Figure 36: Seal impression from Zakros; after CMS II7.36. Catalogue # 48.

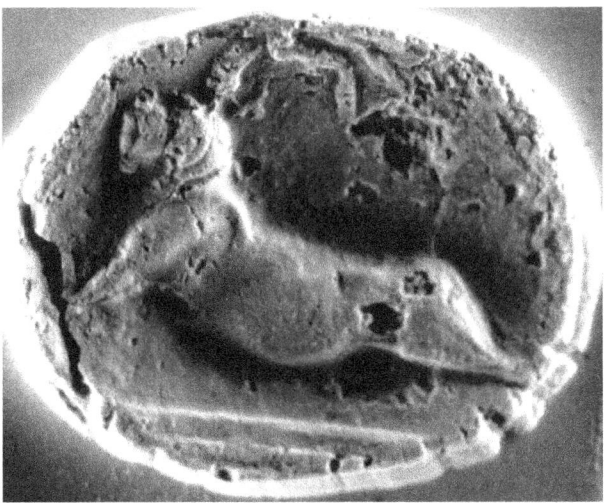

Figure 37: Seal impression from Aghia Triada; after CMS II6.44. Catalogue # 39.

Figure 38: Seal impression from Aghia Triada; after CMS II6.39. Catalogue # 35.

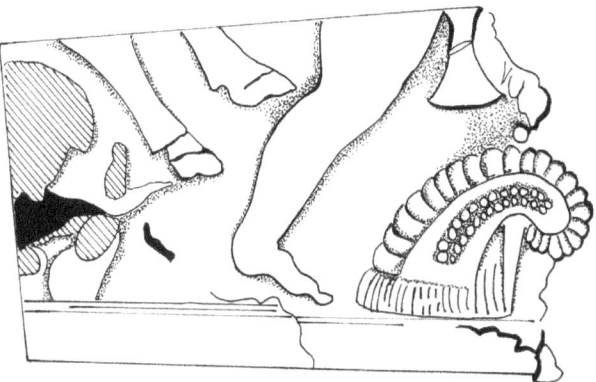

Figure 39: Ivory plaque from Mycenae; after Poursat (1977) fig. 245. Catalogue # 72.

In the following third palace period, there are several examples of bull leaping both from the Mainland and Crete. Beginning with Crete, at Knossos there are three examples of wall paintings of bull leaping found on the walls of the palace. The first is the best known image of bull leaping, the toreador wall paintings found in the Court of the Stone Spout (fig. 9).[89] Remains of three different panels have been found, each framed with a painted variegated rock pattern. The most complete panel illustrates a charging bull with a female bull leaper grasping his horns and a second female bull leaper behind the animal with arms out. A third leaper, male, is upside down over the back of the bull. Another panel shows a female leaper alighting (fig. 40) and another shows a male figure alighting (fig. 41). The last fragment shows the upper torso of another female leaper in frontal view, her head turned to the right as she grasps the horns of a bull (fig. 42). The other two examples of bull leaping in wall painting are miniature, or at least a much smaller scale than the toreador panels. The first, (fig. 43) is the Bull and Tree Grappling Scene from the North-West treasure house and illustrates the hoofs of a charging bull before a large plant and over the area of where the head of bull ought to be (were it surviving) are strands of a bull leaper's tress.[90] The other fragment of wall painting from Knossos is found in the Queen's Megaron (fig. 44) and illustrates a female acrobat springing toward the neck of a bull over which another acrobat, only visible from the hair, is already flying.[91]

---

[89] *PofM* vol. III, 209ff.
[90] *PofM* vol. II.2, 618-622, fig. 389.
[91] *PofM* vol. III, 208-10, fig. 143.

Figure 40: Knossos Toreador panel; after PofM III, plate XXI. Catalogue # 87.

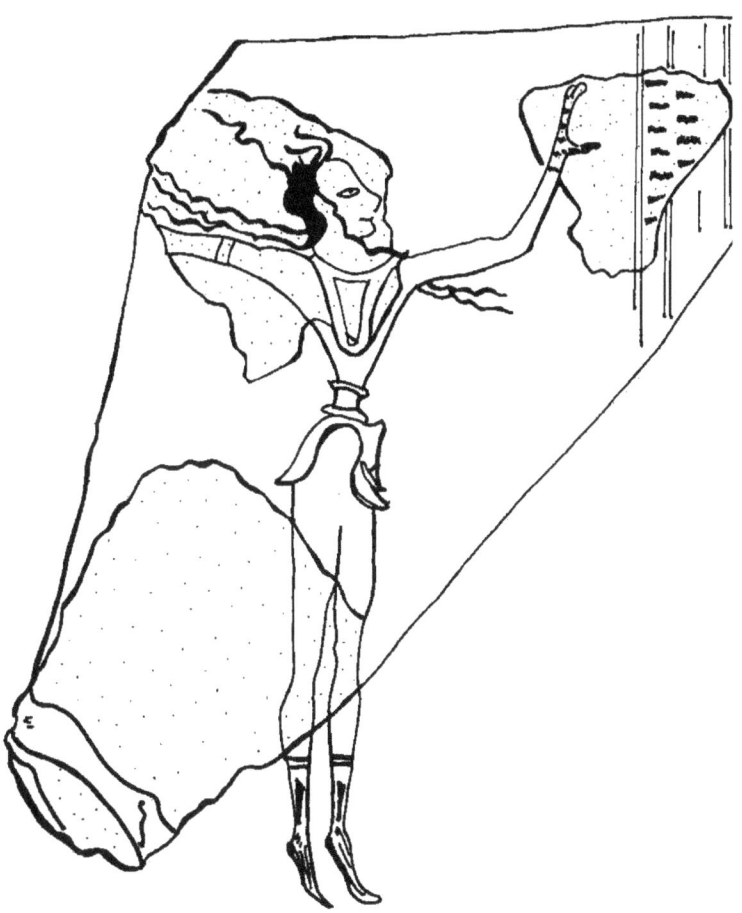

Figure 41: Knossos Toreador panel; after PofM III, fig. 148. Catalogue # 87.

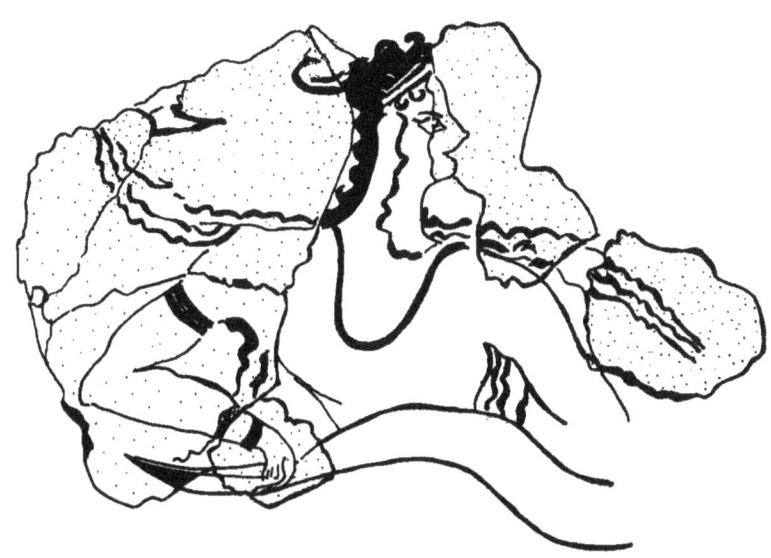

Figure 42: Knossos Toreador panel; after PofM III, fig. 146. Catalogue # 87.

Figure 43: Knossos bull and tree grappling scene; after PofM II2, fig. 389. Catalogue # 86.

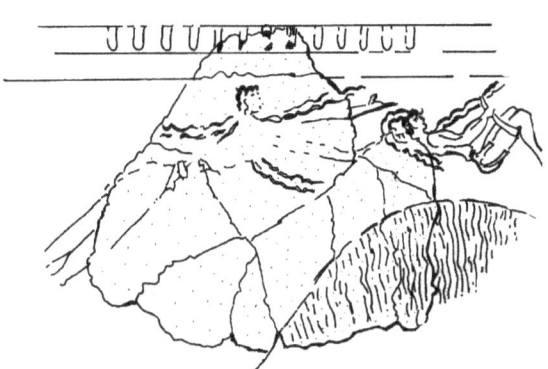

Figure 44: Knossos miniature bull leaping scene from the Queen's megaron; after PofM III, fig. 143. Catalogue # 88.

Figure 45: Agate lentoid seal from Praisos; after CMS II3.271. Catalogue # 27.

Figure 46: **Lapis lentoid seal from Gournes; after CMS II4.157. Catalogue # 28.**

Figure 47: **Seal impression from Knossos; after CMS I8.222. Catalogue # 49.**

are far more examples of bull leaping than in the previous period. As on Crete, there are three examples of wall painting, each from a Mycenaean palace. From Tiryns comes Schliemann's toreador scene (fig. 48) a female bull leaper directly over the back of a charging bull. From Pylos comes a fragment of a bull leaping scene (fig. 49), with only one leaper remaining, the edge of the hoof of the bull from which he has alighted just behind him.[93] At Mycenae a number of fragments of bull leapers and at least one bull were found (fig. 50) although the configuration of this group is difficult to reconstruct.[94] Also from the mainland in the third palace period comes a fragment of a black steatite cylindrical pyxis from the Athenian Acropolis which illustrates a man leaping over the front of a bull (fig. 51), only the horns of which are visible.[95] Finally, on a larnax found at the cemetery at Tanagra (fig. 52) a scene on one side of the sarcophagus illustrates three bulls in a row, each with a leaper in flight above them.[96]

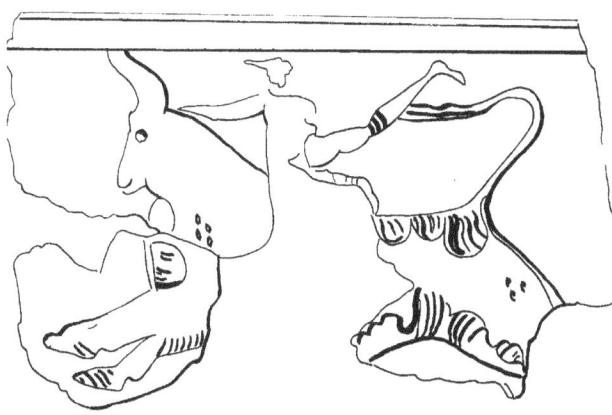

Figure 48: **Bull leaping fresco from Tiryns; after Schliemann (1976), plate XIII. Catalogue # 99.**

Among glyptic finds from the third palace period on Crete there are fewer examples of bull leaping images. The first comes from the necropolis at Praisos, an agate lentoid seal (fig. 45) which illustrates a bull leaper "floating" above a majestic seated bull, who rests on a strong ground line on which a small plant grows. Another seal, a lapis lentoid from Gournes (fig. 46), illustrates another "floating" leaper however, this leaper leaps over a bull who charges. Lastly, there is an oval impression from Knossos which illustrates a bull leaping scene (fig. 47), of a leaper over the back and behind the bull, and which also bears a Linear B sign, 182 Ws, believed to stand for leather thongs.[92]

From the Mainland during the third palace period there

---

[92] Michael Ventris and John Chadwick, *Documents in Mycenaean Greek* (New York: Cambridge University Press, 1956) 51.

[93] M. Lang, *The Palace of Nestor at Pylos in Western Messenia, vol. II The Frescoes.* (Princeton: Princeton University Press) 77; fresco catalog no. 35 H 2, pl. 24.
[94] G. Rodenwaldt, Fragmente mykenischer Wangemälde, *Mitteilungen des deutschen Archäologischen Instituts* 36 (1911) 230ff; W.Lamb "Frescoes from the Ramp House" *Annual of the British School at Athens* 24 (1919-21) 192-4, pl., VII, 406; Maria Shaw, "Bull-Leaping Fresco from Below the Ramp House at Mycenae: A Study in Iconography and Artistic Transmission" *Annual of the British School at Athens* 91 (1996). 167-90.
[95] M. Mayer "Mykenische Beitrage I, *Jahrbuch des deutschen archäologischen Instituts* 7 (1892) 80; I. Sakellerakis, "Mycenaean Stone Vases" *Studi Micenei ed Egeo-Anatolici* 17 (1976) 184, plate XII-32.
[96] Theodore Spyropoulos, "Excavation at the Mycenaean Nekropolis of Tanagra" *Athens Annals of Archaeology* 2, (1970) 184-197, fig. 16.

Figure 49: Bull leaping fresco from Pylos; after Lang (1966), plate 24. Catalogue # 93.

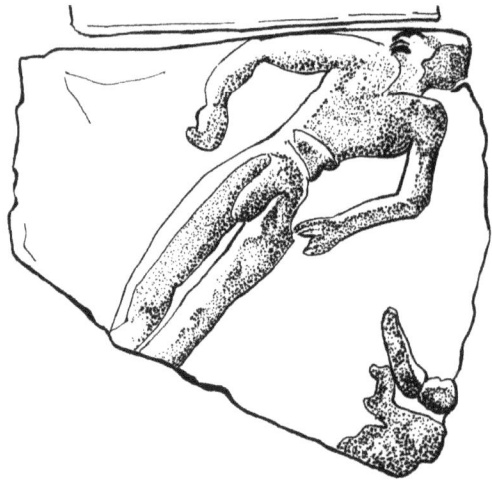

Figure 51: Stone vase fragment from Acropolis; after Sakellarakis (1976), plate XII-32. Catalogue # 66.

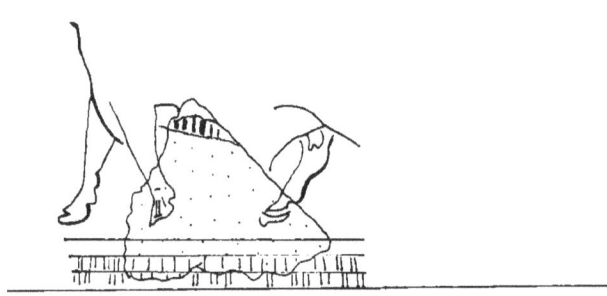

Figure 52: Larnax from Tanagra; after Immerwahr (1990) plate XXII. Catalogue # 96.

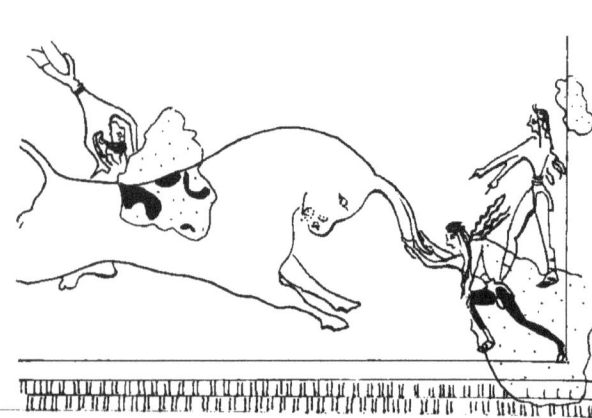

Figure 50: Mycenae miniature bull leaping fresco; after Shaw (1996), plate 1. Catalogue # 80.

Glyptic examples from the third palace period on the mainland are many and can be divided into four groups. The first group, the largest, illustrates a leaper vaulting over the back of a bull but holding on to the creature somehow. This includes an agate lentoid from Dimini (fig, 53), an agate half cylinder from Thebes (fig. 54), a chalcedony lentoid from Koukounara (fig. 55) and a carnelian amygdaloid from Mycenae (fig. 56). The next group is of "floating leapers." This includes an agate lentoid seal from Mycenae (fig. 13) and a carnelian amygdaloid also from Mycenae (fig. 57). The next group illustrates people who are leaping over the back end of the bull. This group includes a gold ring from Asine (fig. 58), a carnelian amygdaloid from Mycenae (fig. 12) and an onyx lentoid also from Mycenae (fig. 42). The last two are unique examples. One, a sealing from Pylos, illustrates a leaper in front of a charging bull with arms raised up (fig. 59) and the other, a gold ring from Anthia (fig. 7) illustrates two leapers, one over the back and one over the head of a charging bull who moves over an elaborate ground line, carved in a double row of hatching.

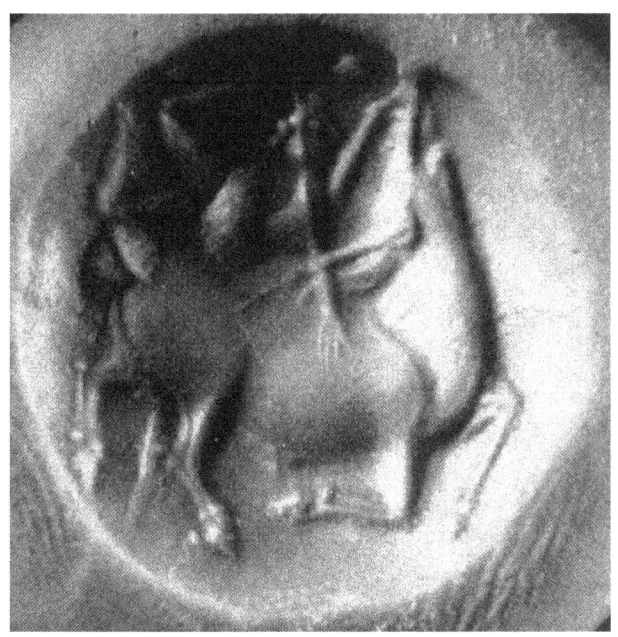

Figure 53: Agate lentoid from Dimini; after CMS I.408. Catalogue # 21.

Figure 54: Agate half cylinder from Thebes; after CMS V2.674. Catalogue # 63.

Figure 55: Chalcedony lentoid form Koukounara; after CMS V2.638. Catalogue # 62.

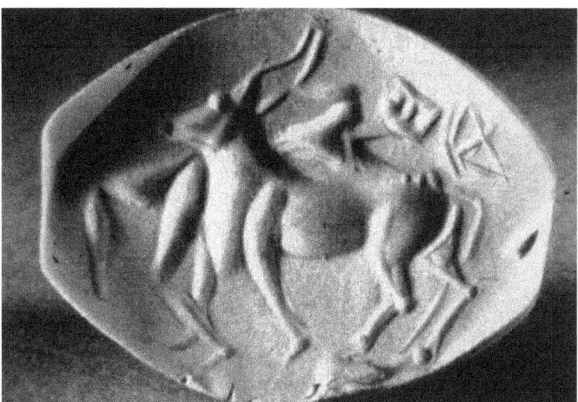

Figure 56: Carnelian amygdaloid from Mycenae; after CMS I.137. Catalogue # 10.

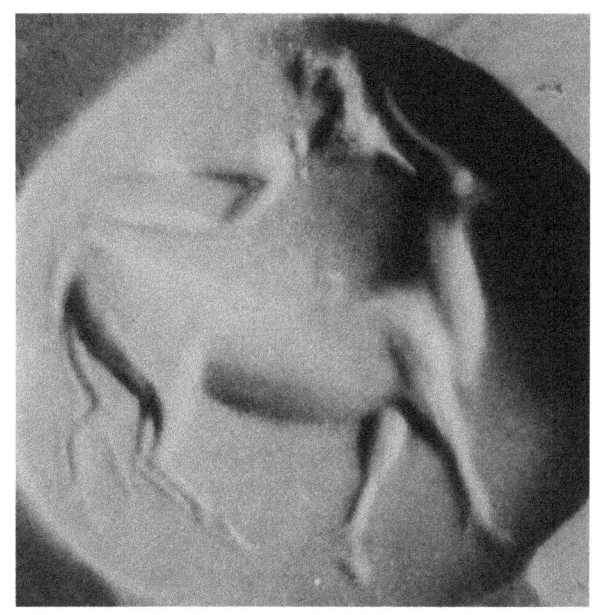

Figure 57: Carnelian amygdaloid from Mycenae; after CMS I.79. Catalogue # 5.

Figure 58: Gold and bronze ring from Asine; after CMS I.200. Catalogue # 14.

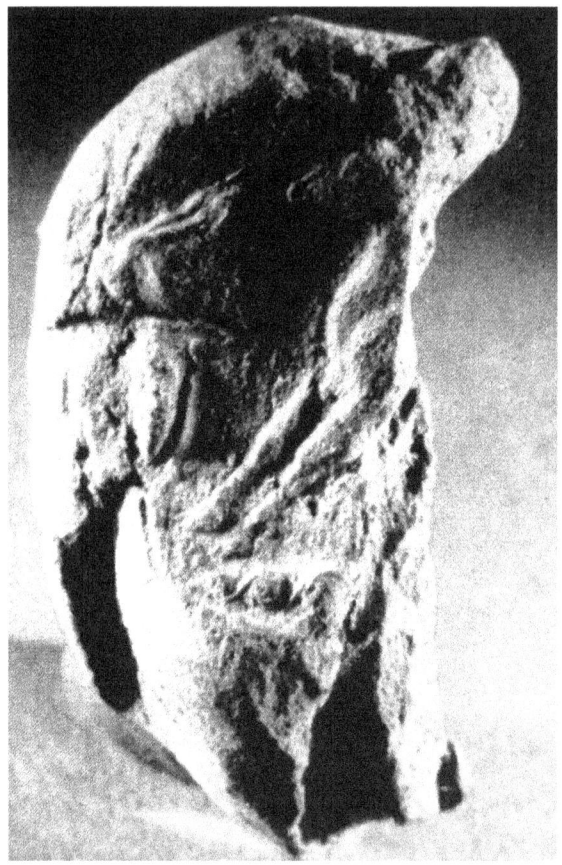

Figure 59: Seal impression from Pylos; after CMS I.305. Catalogue # 18.

* * *

Reviewing the images we have discussed above, it is clear that depictions of bull leaping are strongly consistent. In most cases, one leaper is pictured either in mid-air over the back or in the process of mounting or dismounting from the back or front of a wildly charging bull. Some representations include one or more leapers engaging the same bull; however, these are in the minority. A ground line is sometimes included in representations of bull leaping which surely indicate something about the location where this activity took place, as I shall discuss below. Representations of bull leaping outside of the glyptic media, specifically wall painting and ivory sculpture, tend to show a more complete version of the scene. Without exception, those who participate in bull leaping are young and display all the corporeal characteristics of a male. Despite this, however, the possibility exists that women participated in this activity. As Evans was the first to point out, some of the bull leapers represented in wall painting are illustrated with white or very pale skin.[97] He based his conclusion primarily on the well known ancient Greco-Etruscan and Egyptian color convention of white or pale skin for women and dark or brown skin for men (these specific color values presumably because house-bound women's skin was not darkened by sun exposure). Soon various students of Aegean art pointed out that despite the pale skin, any and all representations of bull leapers looked masculine in every corporeal manner: they are the same size as males, lack breasts and have instead a narrow waist and broad chest.[98] In fact, when the bull leaping scene was discovered at Tiryns in the last century, the first person who examined it, C. Fabricius, noted that yellow lines were visible on top of the white paint which he felt indicated the leaper's masculine musculature and even male sexual organs.[99]

Despite the lack of clarity on the subject, the color conventions have a firm grip in the scholarship however, for the purposes of this work, they do not greatly impact. This is because, as I have argued above, performativity is critical to the construction of gender in the Aegean Bronze Age and, for all intents and purposes, with the exception of the color of the skin in examples of representations of bull leaping which are wall paintings, all bull leapers conform to, perform, masculine corporeal norms: broad chest, muscular legs and arms, narrow waist, etc. Interesting, even Evans acknowledged this performance of masculinity, here repeating the quote from the beginning of chapter one.

> ...girl(s)...had to first undergo a kind of sexual transformation, by divesting themselves of all articles of feminine dress...and by adopting the sporting costume of the male performers, including the universal exterior sign of the masculine sex, the Minoan version of the "Lybian sheath."[100]

Therefore, we can conclude that although the accepted color conventions cannot help in the identification of the gender of most of our representations of bull leaping discussed above, it can be safely assumed that all participants were, if not male, performing a masculine identity.[101]

---

[97] *PofM*, vol. IV.1, 21ff; *PofM*, vol III, 207

[98] Sara Immerwahr, "The People of the Frescoes" in O. Krzyszkowska and L. Nixon eds., *Minoan Society*. 1981, 145; Ibid. *Aegean Painting in the Bronze Age*, 161; J. Younger, "Bronze Age Representations of Aegean Bull-Leaping" American Journal of Archaeology 80 (1976) 131; Silvia Damiani Indelicato, "Were Cretan Girls Playing at Bull-Leaping? *Cretan Studies* 1, (1988) 39-47. Indelicato, interestingly, argues that the use of white to represent some bull leapers in wall paintings refers not to color conventions of gender but rather to the same leaper at a different moment in the process of leaping over the bull. If indeed this is the case, it seems that the Minoans and Mycenaeans chose a poor method to show the passage of time in these quasi-narrative scenes for, in its representation in monochrome media, such as glyptic or metal work or ivory sculpture, one would be unable to identify the "earlier" or "later" leaper.

[99] As Schliemann reported the observations of C. Fabricius. H. Schliemann, *Tirynte* (Paris: Blom, 1885) 284. Sadly, no photograph was taken of the fresco when it was originally found, when these marks were visible. It remains a possibility, therefore, that the observations of Fabricius are erroneous.

[100] *PofM* vol. IV.2, 22.

[101] For an interesting take on cross-dressing in the Aegean Bronze Age see L. Hitchcock, "Engendering Ambiguity in Minoan Crete: It's a Drag to be a King," in M. Donald and L. Hurcombe eds.,

This consistent profile of bull leapers, young and masculine, has lead several scholars to conclude that bull leaping had to do with coming of age ceremonies. This is an important idea and one which I would like to explore here briefly. The first to make such an assertion was Robert Koehl.[102] In his discussion of the important serpentine conical vessel from Aghia Triada, the Chieftain's Cup, which illustrates on one side two men facing each other and on the other side, three men carrying animal skins, Koehl convincingly argues that the scene is not one of military preparedness, as had traditionally been the interpretation, but instead a ritual by which young Minoan men would pass from youthful to adult status, a rite of passage ceremony. At the end of this analysis, Koehl states that a vessel, the Boxer Rhyton, found with the Chieftain Cup, could also illustrate a rite of passage ceremony.[103] This idea was taken up some seven years later by Arnott in a brief article[104] in which he presents an ethnographic analogy to Bronze Age bull leaping in contemporary Ethiopia, among the Oromo people. Arnott explains that male Oromo youths, as a rite of passage into adulthood, run over the backs of several bulls lined up in the center of the village as part of a community-wide ceremony. In this ceremony, young women hold down the bulls horns while the male youths run over their backs. This ceremony is immediately followed by courtship dances and rituals which subsequently lead to marriage. The interpretation of bull leaping as a rite of passage ceremony in association to marriage I will return to in chapter five.

The question still remains: if there were some sort of bull leaping in the Bronze Age Aegean, whatever its configuration or meaning, where would such ceremonies have taken place? Another way to ask this question is, what is the archaeological evidence for bull leaping? This question has traditionally centered around whether bull leaping took place in the central court of the Minoan palaces or outside in some other space.[105] The evidence for locating bull leaping in the central courts is purely circumstantial. There is one seal which illustrates a bull leaping scene which includes a conspicuous stone block, such as has been found in the central courts of Phaistos and Mallia; however, sadly, this seal is from an unknown context, bought from a dealer and therefore we cannot be sure if its authentic.[106] The platform at Phaistos has received some attention as a part of bull leaping equipment, however, this is all necessarily conjecture.[107] The only sensible conclusion is, then, that bull leaping could have taken place in the central courts or elsewhere but it is unknown whether it did. Another paved area of which we are aware in the environs of the palace, the theatral area, might also be a likely candidate.

So, if indeed the practice of bull leaping and, possibly, the place which it was practiced is known, the next question which arises is what was its signification. The following section explores scholarship by Aegean Bronze Age scholars which engage this question.

* * *

Indeed, to contemplate bull leaping is to take up an inescapable aspect of the Aegean Bronze Age. By all accounts, the image best known as an illustration of this activity was unearthed by Evans at Knossos during the 1901 excavation season in the Court of the Stone Spout.[108] Interestingly, this find was not the first in the Aegean illustrating bull leaping; Schliemann had found a fragmentary wall painting depicting bull leaping at Tiryns (fig. 48) two decades earlier.[109] Similarly, Evans' explication of Minoan bull leaping in the publication of the site of Knossos was not the first examination of the activity; A. Reichel wrote a long article in 1909 on the topic.[110] Recently, J. Younger has written a three part reevaluation of the topic.[111] Therefore, we find the development of the scholarly thinking about bull leaping in the Aegean Bronze Age is a long one. The following is a review of such.

In Reichel's study of "kretisch-mykenischen" bull games he gathered all known examples of the images from Crete and the Mainland and grouped them roughly according to the pose of the leaper vis-à-vis the bull. Reichel concluded that bull leaping bore a relationship to cult and likely the worship of Zeus, and that it survived as a cult activity in Roman Thessaly, the taurokathapsiai, and its ultimate expression was in Mithraic religion.[112] Evans, twelve and again twenty-one years later explored the same topic, including several more examples unearthed

---

Representations of Gender from Prehistory to the Present. (New York: Palgrav Macmillan 2000) 69-86.
[102] R. Koehl, "The Chieftain Cup and a Minoan Rite of Passage," *Journal of Hellenic Studies* 106 (1986) 99-110.
[103] Ibid., 109.
[104] W. Geoffrey Arnott, "Bull Leaping as Initiation Ritual," *Liverpool Classical Monthly* 18 (1993) 114-116.
[105] We might assume that bull leaping occurred on a paved space as several examples of its representation include some sort of paving stones under the feet of the charging bull.
[106] V.E.G. Kenna, *Cretan Seals with a Catalogue of the Minoan Gems in the Ashmolean Museum*. (Oxford: Ashmolean Museum,1960) no. 202.

[107] See J. W. Graham, *The Palaces of Crete* (Princeton: Princeton University Press, 1987, revised edition) 73-83. Graham also points to some evidence of the blocking of the central court at Mallia (pg. 77ff.) but, again, there is no way to know securely whether such security was to keep a bull within the confines of the court or for any other purpose.
[108] Arthur Evans, "Knossos 1900" *Annals of the British School at Athens*, (1900-1) 94ff.
[109] Heinrich Schliemann, *Tiryns: The Prehistoric Palace of the Kings of Tiryns*. (New York: Arno, 1967.) 303, plate XIII.
[110] A Reichel, "Die Stierspiele in der kretisch-mykenischen Cultur," *Mitteilungen des Kaiserlich Deutschen Archæologischen Instituts*, 34 (1909), 85-99.
[111] John Younger, "Bronze Age Representations of Aegean Bull-Leaping," *American Journal of Archaeology* 80 (1976) 125-137; "A New Look at Aegean Bull-Leaping," *Muse* 17 (1983) 72-80; "Bronze Age Representations of Aegean Bull-Games, III," *Politeia*. Aegaeum 12 (1995) 507-545.
[112] Ibid., Younger (1983) 97.

by him at Knossos and others elsewhere.[113] In his later analysis Evans reconstructed the various methods by which he believed one could have leapt over a bull in the Bronze Age. He also connected such activities to later antique bull sports as well as modern rodeo. Ultimately, Evans believed that bull leaping was a central ritual of Minoans aristocracy which took place in the central court at Knossos and other palaces. The next new study of the topic was authored by Anne Ward who concentrated not on the form or significance of bull leaping *per se*, but rather its feasibility given the archaeological evidence of the Minoan palaces and various representations of it in Minoan and Mycenaean art.[114] She concludes that the event of bull leaping began with the roping of a wild bull outside the palace, the gathering of an audience in the central court to watch the performance, the performance itself and finally, the sacrifice of the bull.[115]

The last extensive effort to understand the event of bull leaping in the Aegean Bronze Age has been made by John Younger in his series of three articles.[116] Younger provides an encyclopedic listing of all known representations of bulls and bull sports and divides the action among preliminary activities, such as bull-wrestling, bull-leaping and bull-vaulting and discusses locations for bull-leaping, bull leapers and bull-sacrifice. Perhaps most useful in Younger's work, from a taxonomic perspective, is his identification of no fewer than nineteen separate stances and positions represented in bull leaping.[117] Although this does cover the full range of possible positions, it is unclear how useful these identifications are aside from pure classification. And, indeed, classification seems to be Younger's primary concern. Despite his extensive investigation into the motif of bull leaping, his conclusions are few. At the end of his last article on the topic he tentatively identifies the central courts of the palaces as the place where bull leaping occurred and suggests that the activity was part of a ritual.[118]

The generalization can be made that Younger and those others who have pursued the study of bull leaping in the Aegean have been intrepid in their pursuit of *how* Minoans and Mycenaeans might have gone about bounding on or around bulls.[119] Although this line of investigation is interesting, conclusions found along it are frustratingly difficult to prove and, in my opinion, miss the larger point of the cultural importance of the performance and its representation.

Most recently, Eleanor Loughlin has attempted a more integrated approach to the topic of the representation of bull leaping by placing the act within the context of the control of cattle in agricultural, rural and sporting contexts.[120] Not entirely unlike my approach here, Loughlin eschews the temptation to assign specific motions to the representations of bull leaping and instead looks at the motif as a whole, within a social context.

Given this review, it becomes clear that Aegean Bronze Age scholars have provided few integrated theories, as to the meaning of bull leaping. As this is the aim of the present work, we must move forward. In doing this, however, there is the potential for a "theoretical distortion" as Bourdieu has said it in the quote at the beginning of the chapter. That is, in looking for new interpretations for bull leaping, the temptation exists to fall back upon ones that are in our collective knowledge of bulls throughout history. In the interest of being aware of this knowledge or structure, as Bourdieu would say, the following outlines briefly and in historical sequence the most prevalent associations with bulls in, at least, the contemporary western mind.

* * *

As cultural historians have often pointed out, most recently Michael Rice,[121] bulls have loomed large in the religion, culture, sport, art and imagination of man, seemingly from the beginning of his existence. Starting with the Paleolithic cave paintings of Europe, evidence for man's affinity with bulls abounds. This phenomenon is fascinating but difficult to make sense of. Although it is indeed the case since the early prehistoric periods that bulls have been represented in various media all found in various cultural contexts, it would be unwise to assume that the meanings attributed to bulls were the same throughout. The importance, however, of noting these similar representations is to acknowledge the interpretive background brought to the images from the Bronze Age Aegean.

At the Neolithic Anatolian village of Çatal Hüyük, located in modern Turkey, several intricate wall paintings were found dating to the first quarter of the sixth millennia BCE.[122] One is of particular interest here as it may be the earliest representations of a bull leaping scene from the Mediterranean region. The painting (fig, 60),

---

[113] A. Evans, "On a Minoan Bronze Group of a Galloping Bull and Acrobatic Figure from Crete," *Journal of Hellenic Studies*. 41 (1921) 247-259; *PofM*. vol. III, 203-232.
[114] Anne Ward, "The Cretan Bull Sports," *Antiquity* 42, (1968) 117-122. Before Ward's work is an article by Otto Lendle, "Das kretische Stiersprunspiel," *Marburger Winckelmann-Programm*, 1965 (30-37), which does little more than offer a lightly different pose for the leapers than Evans had reconstructed.
[115] Ibid, Ward, 121-2.
[116] Supra note 32.
[117] Ibid. Younger (1995) 527-533.
[118] Ibid 545.
[119] See especially James G. Thompson, "The Bull-Jumping Exhibition at Mallia," *Archaeology News*, 14 (1985) 1-8. Thompson is thoroughly convinced of the reality of bull leaping and, through actual physical trials, proves that a launch or lift of some sort was needed in order for the jumper to be able to clear the back of a mature bull.

[120] Eleanor Loughlin, "Grasping the Bull by the Horns: Minoan Bull Sports." In S. Bell and G. Davvies eds. *Games and Festivals in Classical Antiquity*. BAR International Series, 1220 (2004) 1-8.
[121] Michael Rice, *The Power of the Bull*. (New York: Routledge, 1998). Prior to this, see James Percy, *Bulls, Ancient and Modern* (Dublin: Mecredy, Percy & Co., 1912).
[122] James Mellaart, *Çatal Hüyük* (New York: MacGraw-Hill., 1967) 170-3, fig, 48, 64.

found on the north wall of shrine A.III.i, shows a huge bull (approximately 6 feet long) surrounded by several much smaller people who appear to wear animal skins, or are naked, some bearing weapons. On the wall adjacent to the bull is a hunting scene, yet the people on all sides of the bull do not appear to harm it, some of the figures merely stand on the back of the bull. The painting was found in side a room with another painting, a deer hunting scene, and which also contained a pair of bull bucrania. The excavator designated the room a shrine based upon the topic of the paintings and the bucrania. What makes these finds in Anatolia interesting is the fact that Neolithic Anatolia is thought to be the place whence the people who populated Crete at that time came.[123]

Figure 60: Bull fresco from Catal Huyuk; after Mellaart (1967), fig. 48.

The earliest representation of bull leaping activities also comes from outside of Crete, from Syria. In room 11, level VII of the palace of Alalakh, on the modern Syrian-Turkish border, an archive of cuneiform tablets were found. Domonique Collon published one of the seal impressions found in this archive as an illustration of bull leaping (fig 61).[124] The impression is datable to the late 8th-7th century BCE. At the bottom center of the impression there is a bull with his legs spread out in the "flying gallop" pose and two figures, each with a long pony tail, vaulting on the back of the bull, facing each other. To the right of this scene is a standing robed and bearded figure on one side of a tree below a winged disk; above it is a galloping ibex to the left of a lion and griffin. Another seal, from Tell Leilan in Northern Syria (fig 61), illustrates a figure who grasps a bull by one horn and raises the other arm, another figure stands behind the bull with one knee raised. Iconography elsewhere on the seal shows a cow suckling her calf and a half-kneeling bull before a shrine.[125] Collon proposes that these images,

from Syria, indicate that bull leaping may have originated in that country and therefore the Cretan version may bear some ancient Near Eastern inheritance.

Figure 61: Cylinder seal impressions from Tel Lelan and Allalak; after Colon (1994), plate 2.

In Classical Greece bulls played an important role, not only as victims of sacrifice[126] but as characters in mythology. Interestingly, the more powerful gods of the ancient Greek pantheon are associated with bulls, namely Zeus and Dionysus.[127] Zeus takes the shape of a bull when he abducts Europa from Tyre to Crete and with her begets Minos. In the cult of Zeus the bull was to symbolize his procreative powers.[128] Plutarch recounts a

---

[123] Cyprian Broodbank and Thomas F. Strasser, "Migrant Farmers and the Neolithic Colonization of Crete," *Antiquity* 65 (1991) 233-45, esp. 237-8.
[124] Domonique Collon, "The Seal Impressions from Tell Atchana/Alalakh," *Alter Orient und Altes Testament* 27 (1975), no. 111. See also Domonique Collon, "Bull-Leaping in Syria," *Äypten und Levante* 4 (1994) 81-2. For other examples of Syrian and Aegean glyptic similarities see J. Aruz, "Syrian Seals and the Evidence of Cultural Interaction," *Sceaux Minoens et Mycéniens, Ive symposium international 10-12 septembre 1992, Clermont-Ferrand, Corpus der Minoischen und Mykenischen Siegel*, Beiheft 5 (1995)13-28.
[125] Ibid. Collon 1994, 82-3, fig. 6. Here Collon discusses seven other seals from Syria which include representations of bull leaping however, all of these are from either unknown or dubious contexts.

[126] In fact, the most noble animals sacrificed were bulls. Walter Burkert. *Greek Religion*, trans. John Raffan. (Cambridge: Harvard University Press, 1985) 55-6.
[127] Ibid., 64-5.
[128] Arthur Bernard Cook. *Zeus: A Study in Ancient Religion*. Vol. I. (New York: Biblo and Tannen, 1964) 633-5. Cook traces this association through the belief that on Crete, Zeus' birthplace, bulls were

cult hymn from Elis in which Dionysos is called the one with a raging bull foot[129] and Pausanius, tells of a winter festival in Arkadia where a bull is chosen to represent the god.[130] However, it is Zeus, the leader of the gods, who has the closest association with bulls.

The myth of the Minotaur is possibly the most famous among these and shows a special relationship with Crete, where Zeus was born. Apollodorus reports the birth of the Minotaur in his third book of *The Library* and the story goes that Pasiphae, the wife of king Minos fell in love with a bull that Minos had received from Poseidon and with which he had secured domination of the Aegean sea. Wanting to consummate her love for the animal, Pasiphae had Daedalus construct a hollow wooden cow covered with hide in which she could disguise herself and seduce Poseidon's bull. Asteius was the result of the union, with the head of a bull and the body of a human. In compliance with oracles that Minos consulted, the creature, renamed the Minotaur, was hidden away in another structure of Deadalus' construction, the Labyrinth, an elaborate cage beneath Minos' palace Knossos.[131] The bull of Poseidon continues to play a role in the mythology of the Labyrinth. As Pausanias reports, the bull traveled from Crete to the Peloponnesus and when let loose, traveled further to Attica where he slew, among others, Androgeos, the son of Minos. Minos believed the Athenians had a hand in the death of his son so he sailed his fleet against Athens. It was eventually agreed that in recompense for the death of Androgeos, the Athenians would send seven boys and seven girls to the Minotaur.[132] So we find that the most famous myth concerning a most famous bull is not only about Crete but specifically identifies Knossos as its origin and habitation.

This ancient information is rich with tradition, drama, beauty, heroism, and honor; it also provides another example of romantic contradiction (the violent bull versus the graceful leaper, the rationality of man versus the feral nature of animals, warlike masculine Mycenaeans verses peaceful feminine Minoans) which has marked so much of the study of the Aegean Bronze Age.[133] Indeed, romantic tragedy could not be more firmly affixed to our modern phenomenon of the bullfight. As a result, bull sports have taken on a cathartic meaning in contemporary literature and even art. Perhaps the origin of the romantic evocation of the bull fight dates in the modern era to Freudian psychoanalytical readings of the activity. Two Freudian interpretations for the bull fight were simultaneously in play in the 1920s and 30s, one which read the match as a contest between a father or authority figure (the bull) and the id. The other concerned symbolic gender roles of the two principal protagonists, the bull fighter taking on a female identity, the bull male.[134] These rich symbolic levels of the bull fight no doubt inspired the literary masterpiece on the topic *Death in the Afternoon* by Ernest Hemingway which gave the English speaking world a vivid exposure to the sport.[135]

In academia, anthropologically oriented studies of bull fighting have centered upon how this activity, *los toros*, functions in Spanish society, both historically and today. Interestingly, it has been noted that even within Spain, bulls have several different associations: General Franco, the modern tourist industry, village festivals, Spanish identity within the European Union, fertility and machismo. Perhaps most interestingly for the present study is the more local variation in the meaning of *los toros*. Although the bull fight in the big cities are rather standard, different stories and rituals associated with bulls exist across Spain, each tied to the particular village identity.[136]

Although thinking cross culturally about bull fighting and Aegean Bronze Age bull leaping is fruitful, rodeo may be a closer match as far as the nature of the activity itself is concerned. That is, although there is some evidence for bull sacrifice during the Bronze Age[137] the fact remains that there is no connection between the representation of bull leaping and the death of the bull, the hair raising close to almost all bull fights. Rodeo, on the other hand, is a sport in which man and beast are matched, but the point is not destruction. Therefore, given the great similarity between rodeo and bull leaping, this western American sport is another interesting avenue to explore for cross-cultural parallels.

The rodeo, with its origin among the cattle ranchers of the American west, still perseveres as a reminder and means to honor those 19th century pioneers and entrepreneurs. There are at least two varieties of rodeo, one the roping of a bull and two, retaining one's seat on the animal. Interestingly, the cattle ranching techniques to which these sporting activities bear progenitive relationships were taught to the American pioneers by Spanish and

---

associated with the sun which was associated with fertility. See pgs. 467-9.
[129] Plutarch. *Quaestiones Graecae*, 299 B. Also, in Euripides *Bacchae*, his is referred to as a god bull (theos tauros) 1017-8.
[130] Pausanius (8. 19. 2) describes a sanctuary to Dionysos at Kynaitha in Arkadia where in a winter festival men pick out a bull which the god indicated to them and carry it to the sanctuary for sacrifice.
[131] Apolodorus *The Library*, book III, 1,4.
[132] Pausanias, book I, Attica, XXVII, 10.
[133] See Lucia Nixon's discussion of this reoccurring contradiction, through the lens of gender, in "Gender Bias in Archaeology," in L. Archer, S. Fischler and M. Wyke eds., *Women in Ancient Societies* (New York: Routledge 1994) 1-23.

[134] See discussion in introduction in Carrie B. Douglass, *Bulls, Bullfighting, and Spanish Identities* (Tucson: University of Arizona Press, 1997) 9ff.
[135] Michel Leiris, "The Bullfight as Mirror," *October* 63 (1993) 21-40 sums up this argument. An example of the popularity of bullfighting as a theme in literature, see P. Haining, ed., *A Thousand Afternoons* (Boston: Cowles, 1970); essays about Hemingway and bullfighting and several short stories on the topic.
[136] Ibid. Douglass, 171ff.
[137] For instance, the Aghia Triada Sarcophagus illustrates on one of its long sides a dying bull who is tied to a table before an altar. See C. R. Long, *The Ayia Triadha Sarcophagus: A Study of Late Minoan and Mycenaean Funerary Practices and Beliefs*. Studies in Mediterranean Archaeology 41, 1977.

Mexican colonists in what is now the Southwest United States and California. These skills were apparently greatly prized in Spanish livestock herding traditions and no doubt this sense carried over. Eventually, as the wild west was tamed, rodeo became a part of traveling shows, known as Wild West Shows, which included spectacles, acrobatics and theatre.[138] Rodeo today is exclusively a planned performance, regulated by the Rodeo Association of America (founded in 1929) performed under strict rules and regulations. In a recent examination of a rodeo in Rock Creek, Montana, an ethnologist, Frederick Errington, takes the view that the rodeo functions much like the social drama of Victor Turner. Errington shows how the rodeo, in its strictly contestive nature, functions as a liminal and temporary space in society where the conflicts of the real world are mimicked. The need to move in and out of and work within that liminal space, Errington concludes, is in order to "blow off steam" or work out these tensions. It also gives the participants an opportunity to participate in the excesses and lawlessness associated with the rodeo, which, although less contestive than the rodeo itself, serve to mitigate the tension which is the result of the need to abide by socially acceptable behavior.[139]

* * *

Having now outlined the formal attributes of bull leaping as well as interpretive constructs, I return to the Aegean Bronze Age images to make observations as to their detail giving special attention to those which speak to the social categories of gender, age and social status.

Concentrating on the representation of the performance of the act of bull leaping, I have drawn out three points of visual similarity: movement, danger and strength/vigor. A sense of movement or motion is understood through the recognition of the rigorous activities of bull leaping. However, this sense is furthered in the compositional quality as all action shown is in mid leap, stride or jump. A sense of movement is especially obvious in representations of bull leaping, accentuated by the hair of the leaper trailing behind him (fig. 12). Danger is conveyed more subtly through details such as the hoofs of the mighty bull represented as suspended off the ground which conveys a sense of mortal danger involved in an activity like bull leaping. An impression of strength/vigor is conveyed not only again by the recognition of the activity represented, but also given that limbs are always represented as flexed and muscles swelling, especially in the case of men whose muscles are shown in some detail. This can be found, for example, on the gold ring from Anthia (fig. 7).

What can we make of this information? How do these details impact on the analysis of these scenes? For one, it helps connect these scenes on seals with other media and artistic production. Also, it may serve to highlight interpretive aspects. For instance, a sense of movement in a depiction of bull leaping helps us to understand the physical exertion involved in the actual performance of that act.

Lastly, I believe that information which recalls our social categories can be extracted from these details. First, as most clearly illustrated in the detail of strength/vigor, I believe that the social category of age is clearly depicted. The representation of strength/vigor is necessarily connected to youth. Engagement in danger can also be associated with youth. Typically, only youthful bodies are so strong, flexible, smooth and sensual. Second, not tied to any one of the details outlined above but a part of all of them is the representation of gender as illustrated through an emphasis upon the parts of bodies associated with secondary sexual characteristics.[140] These are a slim waist and hips and broad chest. These particular aspects of men's bodies are often exaggerated in representations of bull leaping and, being secondary sexual characteristics, perhaps even exaggerate or emphasize gender identification.

---

[138] Mark J. Okrant and Paul F. Starrs, "Rodeo," in Karl B. Raitz ed., *The Theater of Sports* (Baltimore: Johns Hopkins University Press, 1995) 296-303.
[139] Frederick Errington, "The Rock Creek Rodeo: Excess and Constraint in Men's Lives," *American Ethnologist*, 17 (1990) 628-645.

[140] See discussion of secondary sexual characteristics in chapter one.

Chapter Three:
Measured Movement: Dance and Procession

"Rhythmically repeated movement, directed to no end and performed together as a group, is, as it were, ritual crystallized in its purest form."
W. Burkert, *Greek Religion* (Oxford: Blackwell, 1985) 102.

"...because the dancer is not limited by the athlete's concrete purposes and the acrobat's single-minded focus, he or she more freely presents us with an ideal vision of ourselves."
D. Jowitt, *Time and the Dancing Image* (New York: Morrow, 1988) 366.

In the introductory chapter, I propose that performance played a major role in social identity and political identification in the late Aegean Bronze Age. One of the most important of these performance was dance. The following chapter presents visual, archaeological and historical evidence for dance in the Aegean Bronze Age, eventually pulling out visual clues for the representation of this activity. Then, the corpus of images of dance and an allied activity, procession, from Minoan and Mycenaean contexts is discussed. Next, means of interpreting these images is explored. Building off this, the chapter ends with a discussion of how details of the representation of dance help to built and reiterate the three social categories of gender, age and social status.

* * *

What proof exists for the actual execution of activities such as dancing and procession in the Aegean Bronze Age? Archaeologically, a variety of evidence might be associated with dance and processional movement. Several structures on Crete (palaces, villas and settlements) include courtyard areas, paved and unpaved, where dancing and processions could have been performed.[141] Although the existence of these spaces does not necessarily indicate that dancing took place there, it does match contexts for illustrations of dance, such as the Grove and Dance fresco, discussed in chapter one, and a number of seals which include details of paving and architecture. Evans was the first to suggest that dancing took place in the central court and theatral area of the palace of Knossos,[142] and as a result, these sorts of spaces at Bronze Age sites have since been associated with this activity. J. W. Graham, in his important study of Minoan architecture,[143] agrees with and amplifies this view. Graham proposes that the central court and paved areas of Minoan palaces, and by extension the open areas of smaller sites, are areas of paramount importance to the function of the building. Although he admits that no doubt these spaces were used for a variety of functions, he believes their most important one was for ceremonies such as dancing.[144]

The connection between dancing such as seen in the Grove and Dance Fresco and the theatral areas or west courts of the palace is greatly strengthened by a comparison of their details. As I noted in the first chapter, in the Sacred Grove and Dance Fresco, there were a number of walkways which divided the space in which the women dance. In plans of the palaces of Knossos (fig. 62), Phaistos (fig. 63), and Mallia (fig. 64) we find in the west courts exactly similar causeways among the paving stones, and in the case of Knossos and Phaistos, steps, for standing observers on two sides.[145] Even at the town of Gournia in east Crete (fig. 65), at the southern limit of the site, there are steps at the edge of the "town court."

There is also evidence for grandstands or viewing platforms, such as those on which the people sit in the Grandstand fresco found at Knossos. Such structures were found to the northwest of the palace, near the remains of an elaborate paved road, referred to as the Royal Road, which leads due east from the northeastern corner of the structure. What was specifically found were foundations of a large building which the excavator believed were grandstands for watching spectacles which moved up and down the Royal road.[146]

The final bit of archaeological context for dancing comes from the site of Knossos itself. In recent excavations at the stratigraphical museum, three low circular structures were discovered to the west of the palace all of which date to the third palace period at the site.[147] It is clear from the excavation that these structures, between three and eight meters in diameter, were platforms with a smoothed paved surface. Sadly, no archaeological evidence which might allude to their use was discovered, but the excavator believes that they were used for dancing, based on iconographic parallels of circular dance (for instance the Palaikastro figures, fig. 66) and the existence of historical evidence which associates Crete with a very old dancing tradition.[148]

---

[141] Buildings with courts or court yards on Crete are Ayia Triada, Gournia, Knossos, Kommos, Mallia, Zakros, Phaistos, Tylissos, Vasiliki, Archanes-Tourkoyeitonia, Chamaizi, Makryyialos, Myrtos-Pyrgos, Odigitria, Platanos, Pseira, Syme, Vathypetro. For plans and photos, see J. Meyers, E. Meyers and G. Cadogan eds., *The Aerial Atlas of Ancient Crete* (Berkeley: University of California Press, 1992)
[142] See his description of dance on Crete centered around the Sacred Grove and Dance Fresco, *PofM*, vol. III 66-80.
[143] J Graham, *The Palaces of Crete* (Princeton: Princeton University Press, 1987, rev. ed.).

[144] Ibid., 73-5.
[145] Nanno Marinatos, ("Public Festivals in the West Courts of the Palaces," *Function of the Minoan Palaces*, Skrifter utgivna av Svenska Institutet I Athen. (1987) 138-41) proposes that there were shrines in the vicinity of these paved areas which were used for seasonal festivals. Sadly, as with so many of Marinatos' theories, this is based largely on conjecture and assertion.
[146] H. W. Catling, "Central Crete," *Archaeological Reports* (1972-3) 27-30.
[147] Peter Warren, "Circular Platforms at Minoan Knossos" *Annals of the British School at Athens* 79 (1984) 307-323.
[148] Ibid., 319ff.

Figure 62: Plan of Knossos.

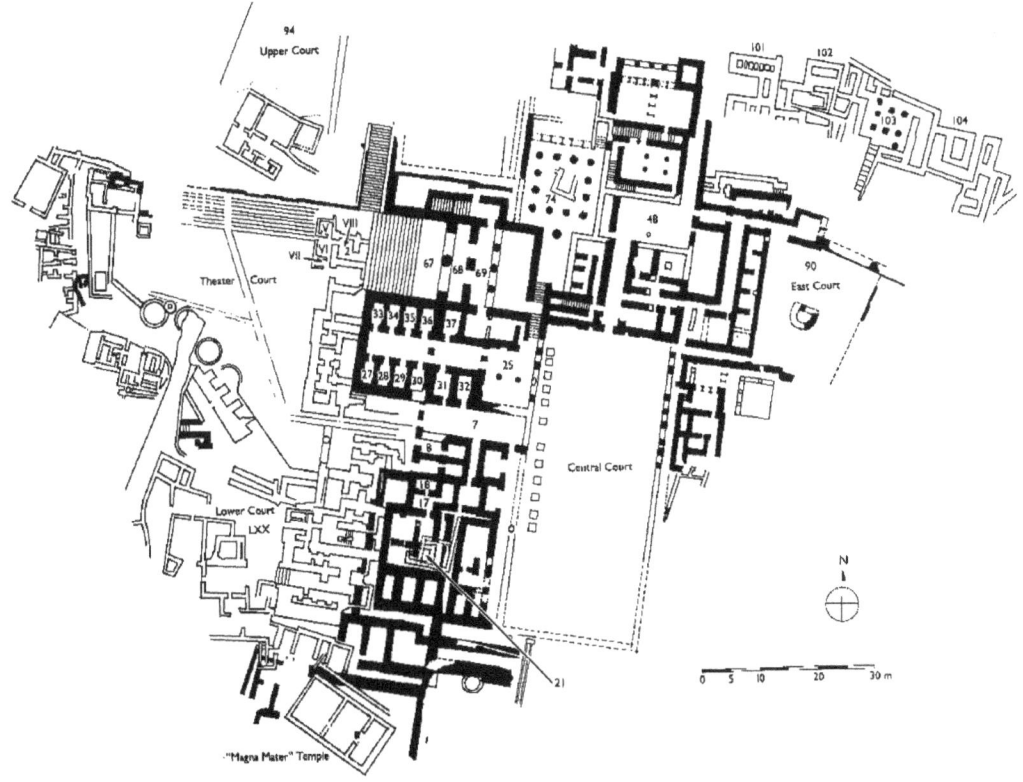

Figure 63: Plan of Phaistos.

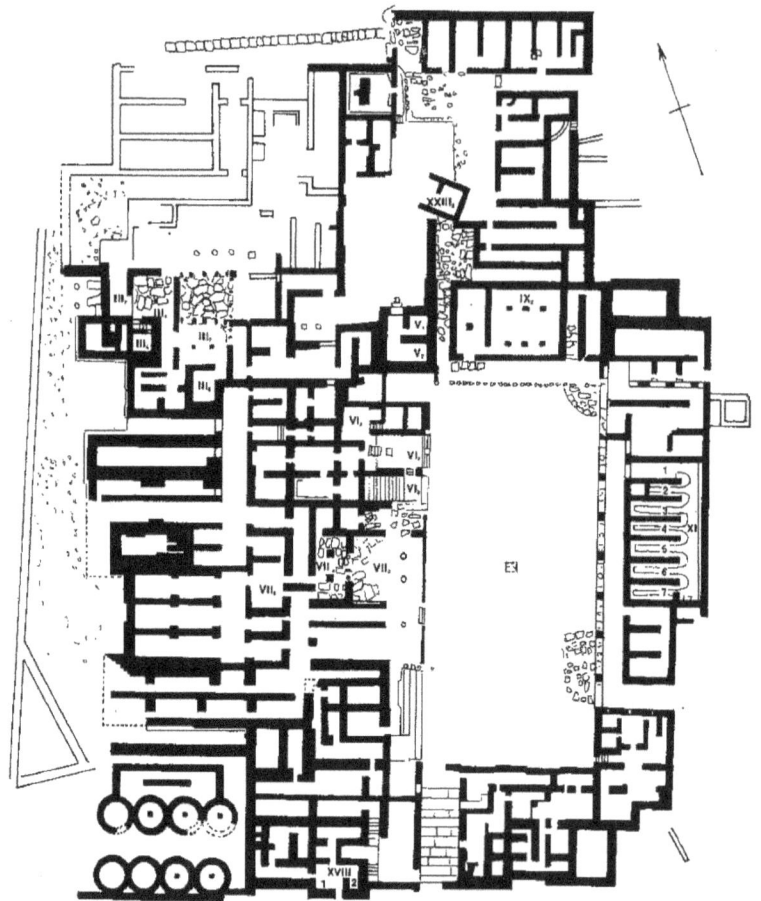

Figure 64: Plan of Mallia.

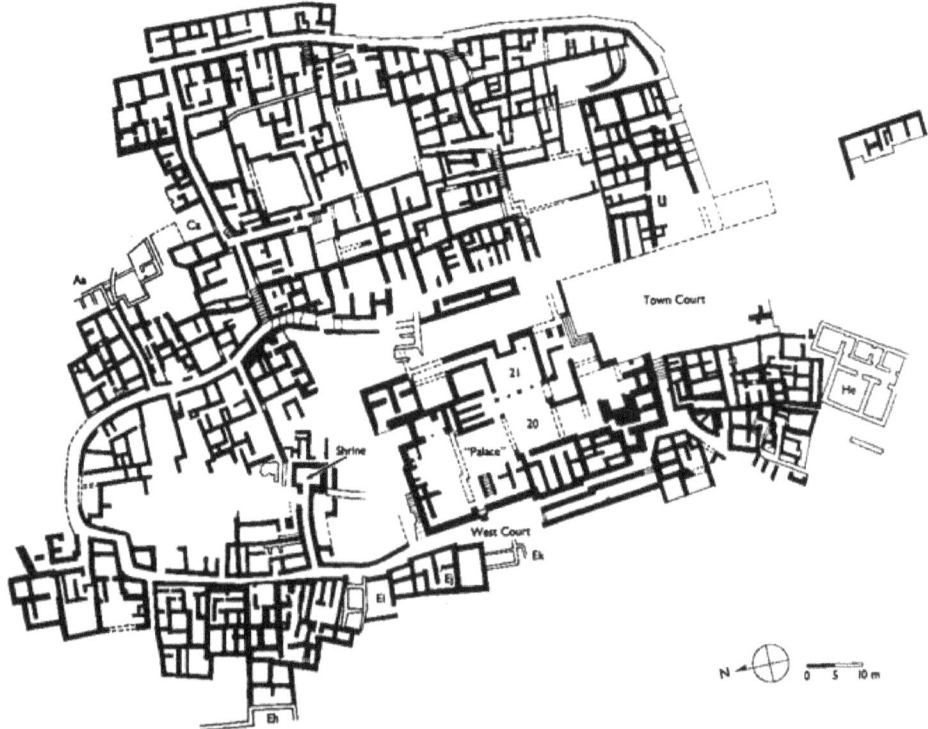

Figure 65: Plan of Gournia.

Figure 66: Figurines of dancing women from Palaikastro; after Warren (1984), plate 35. Catalogue # 84.

The interest in identifying the circular spaces near Knossos as platforms for activities such as dancing would not be so great were it not for a passage from Homer. Book eighteen of the Iliad describes Achilles' shield made by Hephaestus at Thetis' bidding:

> And upon the shield the illustrious smith, lame in both legs, hammered out a dance, similar to (what took place) on the dance floor Daidalos once made in broad Knossos for Ariadne with intricately plaited locks. There were youths dancing and maidens of the price of many cattle, holding their hands upon the wrists of one another. Of these the maidens were clad in fine linen, while the youths wore well-woven tunics faintly glistening with oil; and the maidens had fair chaplets, and the youths had daggers of gold hanging from silver baldrics. Now would they run round with cunning feet exceeding lightly, as when a potter sits by his wheel that is fitted between his hands and makes trial of it whether it will run; and now again would run in rows toward each other. And a great company stood around the lovely dance, taking joy therein; and two tumblers whirled up and down through the midst of them as leaders in the dance.[149]

Hephaestus, we read, creates a whole scene with dancing and acrobatics, and as part of it, he includes a great audience. This excerpt from the Iliad which describes a representation of a performance shows not only that dance was performed and watched but, the scene as described sounds very similar to that of the Sacred Grove and Dance fresco: several people gathered watching a group of well dressed women dancing. This evidence is tantalizing and it is hard to resist making a direct connection between the Iliad and representations which survive from Minoan Crete.

From the Odyssey, there are a number of references to dancing at the royal houses of Menelaus and Odysseus. This activity was always accompanied by eating, music and acrobatics, and was regarded as the highlight of the meal.[150] Dancing is among the activities at a great marriage celebration hosted by Menelaus for the double wedding of his son and daughter.[151] Dancing in the Homeric world, we might conclude, was part of important social events, and perhaps especially associated with Crete. In the melee of battle, in book 16 of the Iliad, Aenaeus comments to Meriones, who has just avoided his spear, that it is on account of his dancing skills that his life was spared;[152] Meriones is introduced in book 2 as slayer of men and native of Crete.[153] However, one must carefully consider the later Homeric source.[154] Although it is generally agreed that Homer preserves some memories, albeit dim, of pre-Classical Greece, it is furthermore agreed that most of these recollections are of the Dark Ages which follow the Bronze Age.[155] In essence, the possibility of anachronism in the use of these data is high and therefore we must proceed cautiously.

Caution notwithstanding, the association between dancing and Crete persists into the classical period in mythology and literature. Lucian, a second century AD philosopher and historian recorded the myth of how Rhea, the mother of Zeus and wife of Kronos, taught the art of dance to, among others, the kouretes, who lived on Crete. The kouretes, a name which literally means young men, later protected the baby Zeus. Rhea fled to Crete and delivered Zeus there and hid him in a cave for fear he would be eaten by his father. In order to drown out the sounds of the baby Zeus' crying, the kouretes leapt and danced around with such vigor that Kronos did not hear him and the child was saved.[156] Most likely it was as a

---

[149] *Iliad*, book 18, 590-606. Loeb translation, A. T. Murray.

[150] *Odyssey*, Book 1, line 125.
[151] *Odyssey* Book 4, lines 17-19.
[152] *Iliad*, book 16, 616-9.
[153] *Iliad*, book 2, 650-1.
[154] For a full treatment of this passage and its possible relationship to Minoan Religion see S. Lonsdale "A Dancing Floor for Ariadne (*Iliad* 18.590-592): Aspects of Ritual Movement in Homer and Minoan Religion," in J. Carter and S. Morris eds. *The Ages of Homer: A Tribute to Emily Townsend Vermeule*. (Austin: University of Texas Press, 1995) 156-64.
[155] For instance, Linear B archives reflect a quite sophisticated political and economic hierarchy which stands at a great distance from the simple oligarchic system reflected in Homer. See Killian's "The Linear B Tablets and Mycenaean Economy" in Morpurgo Davies and Y.Duhoux eds. *Linear B: a 1984 Survey* (Louvian-la-Neuve: Institute de Linguistique de Louvain, 1985) 45-52, for a description of the Mycenaean economy and by extension political hierarchy as represented in the Linear B texts.
[156] *Salt.* 8.

result of this myth that ancient authors frequently referred to Cretans as those who originally developed the art of dance and taught it to others.[157]

The scholiast on the Iliad passage describing Achilles' shield describes the dance in question as known by Theseus. He explains that Theseus, after escaping from the Labyrinth with the help of Ariadne, was instructed by Daidalos in a circling dance. This dance was performed for the gods by him and by the youths and maidens he had rescued and was supposed to resemble in its steps his own wanderings in the labyrinth.[158] Plutarch describes a similar sort of dance which Theseus performed on Delos when he visited that island to dedicate the image of Aphrodite which he had received from Ariadne. We learn that the dance survived to the time of Plutarch and imitated the turns and twists of the Labyrinth.[159] Sophocles' chorus in the *Ajax* mentions a Knossian dance; although we don't know what it looked like, it is referred to as vigorous, high and excited.[160] No doubt, these reflections of Homeric Cretan dancing perpetuated in the later Classical period were only strengthened by the continued practice up to the Iron age on Crete of certain initiation rituals which included dancing. Strabo reports that young men were organized into herds and, among their activities were group dances. In Spartan social practice, noted since antiquity for its strong resemblance to Cretan,[161] women were herded together as well and also were trained in sports, dancing and music.[162]

Therefore, we can see that there is ample later Classical context for connections between Crete and dancing. Specifically, dancing as we read in Homer, was connected with large social celebrations. Dance in Aristotle and Strabo is associated with age and aristocratic activities. And, in both Homer and Sophocles we see that dance was used as a means of identification for people from Crete. We might wonder if dancing at large celebrations, such as a marriage, during the Bronze Age was the origin for these later classical reflections. This is an idea to which I shall return in the fifth chapter.

---

[157] Athenaeus 181b; Strabo 10.5.18; Lucian, Ibid. Lillian Lawler, based on these sources asserts that the Minoans invented dance and were highly developed before the Homeric period. See "The Dance in Ancient Crete," in G. Mylonas ed. *Studies Presented to David Moore Robinson* Vol. I (St. Louis: Washington University Press, 1951).
[158] Schliast A. B. on *Iliad* 18 18.590m as cited in A. B. Cook, *Zeus*, vol. I, (London: Cambridge University Press, 1914), pg. 481.
[159] *Thesus* 21.
[160] *Ajax*, l.700.
[161] Aristotle (Politics II. 127 B 40-1272 A 4) argues that the Spartan constitution was derived from the Cretan and Herodotus (Book I, 65. ii-66.i), Strabo (book 10, 4.17-19) echo this. Several authors both antique and modern take this similarity in legal systems to reflect commonality in social practice. See Willetts, Cretan Cults and Festivals (London: Routledge, 1962) 39-53. One ancient author, Ephorus (FGrH 70, F149) argues the opposite and he might find sympathy with much of modern scholarship. Although Ephorus claims that those who wrote the Cretan constitution came from Sparta, those writing history today attribute the similarity in legal systems to the shared domination of both Crete and the Peloponese (indeed, all of Greece) by the Dorinas.
[162] Ibid. Willetts, 46.

* * *

Having now established the existence of dance in the Aegean Bronze Age, we might turn now to the question of the identification of its representation. How does one determine that an image on a seal is dancing and not acrobatics or some other activity? In approaching this problem it may be fruitful to examine the way in which dancing is identified in the art of other cultures. The goal in this exercise is not so much to discover how dance is represented elsewhere in the hopes that it is the same in the Bronze Age evidence, but rather to understand the ways or codes with which other artists have approached the static representation of patterned movement.

Figure 67: Poussin, Dance to the Music of Time; The Wallace Collection, London. By perrmission of the Trustees of the Wallace Collection.

Nicolas Poussin's *A Dance to the Music of Time* (The Wallace Collection, London; fig. 67) is a typical example of Baroque classicism in style, theme and iconography. Set in an idealized landscape father-time himself sits at the far right of the canvas playing the music to which four women dance in a circle at the center of the canvas. Two putti recline at either lower edge of the scene; one accompanies the song of Father time with a small wind instrument. At the far left is a double headed herm hung with a garland. The way in which Poussin has posed the dancing women ensures the viewer's ability to identify the scene as one of dance. Specifically, the four women hold hands in a circle facing outwards, two with clasped hands raised, two arms down. Each woman has her weight squarely on one foot and the other is bent and out, toes pointed, in mid step. The robes of the women swirl around them ruffled as they catch the air or flat against their flesh, reacting to the ebb and flow of the dance. Lastly, each of the women's heads are extended up and or out in a dramatic pose as if they bend in alternate direction to their bodies. Poussin's inspiration for the billowy movement of the robes of the dancers and the motif of women together dancing is unmistakably Classical art, specifically images of muses and the three

Figure 68: Screen painted with Kabuki dancers; Victoria and Albert Museum, London.
By permission of the Trustees of the Victoria and Albert Museuum.

graces. Reinforcing these classical sources is the herm hung with garlands, a symbol for Dionysus, *de rigeur* for any classical revelry in which there was always ample dancing. Yet, aside from these visual clues for dancing, viewers contemporary with Poussin would have recognized the scene because the dance performed by the women in a ring, called the gavotte, was popular in France and Italy in the 17th and 18th centuries.[163] Thus we see that in Poussin's *A Dance to the Music of Time*, several clues help the contemporary viewer to be able to understand the main activity as dancing.

Japanese block prints illustrating Kabuki dancing are another excellent example of the representation of dancing which is accomplished through the use of visual clues. Kabuki, which consisted of music, theatrical performance and dancing, was conceived in Tokugawa Japan during the 17th century and rapidly became one of the most important forms of entertainment.[164] Because of the huge popularity of Kabuki, its illustration was rapidly taken up by contemporary artists and soon block print scenes of performances and individual performers were popular as well. In one illustration of Kabuki, this one painted on a screen now in the Victoria and Albert Museum (fig. 68), we see the elaborate stage, an audience seated before it, musicians and a line of Kabuki artists dancing. The straight-forward setting of stage, musicians and audience lend the most effective clues to the identification of the scene as Kabuki dancing. However, the dancers themselves, in the way they are represented, offer some clues as to the topic of the image as well. Firstly, the dancers are evenly spaced and generally are grouped in pairs facing each other. Each dancer is in profile and holds one hand up to his head and the other down behind his back. Similarly, each has a foot raised and one on the stage, often matching the raised and lowered hand, creating an almost diagonal or tilting effect of the body. Lastly, the long robes of the dancers sway down from and around the extended limbs of each in such a way as to create a double curved shape, like an "S". All of these repetitively, antithetically, and evenly spaced characters create a rhythmic effect which, in combination with the clearly theatrical venue, corroborates an interpretation of dancing for the scene. Much like the Poussin painting above, the Tokugawa artist has employed a set of culturally specific visual codes which help to illustrate dancing.

Thus, we find that visual clues are immensely helpful in distinguishing activities such as dance in status images. It important to note, however, that such visual clues for dancing can exist in an image which, in fact, does not illustrate dance. For instance, imagine a photograph of a person hailing a cab in a city, one arm out and perhaps even their body leaning towards the oncoming traffic. A position of the body frozen in such a way, arm raised, torso extended, a sense of deliberate direction, could easily be interpreted as part of dance. Like distinguishing dance movements from gymnastics described above, context is critically important, and, even with that, errors are possible. The point being made here is that there is room for the erroneous identification of images of dance

---
[163] Joan Cass, *Dancing Through History*, (Englewood Cliffs: Prentice Hall, 1993) 114-7.
[164] Benito Ortolani, *The Japanese Theatre: from Shamanistic Ritual to Contemporary Pluralism*. Princeton, Princeton University Press, 1995) 45-51.

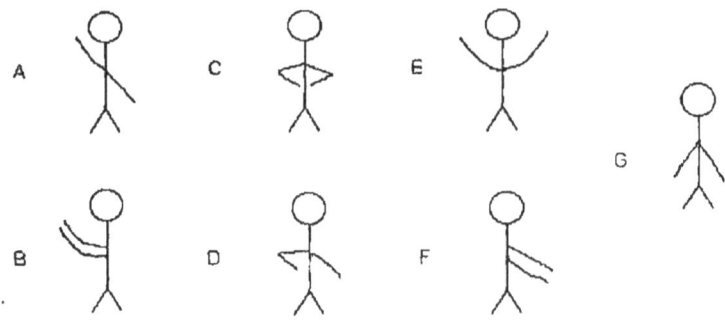

A: One hand front, one back,
B: both in front,
C: arms up at side,
D: one arm up at side the other out.
E: both hands in the air
F: hands held
G: both arms down

Figure 69: Diagram of dance steps.

even in our own culture. It is, of course, possible that such an error can be made with the culturally and temporally remote Aegean Bronze Age materials. Basically, in order to assign an identification of dance to images from that era, a leap of faith is in order.

What about the visual codes used by Aegean Bronze Age artists? The most important visual codes to indicate dance are arm gestures, specifically seven individual ones. These might be called dance steps, however they only involve the movement of the arms. The following is a description of these gestures (see figure 69 for a diagram) By far, the most frequent gesture, A, is one arm up and in front of the body and one arm behind. A sealing from the East Wing of Knossos (fig. 70) is a good example of this pose, featuring two women. The second pose of dance, B, is holding both hands in front. A gold ring from the Isopata cemetery at Knossos (fig. 6) shows two woman striking this pose. The next example, C, consists of both hands held up at the sides. A good example of this pose can be found on a sealing from House A at Zakros (fig. 71), illustrating three men. The next is a pose, D, consisting of one hand up at the side, like the previous pose and one hand down. An example of this comes from a gold ring found at the Aidonia cemetery (fig. 72). In this scene three woman are dancing and the last one on the right performs this step. Another step, E, is both hands in the air, found on a sealing from the House of the Oil Merchant (fig. 73). The next step, F, is both arms out and down, always found in antithetical pairs, like two people holding hands. An example of this step can be found on a sealing from Chania (fig. 74). The final pose, G, a rare one, is both arms down at the sides. This is found on a seal from the cemetery of the Lower town at Mycenae (fig. 75). The woman who dances this step is one of three, the last on the right side.

Figure 70: Seal impression from Knossos; after CMS II8.226. Catalogue # 50.

Figure 71: Seal impression from Zakros; after CMS II7.17. Catalogue # 46.

Figure 72: Gold ring from Aidonia; after CMS V.Sup.IB.115. Catalogue # 58.

Figure 73: Seal impression from Mycenae; after CMS I.162. Catalogue # 12.

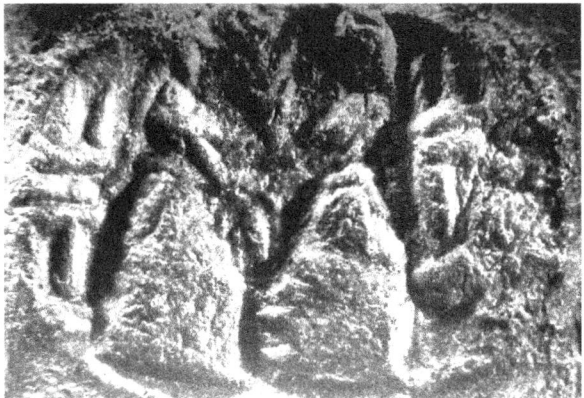

Figure 74: Seal impression from Chania; after CMS V.Sup.IA.178. Catalogue # 54.

These visual clues, or steps, help to identify dancing. Interestingly, these same visual clues not only circumscribes the representation of dancers but, by and large, serve to describe representations of processions as well. One might ask exactly what the difference is between a procession and dance. A procession is movement in succession on any continuous course, in essence not very different from dance but with an intended spatial goal or end point. Objects are also often carried in a procession. Recalling the illustration of the Kabuki dancers (fig. 68), were it not for the inclusion of the musician at the right extreme of the stage, one might believe the other characters on stage were engaged in a procession. In other words, as we have said of dancing above, one needs to understand all the visual clues of processions and the large complex of the activity in order to be able to identify its representations.[165]

The visual similarities between scenes of dancing and processions are strong. For instance, a restored wall painting from Pylos (fig. 76) found on the Northwest slope of the palace illustrates two women who are in the A and G positions, but they carry bouquets of flowers, making it more likely they participate in a procession and are not merely dancing. Another image, a gold ring from the treasury acropolis at Mycenae (fig. 19), shows two women, both in position D and both carrying objects, one a bouquet of lilies and the other a double axe, approaching another woman who sits at the base of a tree. Two aspects of this images lead one to think this represents a procession and not dancing. First, the two women who strike the D pose are carrying objects. Second, we can see that they are processing toward a goal, the woman seated at the base of the tree. Therefore, the only important difference between images of dancing and procession is that some who participate carry objects and some procession/dancing scenes move toward a goal, often a character who is seated facing the action.

Figure 75: Quartz lentoid from Mycenae; after CMS I.132. Catalogue # 9.

---

[165] One study of procession, in wall painting exists. Suzanne Elaine Preston. *Wall Painting in the Aegean Bronze Age: The Procession Frescoes*. PhD Dissertation, University of Minnesota, 1981. The Dissertation seeks to identify all occurrences of processions and concludes that it was a form borrowed from Crete and taken to the mainland and that it bears a relationship to Linear B tables which describe offerings being brought to female deities.

Figure 76: Pylos women fresco; after Immerwahr (1990), plate 57. Catalogue # 92.

The earliest representations of dance come from Crete, specifically from the old palace of Phaistos (fig 77). The first example is an image painted within a bowl found in a room opening out onto the West Court of the Old or first palace.[167] The rather abstract scene shows a figure at the bottom center of the field who wears a long dress which covers all of the body. Two more figures surround this first one, each wearing a petal-shaped tunic and holding one arm up and one down, pose A. The alternating curve of the arms of these surrounding figures coupled with the swoosh of their clothing gives the impression of whirling, almost rhythmic movement. This impression is heightened by the compositional placement of the figures surrounding the central one and by the location of them on the upturned inside of the round bowl. This scene has traditionally been interpreted as two dancers surrounding a goddess.[168] While there is little compelling reason to identify the central character as a goddess, an identification of dancers seems plausible given their formal attributes. If these are indeed dancers, what clues might we find in their representation that helps up identify them as such? An overall sense of movement is conveyed with their body and limbs, a compositional position in relation to one another which indicates shared or simultaneous movement, and arms raised.

However, as the ring from Mycenae illustrates, there are some images which in some ways look like dance (participants strike a dancing pose) but at the same time, they appear to be engaged in a procession (they are carrying an object).[166] How can we tell one from the other and what different meanings might dance and procession have? I believe for these images which exhibit aspects of dancing and procession it is, for all intents and purpose, impossible to determine which activity is being performed. And, indeed, the question must be asked that if they are so similar visually, perhaps, to the Minoans and Mycenaean, there was no difference. This too is a question that cannot be answered. What we can say is, lacking certain facts of cultural contexts, differing interpretations of images as both dancing and procession, are possible and, indeed, must be afforded. Given this, for the purposes of this book, I consider the images of dancing and procession together as a group.

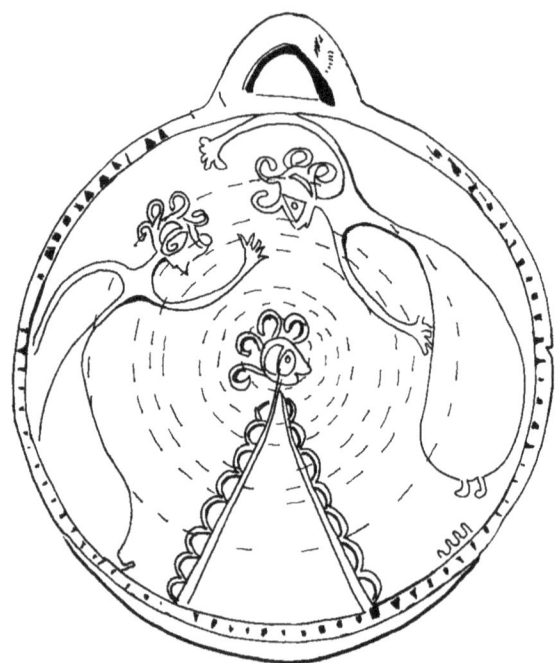

Figure 77: Bowl with dancing women from Phaistos; after Levi (1976), plate LXVII. Catalogue # 82.

* * *

If we can, with some confidence, identify images of dancing and its allied activity, procession, let us move on to examine the corpus of these images as found in various media on Crete and the Mainland.

All these visual clues which identify dancers can be found in another vase (fig. 78) from the same room opening out onto the West Court of the Old palace at

---

[166] Indeed, Lillian Lawler, *The Dance in Ancient Greece*, (Middletown: Wesleyan University Press, 1964) 35, believes some dances were performed while carrying objects.

[167] D. Levi, *Festos* I (Athens: Scuola archeologica di Atene e delle Missioni italiane in Oriente) pl. LXVII.
[168] S. Immerwahr 1990, 33.

Phaistos.[169] This vase shape, essentially a plate elevated on a footed stand, is called a fruit stand, no doubt named such because of its resemblance to modern table serving pieces; its ancient use is unknown. The scene painted on the plate consists of a central character with both hands raised, pose E, holding flowers flanked by two other characters, both with one hand raised up and the other down, pose A. On the foot of the stand, four more characters are painted each of whom wears a petal shaped tunic and holds their hands down at the waist, pose C.

move from left to right. But, in later volumes of the CMS, for instance, volume II3, edited by I. Pini and N. Platon, roughly identically posed men and women are referred to as figures with arms raised (fig. 79 and fig 80). J. Younger, in his volume on late Bronze Age glyptic iconography, refers to the figures as people who are saluting.[170] What becomes obvious from even such a brief review of the historiography of these images is that their static nature has been stressed by past scholars despite the dramatic poses and grand gestures.

Figure 79: Serpentine cushion seal from Knossos; after CMS II3.17. Catalogue # 23.

Figure 78: Fruitstand with dancing women from Phaistos; after Levi (1976), plate LXVI. Catalogue # 83.

In the second palace period, it is again the case that all illustrations of dancing come from only from Crete; however these illustrations are found not on pottery but carved on stamp seals and painted on plaster walls. The dancing image represented on the old palace bowl from Phaistos, two figures in complimentary positions, giving a sense of movement with one arm raised and one down, pose A, remains a popular type in the second palace period, represented in several examples of seals, rings and seal impressions. It is interesting to note that most of these illustrations of dancing found in the medium of glyptic, have been called anything but dance by past scholars. For instance, in A. Sakellariou's description of seals which show dancing in the first volume of the CMS in 1964, she calls them adorants or simply figures who

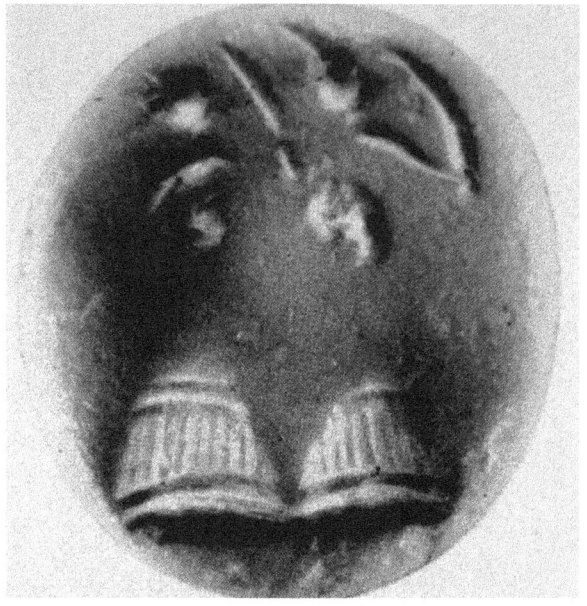

Figure 80: Serpentine lentoid from Gournia; after CMS II3.236. Catalogue # 26.

---

[169] D. Levi, *Festos* I, pl. LXVI.

[170] J. Younger. *The Iconography of Late Bronze Age Glyptic*. Bristol (1992) 217. See pg. 135 where he identifies fig. 25 as "saluting to the left."

Perhaps the most elegant and finely executed example of dancing from the second palace period is a seal impression from Aghia Triada (fig. 81) which illustrates two women facing right in the same pose: one arm raised before them, one behind, both striking pose A, hips back, chest out. Two seal stones, one from Knossos (fig. 79) and one from Gournia (fig. 80) shows very similar scenes and a seal impression from Pylos (fig, 82) can also be included in this group but includes three women, each holding one hand up and one back, in the same swaying, type A pose. A variation on this type, more similar to the characters on the base of the fruit stand from old palace Phaistos, is found on a second palace period seal impression from Aghia Triada (fig. 83). This shows a large woman flanked by two smaller women, each holding their hands at their hips, pose C, swaying torso, moving in tandem. This scene includes some interesting architectural elements: paving beneath the feet of the women and a structure at one end from which a tree or great plant grows. The last example of this group (fig. 74) is of two women who face each other, both in pose F antithetically. Behind each is architecture shown as a post and lintel. The architectural elements in these seals and sealings remind us of the elements of archaeological context associated with dancing discussed above.

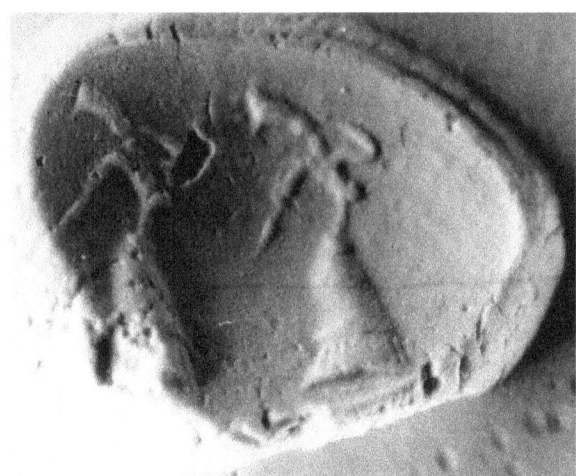

Figure 81: Seal impression from Aghia Triada; after CMS II6.13. Catalogue # 33.

Figure 82: Seal impression from Pylos; after CMS I.313. Catalogue # 19.

Figure 83: Seal impression from Aghia Triada; after CMS II6.1. Catalogue # 29.

These same visual clues which help us identify the women on seals, sealings and rings as dancers are used in the Sacred Grove and Dance fresco (fig. 8), discussed in chapter one. Although fragmentary, the fresco shows women with their arms raised, and bodies poised in the same swaying motions, pose A So, during the second palace period, visual clues which help identify people as dancers include figures in complimentary positions, giving a sense of movement, arms raised, and sometimes in a built environment. As we have also discussed, representations of procession are very similar.

The most famous representation of a procession from the Aegean Bronze Age, the procession fresco, comes from Knossos.[171] Originally lining both sides of the walls of the west entrance passage,[172] the fresco illustrates several figures, men and women, moving toward each other. Sadly, the vast majority of the fresco is gone with the exception of many of the figures' feet and a few characters in the scene.[173] The best preserved, the cup bearer (fig. 5) is a man who carries a large conical vase, or rhyton, in a variation of pose C.[174] The torsos and legs of two other figures are also preserved and together with the cup bearer, the sense of the procession can be imagined (fig. 4)[175] and, indeed, seems somewhat similar

---

[171] I use the procession fresco here as an example of second palace period wall painting. Evans' original publication of the fresco was ambiguous about its date, reporting a third palace period destruction context, but claiming that it was based upon an earlier painting in the same spot, for which there is no archaeological evidence. Although a third palace period date is in general preferred; see E. Davis "The Cycladic Style of the Thera Frescoes," in L. Hardy and C. Renfrew eds. *Thera and the Aegean World III*, 1990) 214-227 has recently suggested that the fresco might be datable to LMIb, the second palace, based on the vessels carried by the participants.
[172] *PofM* vol. II.2, 679-684. Evans first reconstructed the scene as two friezes one above the other.
[173] Christos Boulotis, "Nochmals zum Prozessionsfresko von Kossos: Palast und Darbringung von Prestige-Objekten," *Function of the Mionan Palaces* (1987) 145-155. In this article Boulotis proposes a new reconstruction for the fresco (Boulotis fig. 8) not as a continuous procession towards a female figure at the north end of the east wall of the corridor, as Evans did, but instead as a procession in which the female is at the center and discrete groups move toward her.
[174] *PofM* II.2, fig. 443; Ibid. Boulotis' fragment group H.
[175] Ibid, Boulotis fragment group D, fig.5.

to illustrations of dancing discussed above. Specifically, characters share pose and gesture and these suggests measured purposeful movement. No doubt, there are differences between commonly known contemporary examples of dancing and procession, such as square dancing and the procession to the altar in a church. However, how different really is the basic appearance of these two activities? Considered in these visual terms, similarities between dancing or processions seem greater than differences and one is compelled to couple the two in the same general category. The discussion of other examples of processions will help make this point clear.

A seal impression from the second palace period palace of Zakros (fig. 84) shows two men, legs apart, seemingly in mid-step, both striking the same pose, one hand carrying an object, the other arm away from the torso or, in pose D. One man carries a double axe, the other a large piece of cloth. Like the representations of dancing discussed earlier, there is a sense of movement and the poses are complimentary. Two impressions of the same date from Aghia Triada illustrate very similar scenes; one (fig. 85) shows a man and a woman, his arm raised carrying a double axe, her arms raised too, possibly carrying the same object, although this is unclear. Their movements compliment one another, arms raised in the same pose, and her hips and his skirt swaying. The other sealing (fig. 86) illustrates three men in procession, each with arms raised carrying objects, in various poses, B, C and D from left to right, all the while swaying back, feet apart, as they move to the left.

Figure 85: Seal impression from Aghia Triada; after CMS II6.10. Catalogue # 31.

Figure 86: Seal impression from Aghia Triada; after CMS II6.9. Catalogue # 30.

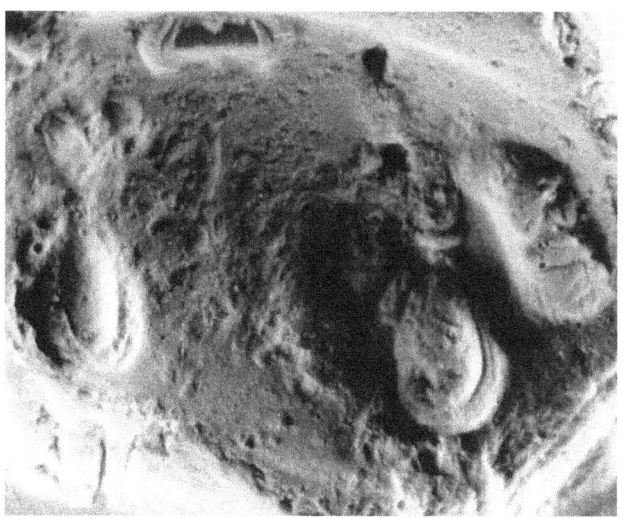

Figure 84: Seal impression from Zakros; after CMS II7.7. Catalogue # 40.

As mentioned above, a variation on this type of procession is when characters who move in procession carrying things to someone who is seated. A good example of this can be found on a seal impression from Zakros (fig. 87) which illustrates two women, the first one of whom carries a two handled vessel, a variation on pose B, moving toward another woman who is seated at the far right. The second woman in the procession is very difficult to see because of damage to the impression. Another glyptic representation of a procession which dates to the second palace period comes from the Mainland and, in fact, is the only example of a procession dating to the second palace period not from Crete. The piece is a gold ring (fig. 19) found in the Treasury Acropolis at Mycenae south of the grave circles. The ring is excellently preserved and offers many interesting details. There are three main characters in the scene, two women who move from right to left, the one in front carrying a double axe and the one behind flowers, and another woman who is seated at the base of a tree, herself holding flowers. In addition to these three, there are three diminutive characters, one of whom, female, leads the procession and carries flowers as well, one behind the tree with her arms raised, and a smaller man wearing a figure-eight shield who appears suspended above and between the two women who move toward the seated character. No doubt, this ring illustrates a specific idea, story or ceremony, sadly lost to us today. I would argue, however, that procession is a component of it, given the way in which the two woman are depicted moving toward the seated one, each in the same pose, hips back, and carrying an objects, both in pose D.

Figure 88: Seal impression from Zakros; after CMS II7.15. Catalogue # 44.

Figure 87: Seal impression from Zakros; after CMS II7.8. Catalogue # 41.

All of these examples of procession include men and women who carry objects. In fact, it is this detail which is most important in differentiating these images from those of dancing, for we have seen that they otherwise share important visual codes. There is yet another group of images which share these visual codes of procession and dancing but do not feature objects in the hands of the participants. This is a small group, comprised of only seals and sealings, and interestingly, it disappears entirely in the following third palace period. Perhaps the clearest example of this group is a sealing from Zakros (fig. 88). This impression shows three men, all in the same pose, legs apart, arms held up at their waists, all in pose C, moving as a group from left to right. The carver of the stone which created the impression overlapped the back two figures and, as the three men strike exactly the same pose as they move along, the effect is almost rhythmic, just as that found in representation of dancing. Two other sealings (fig 89 and fig. 90), also from Zakros, illustrate very similar scenes, but feature only two men. A serpentine seal from the villa site of Nerokourou can be grouped with these sealings in pose C (fig. 91). It illustrates five women in tight profile procession, each wearing a long skirt and elaborate jacket. Interestingly, as with some examples of dancing, they are shown walking on a paved surface to which a special detail has been added, a hatched texture.

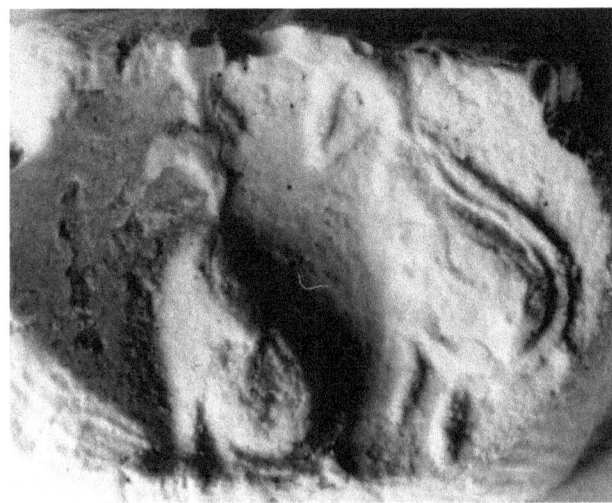

Figure 89: Seal impression from Zakros; after CMS II7.13. Catalogue # 42.

Figure 90: Seal impression from Zakros; after CMS II7.14. Catalogue # 43.

Figure 91: Serpentine lentoid from Nerokourou; after CMS V.Sup.1A.186. Catalogue # 45.

The last subset of this group of glyptic representations of men and women not carrying objects, is one which features people walking in the same direction but who do not hold their arms in the same way. What gives the impression that these representations are of processions is only that two people are shown moving in the same direction; they don't look similar in the way in which the other men and women in representations of procession and dancing do. The first two examples are two identical impressions (fig. 92; cat.#45; fig. 93; cat.#46), no doubt made with the same seal, from Zakros. This scene shows a woman and another character, likely a man, both legs apart, both arms forward moving from right to left. The woman holds her hands up to her waist, pose C, and the other character holds his arms out before him in pose B. The last example of this type (fig. 93) comes from Aghia Triada and is quite fragmentary. Despite its state of preservation, one can make out that there are two men, both legs apart, moving from right to left, the one in front holding his hands to his waist, pose C, and the man behind apparently wrapped in a robe, likely his hands at his sides beneath the cloth, pose G.

During the third palace period, representations of dancing and processions continue to be popular with some notable changes. First, the last type discussed above, men and women in procession empty-handed is not found. Second, representations of both processions and dancing abound on the Mainland, a great change from the previous second palace period which featured only one representation of a procession. Third, there are several more examples of these representations in wall painting.

On Crete during the third palace period the only representation of dancing found in wall painting comes from the Queen's Megaron at Knossos (fig. 94). This fresco is only preserved to show the top half of a woman who has her arms out in front of her, pose B, and her hair flying around her shoulders as she moves. Although the lower half of her torso and therefore part of the shape of her pose is lost, the indication of her flying hair and the pose of her arms can safely lead us to believe that this is a painting of a woman engaged in dance. The three remaining representations of dancing from Crete during the third palace period come from Knossos. The first is a seal impression (fig. 70) from the East wing of the palace which shows a now familiar scene of three women each holding one hand up and one back and behind and all sharing the same swaying pose, A. The next example, a gold ring from the Isopata cemetery (fig. 6) is a more complicated composition and recalls the Sacred Grove and Dance fresco where a number of women are spread across a field, posing in various positions. On this seal, one woman occupies the top of the field, holding one arm up and forward and the other back and down, pose A. She faces another who stands with her arms raised up and out, pose E. At the right stand two women both holding their hands up in the air before them, pose B. All the women stand in the familiar swaying pose of dance. One diminutive figure hangs in the air above the pair with their arms raised, her arms out and facing the woman at the top of the scene. Scattered throughout the field lilies bloom, creating the sense that the scene takes place outside and in an area that stretches around them. Much like the second palace period ring from Mycenae discussed above, the meaning of this complicated scene is lost to us today. However, it appears that dancing is part of the story. The last glyptic example of a representation of dancing which dates to the third palace period on Crete is an electrum ring (fig. 95; cat.#25) from the Isopata cemetery near the palace. In this scene, two women face each other arms out and touching, both in pose F, with a post and lintel architectural element behind them.

Figure 92: Seal impression from Zakros; after CMA II7.16. Catalogue # 55.

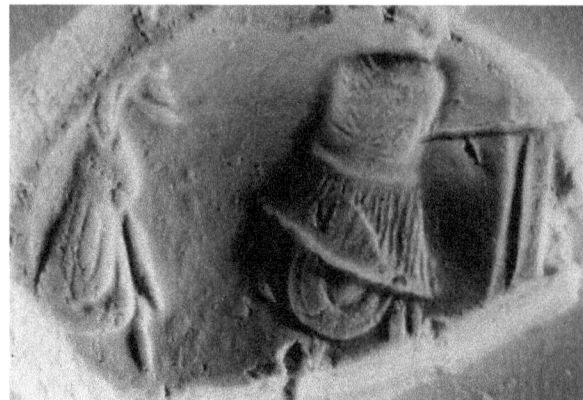

Figure 93: Seal impression from Aghia Triada; after CMS II6.11. Catalogue # 32.

Figure 94: Dancing woman fresco from Knossos; after Immerwahr (1990) plate 43. Catalogue # 76.

Figure 95: Electrum ring from Knossos; after CMS II3.56. Catalogue # 25.

The only other representation of dancing dating to the third palace period on Crete is a small terra-cotta group found at the site of Palaikastro, block Delta (fig. 66). This scene shows three women, each with her arms out to hold the hand of another, forming a ring. In the middle of the scene is a lyre or kithara player. The scene is no doubt a ring dance, complete with musician.

There is only one representation in wall painting of a procession dating to the third palace period on Crete, and it comes from Aghia Triada, on the Aghia Triada sarcophagus (Fig. 96). Although enigmatic in interpretation, it clearly shows at least two men moving from left to right, each holding animal, each in a variation of pose C. However, given the similarity to, for instance, images like the impressions from Aghia Triada (figs 86 and fig. 85) which show two figures moving together carrying objects, it seems likely that the painting on the sarcophagus depicts a procession as well.

Figure 96: Aghia Triada sarcophagus; after Long (1977), plate 13. Catalogue # 73.

Turning to the Mainland during the third palace period, as mentioned above, representations of dancing and processions are many. There are no fewer than eight examples of dancing found illustrated on seals, sealings and rings. As a group, these images are rather homogeneous. Three examples, a gold ring from Mega Monastiri (fig. 97), and two impressions, one from the House of the Oil Merchant at Mycenae (fig. 73) and the other from Room 98 at the palace of Pylos (fig. 82), are excellent examples of dancing that employ the visual codes in use since the old palace period. In each, all the women strike exactly the same swaying pose, and each holds her arms identically, either one hand before the face and one down or both hands raised up, the popular pose A. Interestingly, the ring from Monastiri places the dancing women in the proximity of a post and lintel structure. Three more examples, all gold rings, one from a chamber tomb within the necropolis of the Lower Town at Mycenae (fig. 98) and two from A chamber tomb at Aidonia (figs. 11 and fig 72) are very similar to one another because they all feature three dancing women facing a post and lintel architectural structure. The ring from Mycenae is damaged and the bottom of the scene is invisible however, the poses of the three women are clear: the first in pose C, second pose A and the third in pose G, from left to right. The first example from Aidonia (fig. 11) shows outstanding detail, both in the paving stones beneath the feet of the women and in the architecture they face. They strike poses, A, E and D, from left to right respectively. The last of the three (fig. 72) features a post and lintel structure at either side of the group of three women, who dance in pose B, A and D, from left to right. A nice detail of this otherwise crude ring is a line of paving blocks beneath the feet of the dancers. The final example of representations of dancing in glyptic dating to the third palace period from the Mainland is somewhat unusual. It is a quartz seal stone from a chamber tomb in the Lower Town at Mycenae (fig. 75) and illustrates two women, both in pose D, and one man, in pose G, dancing in tandem facing to the right. Unusual are two figure-eight shields floating in the field around the dancers.

Figure 97: Gold ring from Mega Monasiri; after CMS V2.728. Catalogue # 64.

Figure 98: Gold and silver ring from Mycenae; after CMS I.108. Catalogue # 8.

The largest group of images of dancing and procession dating to the third palace period from the Mainland depicts men and women in procession carrying objects; some of the most vivid representations in this group are wall paintings. One of the better known and often reproduced is the frieze from the Kadmeia at Thebes (fig. 99). Restored by Reusch[176] the procession includes somewhere between nine and twelve life-sized women facing left and right, with both frontal and profile bodies. Although apparently there is a variety of poses, almost all the woman hold objects ranging from flowers to vessels to pyxides, and the women all strike variations of poses B and D. Very similar to this procession is the one found at Tiryns (fig. 100). This procession consisted of as many as eight life-sized women each of whom carried objects such as vases and even a figurine; again, all women strike poses in some variation of B and D. Yet another very similar fresco comes from Pylos (fig. 76), again of life-sized women carrying objects, in this case flowers, but in a variation of pose A, one hand up and one behind. These figures are somewhat different from the other two examples as the women seem very close together, almost overlapping. Also from Pylos, from the vestibule of the late palace, comes a frieze of men (fig. 101), less than life-size, however, carrying, apparently, a different range of objects, such as woven baskets and a palanquin, or pole suspended between them. These figures strike a variation of pose B. From Mycenae comes the last example of this group (fig. 102). This procession fresco, also featuring men, comes from the floor beneath the main corridor of the House of the Oil Merchant. The scale is much smaller than that of the other three examples, but not quite miniature, and features men carrying objects on a palanquin, again in a variation of pose B.

Figure 99: Procession fresco from Thebes; after Reusch (1948-9), fig. 11. Catalogue # 68.

---

[176] H. Reusch. "Der Franenfries von Theben." *Archaeologische Anzeiger* 63-64 (1948-49) 240-253. The reconstruction that Reusch proposes is based on several fragments which were found in a disturbed context. The reconstruction, then, must be used cautiously.

Figure 100: Procession fresco from Tiryns; after Immerwahr (1990), plate 56. Catalogue # 100.

Figure 102: Palaquin fresco from Mycenae; after Wace (1956), plate 9. Catalogue # 81.

Processions featuring people carrying objects are also found in the third palace period in the glyptic arts. Three sub groups stand out. First, three rings and one ring mold all feature women in groups of two or three processing adjacent to architecture, carrying flowers or some sort of vegetation, all in pose A, one hand before them and one behind. The first (fig. 103) an extraordinary gold ring from a tomb at Aidonia, gives perhaps the most detail, including the women's hair flowing down from their shoulders, carefully paved stones beneath their feet, and even the stamens of the lilies they carry. The next ring (fig. 104), also gold from a chamber tomb at Dendra, shows the same sort of scene but with less detail; not only is the ring clearly made by a different artist, but it is much more the worse for wear. Nonetheless, the free-flowing hair of the women and details of the architectural framework before them and beneath their feet is very similar. The next ring of this group (fig. 105), another gold ring, this one from a chamber tomb in the Lower Town at Mycenae, shows the same scene but features three women what they carry looks much more like branches than blossoms. However, great detail is given to the pavement beneath their feet and even to their facial features which is somewhat unusual in this medium. Last of this group is a steatite block into which is carved a mold which was likely used to form the bezel for a ring (fig. 106). Although the representation is crude, one is able to make out the structure towards which the two women process and the vegetation which they hold in their hands.

Figure 101: Miniature procession fresco from Pylos; after Lang (1966), plate 4-6. Catalogue # 94.

Figure 103: Gold ring from Aidonia; after CMS V.Sup.1B.113. Catalogue # 56.

illustrates two women together moving in a procession, one arm up before them, the other down and behind, pose A. However, the woman in front is carrying an animal of some sort over her shoulder. The impression from Pylos (fig. 108), although fragmentary and further marred by a linear B inscription on its face, appears to bear a striking resemblance to the theme of the gold ring from Mycenae (fig. 19) dating to the second palace period: two women approaching in procession a woman seated at the right. Despite the difficulty in reading the images, one can perhaps see that the woman directly in front of the seated woman is carrying a small object, perhaps a vessel of some kind and is in a variation of pose B. This is again similar to the seal impression from Zakros dating to the second palace period (fig. 87).

Figure 106: Steatite lentoid from Eleusis; after V2.422. Catalogue # 60.

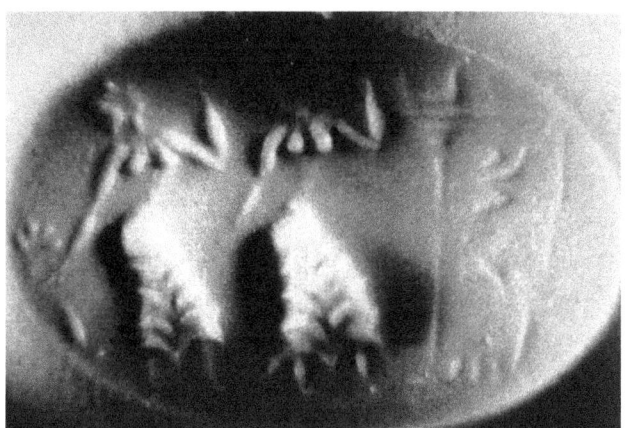

Figure 104: Gold ring from Midea; after CMS I.191. Catalogue # 13.

Figure 105: Gold ring from Mycenae; after CMS I.86. Catalogue # 7.

Two more examples remain in the category of glyptic examples of figures in a procession carrying objects, dating to the third palace period from the Mainland: a seal stone from the beehive tomb at Vaphio and a sealing from Pylos. The seal stone from Vaphio (fig. 107)

Figure 107: Chalcedony lentoid from Vaphio; after CMS I.220. Catalogue # 15.

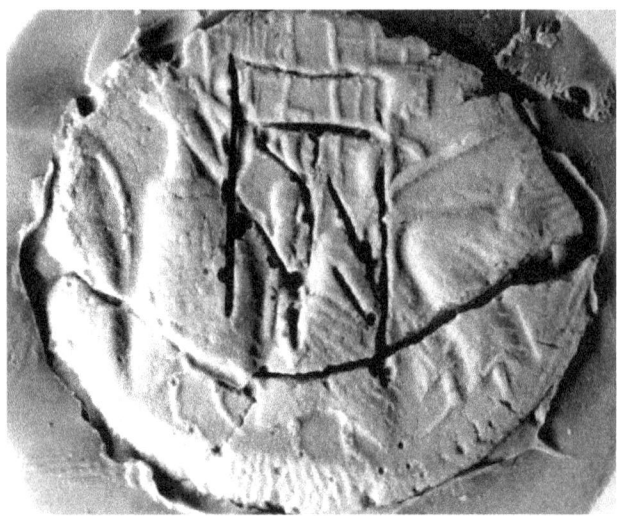

Figure 108: Seal impression from Pylos; after CMS I.361. Catalogue # 20.

This examination of images of dancing and procession give an understanding of the formal qualities and historical development of these images. Abstracted representations of dance comes first at the old palace of Phaistos followed by an explosion on Crete during the second palace period where images of dance and its sister motion, procession, become rather standardized. Interestingly, there appear to be no wall paintings which illustrate processions. A gold ring from Mycenae is the only example of this motif on the mainland during this period. In the following third palace period, however, images of dancing and procession on the mainland outnumber those on Crete by more than two to one with no fewer than five examples of wall painting, all processions. Glyptic evidence from the third palace period on the mainland is still, though, the majority. On Crete during this period, there are nearly equal numbers of examples of wall painting and glyptic representations of dancing and procession, and on the mainland, among wall paintings, processions prevail.

* * *

Having now established the existence of dance and procession and having reviewed the development of these images on Crete and the Mainland during the late Bronze Age, we might now turn to issues of interpretation. Perhaps the best starting point for such a discussion is with the meaning of dance itself.

Dancing can describe small or large actions, whimsical or tightly choreographed, one person or a line of Rockettes. For some, dance is an event of high culture executed on a stage in leotards; for others it is spontaneous, enjoyed barefoot on a dirt floor, surrounded by friends and family. Despite wide variations, dance is an activity that all cultures share; the range of actions, circumstances, and rules of dancing in the cultures of today's world is vast. There is no reason to assume that dancing in the past wasn't equally diverse, nor is there any reason to think it bears any relation to our own today. Thus, when thinking about dancing as a category of description for images dating to the late Aegean Bronze Age, one must be careful that the construction of that category is based as much as possible upon a range of definitions of dancing culled from cross-cultural and transhistorical study and as little as possible upon the thin sliver of our own modern experiences.

But, what is dance? Like most definitional questions, the asking is embedded in specific interpretive modes and an expectation of a certain range of answers. I pose this question here in order to get at the variety of meanings dance might have had in the past. As with all questions about history, we approach this one from the bias of our modern perspective and experiences.[177] In short, a definitive definition of dance is impossible and not particularly desirable because it would, inevitably, be in some way lacking.

It is perhaps more useful to try to think about the various components of such a definition. First might be the aesthetics of dance. This is to see dance as a kind of art which can be appreciated and judged as such. This view of dance, which brings to bear aesthetic concepts such as beauty and harmony, can be contrasted with an artistic approach to dance which involves specific knowledge of the art, such as form, style and meaning.[178] In other words, there is the aesthetic definition of dance, "it is exciting and beautiful, and the artistic, "it is tightly executed rings of tourne-jétés." One is ruled by subjective measures of pleasure and beauty and the other by a shared body of knowledge, history and meanings. To approach dance from the point of view of aesthetics can be limiting, as invariably whatever dance is deemed an aesthetic success is merely one which is in accordance with contemporary definitions of beauty. Artistic approaches to dance offer more as they involve a larger and more regularized set of standards. As anyone who has read a dance review in the newspaper can attest, although the author's opinion of the "prettiness" of a given dance performance might be interesting, one's judgment of the form, style and historical contribution is more critical.

Another approach to dance is phenomenological, its meaning generated within the context of a field of action. Aristotle's view of dance is an example of such, seeing it as the movement of the limbs in relation to what remains the static center of the dancer's being.[179] In phenomenology, then, dance is an activity which serves, in part, to create a being or identity of the dancer. This experience is expressed elegantly by Mary Coros, in her discussion of liminality and the phenomenological exploration of Cretan dance:

---

[177] Cf. discussion of Bourdieu at the beginning of chapter two.
[178] Graham McFee, *Understanding Dance*. (New York: Routledge, 1992) 42.
[179] On the Soul, III

On the Way to the Dance Floor
I am not as I have just been and
I am not as I am about to be
My body-being is on its way...to it knows not what...
My body-being is moving away from what is known, from what is comfortable...
To the Unknown...
My body-being is on it way to risk...
My body–being doesn't Recognize itself...
My body-being is moving out of the mundane kinetic mode but does not know what to be-come or how to be-come or when to be-come...[180]

In other words, Coros sees dance as an action which works to define the self. Some philosophers see this as a promising new direction in dance philosophy.[181] Indeed, perhaps this approach to dance, so closely rooted to physical activity and ultimately tied to issues of meaning and self creation, is the most fruitful to keep in mind in the following chapter. Specifically, what were the dances that might have taken place in the Bronze Age Aegean, what did they look like and how did they work to create meaning for the participants?

In order to pursue this sort of approach to dance, the nuts and bolts of dance, the movement itself, must be explored. At its most basic, dance is the movement of the body through time and space as an end in itself; a non-utilitarian body movement. But, what is dance and what is not? How can one tell the difference between a gymnastic display and dancing? As Graham McFee has pointed out in her discussion of this same question, it is only through the knowledge of the relationships that a set of movements has to other things one understands that allows one to be able to identify the difference.[182] For instance, indeed, there is little difference between a number of the physical actions of an acrobat and a dancer. However, the association the same act has with the different consumes, venues, staging and music, easily distinguishes it. Because one knows other actions and circumstances of dance and gymnastics, one is able to distinguish a movement shared by both of these activities as one or the other. Furthermore, there are sets of rules which are different for gymnastics and dance. Again, because of a shared knowledge about the practice of gymnastics and dance one is able to distinguish one from the other. In all cases, these distinctions can be made visually. In short, visual clues, the likes of which we have explored above, help us determine what is dance and what is not.[183]

But, how can we begin to understand the signification of these images? Three approaches are worth exploring to interpret dance: post-modern, anthropological, and religious. Each one of these approaches offers important insight to the representation of dance.

Post-modern scholars approach dance in cross disciplinary studies which employ the now massive literature on the body and gender. These studies approach dance and the body with an emphasis on corporeality and physical interaction, moving away from the idea of dance as social event embedded within a specific cultural practice but instead embracing it as non-verbal text, something that can be independently examined and interpreted.[184] This sort of approach to dance offers the reintroduction of the body itself into thinking and thus, an essentially physical, corporeal self-consciousness of our own bodies in the reconstruction of past and present knowledge.[185] Ultimately, through these works, the concept of dance, and dance itself, emerge as a vital component of self conscious culture-creation and not merely corporal manipulation. Furthermore, this reconsideration of dance makes the examination of it, especially in the remote past, vastly more rich.

But, what can a post-modern approach to dance offer Bronze Age studies? Broadly, it casts dance as a key component in cultural history as "socially structured movement,"[186] able to be interrogated and interpreted like any other sort of historical text. More specifically, this approach opens the possibility that embedded within, swirling around, dance are elements that influence and are reactive to ambient society.

The meanings of dance are interpreted by anthropologists as aspects of human behavior and ritualized action.[187] Concentrating on the way in which dance functions as metaphor for or representative of tensions, narratives or celebrations within cultural systems such as rites of

---

[180] Mary Coros as quoted in Francis Sparshott, *Off the Ground: First Steps to a Philosophical Consideration of the Dance* (Princeton: Princeton University Press, 1988) 345.
[181] Ibid, Sparshott 131-2, 239-240.
[182] Ibid, McFee, 53.
[183] Another form of performative body movement for which there is some visual evidence (see for instance CMS II3.10) is acrobatics. This images of acrobats and this activity has been discussed by W. Deonna, *Symbolisme de L'acrobatie Antique*, (Paris: Boccard, 1953) and O. Pelon, "L'acrobate de Malia et L'art de l'epoque Protopalatial en Crete" in R. Laffineur ed. *Iconographie Minoenne*, (Athens, Ecole francaise d'Athens, 1985). I regard acrobatics as distinct from dancing because this is an action for which an extensive amount of training is needed and therefore performed by a special group of people. Indeed, images of acrobatics, compared to bull leaping, dancing or procession are rare and no doubt reflect the exclusivity of this activity.
[184] See especially Susan Leigh Foster ed. *Representation Corporealities: Dancing, Knowledge, Culture and Power* (New York: Routledge, 1996) and Judith Lynne Hanna *Dance, Sex and Gender: Signs of Identity, Dominance, Defiance, and Desire* (Chicago: U. Of Chicago Press, 1988)
[185] Further on this ideas of the reintroduction of the corporeal body to studies of the body see Caroline Bynum, "Why All the Fuss About the Body? A Medievalist's Perspective" *Critical Inquiry* 22 (1995) 1-33.
[186] Norman Bryson, "Cultural Studies and Dance History," in Jane C. Desmond ed. *Meaning in Motion: New Cultural Studies of Dance* (Durham: Duke University Press, 1997) 61.
[187] For an excellent introduction to the topic see Anya Peterson Royce *The Anthropology of Dance* (Bloomington, Indiana University Press, 1977), especially chapters two and nine which discuss anthropological approaches and meaning. L. Ager Wallen and J Acocella eds. *A Spectrum of World Dance: Tradition, Transition and Innovation* (Boston: Cord 1987) gives a good overview of the variety of dances today all over the world.

passage, rituals of warfare or feasts, anthropologists have located dance as part of the configuration of, among other things, societal traits, non-verbal communication, theater or entertainment. Thinking about dance in these ways transcends issues of technique and form and instead starts to get at the ways dance can take on meaning in the lives of individuals and groups.

Paul Spencer, in his introduction to a volume on dance and anthropology lists a number of themes recurrent in anthropological works on dance.[188] First, there is the notion that dance functions as a sort of society-wide catharsis, releasing pent-up emotions within social groups. This notion is, obviously, very similar to Victor Turner's idea of social drama.[189] The second notion is dance as a means of social control. This is that dance is used as an educational technique, or passage rite. A variation on this is the notion that dance is part of the maintenance of sentiments. In other words, this means that dance can be seen as a mechanism through which cultural sentiments or collective emotions, are communicated. An example of this might be a joyful dance at a celebratory ceremony. Lastly three is the notion that dance functions as an element of competition and boundary display. Obviously, in no culture is dance one or all of these things however, these themes, offer an excellent starting point for approaches.

Religion is the lens through which Aegean prehistorians have most often viewed to dancing and processions. Evans was largely the progenitor of this thinking. He devotes a chapter in *The Palace of Minos* to the discussion of processions which begins with the great procession fresco at Knossos (fig. 5).[190] Evans seems split on the significance of processions, partially interested in how they seem to imitate tributary processions often illustrated in contemporary Egypt,[191] and their ritual function. Evans devotes another full chapter to a discussion of dancing in the third volume of *The Palace of Minos* and in it, working from the representation of the Sacred Grove and Dance fresco, he outlines the religious function of dance, describing it as orgiastic and ecstatic. Evans' descriptions of dance belies his period's belief in the primitive and feral nature of preliterate cultures. The ultimate goal of these frenzied and, to his 19th century eye, somewhat indecent performances was to cause an epiphany of the divinity.[192]

As with so many of Evans' ideas, especially about religion, his interpretation of dancing and its role in religious ritual was, without criticism, picked up by later scholars and built upon.[193] Some thirty years after the publication of *The Palace of Minos*, in a book dedicated to dancing in ancient Greece, one reads that dancing was central to Cretan religion, yet little more than Evans' musings can prove this.[194] The result is that dancing is now exclusively associated with goddesses or religious ritual in the literature and, like many aspects of Bronze Age religion, is regarded as an enigma.[195] The infamous mother-goddess cult of early Greece which grew in tandem with Evans' belief in matriliny and matriarchy in Bronze Age Crete has lately suffered a certain amount of criticism or at least historicizing.[196] Briefly stated, these recent critical works deconstruct Evans' interpretations of archaeological remains which pertain to women, mostly representations of them in art, placing them within his turn of the century British bourgeois idea(l)s of femininity and his interpretations of women's status in Homer.

Although some of Evans' ideas about dance and Minoan religion may indeed be correct, the lack of critical thinking about Minoan dance precludes acceptance of this. If a critical analysis of dance, such as I hope to accomplish here, would indicated the usefulness of a religious approach to dance in the Aegean Bronze Age, Evans' and other's works would gain strength and renewed importance.

* * *

Having now outlined the formal attributes of dancing and procession as well as interpretive constructs of these activities, I return to the images again to make general observations in order to see how they convey ideas about our three social categories, gender, age and social status.

Concentrating on the basic nature of the representations of dance performance and procession, I have drawn out three points of detail which the images share: movement, strength/vigor, and balance/torsion. A sense of movement or motion is understood through the recognition of the sometimes rigorous, always active forward movement in dancing and procession. A sense

---

[188] Paul Spencer, ed. *Society and the Dance: The Social Anthropology of Process and Performance* (New York: Cambridge University Press, 1985).
[189] See discussion of this in the introductory and first chapter.
[190] *PofM*, vol. II.2, 720-763.
[191] Ibid., 746ff.
[192] Ibid., vol. III, 68ff.
[193] See G. E. Mylonas, *Mycenae and the Mycenaeans Age* (Princeton: Princeton University Press, 1966) 140-5, 149, 150, 165 and 168.. N, Marinatos *Minoan Religion: Ritual, Image and Symbol* (Columbia: University Of North Carolina Press, 1993) passim and P. Warren, *Minoan Religion as Ritual Action* (London: (Cambridge University Press, 1988) passim
[194] Ibid Lawler, 28-9. See also Steven H. Lonsdale, *Dance and Ritual Play in Greek Religion* (Baltimore: Johns Hopkins University Press, 1993) 115-6 for much the same, another thirty years later.
[195] See the recent work of Lonsdale (1993) which takes up with new vigor the connection of dancing and religion in the Bronze Age from the perspective of Homer.
[196] See for instance the second half of chapter IV in Dimitra Kokkinidou and Marianna Niklolaïdou. *Archaeologia kai H Koinonike Tetoteta tou Felou: Prosegises sthn aigaike Prestoria [Archaeology and Gender: Approaches to Aegean Prehistory]* (Thessaloniki: Banias, 1993); Lucia Nixon, "Gender Bias in Archaeology" in Archer, S. Fischler and M. Wyke eds. *Women in Ancient Societies*, Routledge (New York: Routledge, 1994), Sarah B. Pomeroy, "Selected Bibliography on Women in Classical Antiquity: The Bronze Age" in J. Perodotto and J. Sullivan eds, *Women in the Ancient Word: The Arethusa Papers* (Albany: State University of New York Press, 1984) and L. Talalay "A Feminist Boomerang: The Great Goddess of Greek Prehistory" *Gender and History* 6 (1994) 165-83.

of movement is especially obvious in representations of dancing where feet are spread as in mid stride, such as seen on a sealing from Zakros (fig. 88). A feeling or sense of softness or richness is conveyed by the bulging fleshy bodies of the women engaged in dance and procession. Lastly, an effect of balance/torsion is found in the composition of the representations of a number of the seals, especially those depicting dancing. For example, on a gold ring from Aidonia (fig. 103) which illustrates two women dancing among lily plants and around architecture, the "S" curve of their bodies is met with the oppositionally curving flowers equally spaced between them. The motion of their arms and their long hair swinging out from their heads at complimentary angles heightens the sense of turning and curving. This effect is very similar to that of Kamares ware, a brilliant polychrome pottery made at the first palaces on Crete in the MMII period. Kamares ware is notable for its quality of all over symmetry and balance within the painted abstract composition as well as in its relation to the shape of the object.[197] This sense of balance/torsion may be a hold-over from Old Palace styles.

What can we make of this information? How do these details impact on the more strict formal analysis of these scenes? For one, it helps connect these scenes on seals with other media and artistic production, such as the example of Kamares ware above. Also, it may serve to highlight interpretive aspects. For instance, a sense of balance/torsion in a depiction of dancing helps us to understand the motion of dancing as perhaps circular. A step beyond the basics of composition, these details add to interpretive information.

Information which recalls our social categories can also be extracted from these visual clues. First, not tied to any one of the visual inflections but helping to create all of them is the representation of gender as illustrated through an emphasis upon the parts of bodies associated with secondary sexual characteristics. These are swelling hips and breasts with an in-curving waist. These particular corporal details are often exaggerated in representations of dancing and, being secondary sexual characteristics, might indicate exaggerated or emphasized gender identification. Interestingly, taking images of dancing and procession together as a group (as I do here), like bull leaping, it would appear that both genders are engaged in this performed act. This corporeal detail, which stresses a youthful body, I argue, stresses the social category of age as well. Lastly, images of procession in which characters carry objects I believe invoke the social category of social status. This is because the objects which are carried of a high value, such as a double axe shown carried in a sealing from Aghia Triada (fig. 85), a large portion of cloth on another sealing, this one from Zakros (fig. 84) or even an animal, seen on a seal from Vaphio (fig. 107).

---

[197] See G. Walberg *The Kamares Style: Overall Effects* (Uppsala: University of Uppsal, 1978) and *Kamares: A Study of the Character of Palatial Middle Minoan Pottery* (Uppsala: Univeristy of Uppsala, 1976. Specifically, compare CMS II8.202 described above with the famous narrow necked jar from Phaistos with a quadruple spiral motif. E.H. Hall, "The Decorative Art of Crete in the Bronze Age," *University of Pennsylvania Transactions of the Department of Archaeology, Free Museum of Science and Art* 2 (1906-07) pl.1, no.1.

Chapter Four:

Issues of Archaeological Context and Interpretation

"The Palace of Knossos was my idea and my work, and it turned out to be a find as one could not hope for in a lifetime or in many lifetimes..."
Letter from Sir Arthur Evans to his father transcribed in Joan Evans, *Time and Chance* (London: Longmans, 1943) 335.

The following chapter considers the archaeological contexts from which the objects discussed in this book were extracted. Implicit in the presence of this chapter are two things: first, these objects bear specific contextual information and, second, this context is important in the development of an understanding of these materials and in turn of performance in the Bronze Age Aegean. Time is taken here to make this seemingly obvious observation in order to set this study apart from the many which use glyptic data from dubious contexts or which ignore contextual information even when it is available.[198] Yet, the use of these data is not uncomplicated. The significance of context to the interpretation of cultural remains is complex: woven from theoretical orientations, the nature of the contexts themselves, their state of preservation, and the kinds of questions asked of them. Furthermore, the use of context in the interpretation of archaeological remains exists at the center of archaeological theory and therefore, whenever consciously discussed, begs for the promotion of one theoretical framework or another. I begin this chapter with a brief history of the approach to of archaeological context and its role in the interpretation of cultural remains, then turn to my particular use of it in the present project with special attention to its role in performance studies. Next, I discuss images of bull leaping and dancing in groupings of general archaeological provenience, namely, palatial, burial, storage/administration and settlement. Based upon this, two general conclusions are drawn: first, that images of bull leaping and dancing come from elite contexts and second, that they can all be associated with the prestige of the palaces, palatial administration, or personal wealth. More specifically, it is revealed that images of bull leaping and dancing are found only on Crete during the second palace period and mostly in settlement and storage/administration sites, and there is a relatively equal distribution of images of bull leaping and dancing. During the third palace period fewer images of bull leaping and dancing are found on Crete, but their numbers dramatically rise on the mainland, found mostly in burial and palatial contexts and equally distributed between images of bull leaping and dancing.

* * *

The notion of context, in general, is quite broad within the discipline of archaeology and bears a special significance because of the nature of archaeological field work. Artifacts found in the process of archaeological excavation (found *in situ*) are extracted from three-dimensional spaces, surrounded by other objects ceramic, metal, faunal or microbotanical and embedded in an earth matrix. Often beginning with the label of an artifact's horizontal and vertical location in relation to a fixed datum point, meaning begins to be ascribed. Yet, this is only in relation to what we know and can see today. Archaeological sites are mute, the people who inhabited them unobservable, and at most sites written records are rare, and contexts which archaeologists uncover bear only that which has survived destruction, abandonment, burial and decomposition. Therefore, the invariably abbreviated picture of a rich cultural context in the past represented by the modern archaeological record takes on an inordinate importance in the interpretation of individual finds. The question is, exactly what does the information of archaeological context offer to the interpretation of an object?

The question of how archaeological context informs the meaning of an artifact is at the heart of archaeological interpretation and approaches to this question are basic to all schools of archaeological theory and practice. When archeology was in its infancy, contexts for objects were regarded as unimportant because archaeologists were merely interested in uncovering the monuments of the remote recorded past, such as Schliemann at Mycenae or Layard at Nineveh. This positivist approach[199] was useless, however, to later archaeologists who were interested in the remains of undiscovered prehistoric cultures, primarily those outside of central Europe. Because no historical facts could be linked to the remains found at these sites, a new approach was needed to understand their remains. This new approach, called scientific archaeology, valued the context of archaeological discoveries, such as pottery, as it helped to date them.[200] However, by the mid-20th century, new questions began to be asked of past cultures, having more to do with people than objects, questions which couldn't be answered by means of this scientific approach. The New Archaeology sought to answer these questions with a strategy influenced by social anthropology. In short, the New Archaeology, colored largely by the processual theories of Lewis Binford, argued for the recognition of strong universal similarities of human behavior and that through the study of human behavior, processes of cultural development and change could be explained and recognized in the archaeological record.[201] Within this

---

[198] See discussion of Niemeier below.

[199] Often referred to as the historical approach which was typical of the field from the 18th century through to the beginning of the 20th century. This is the belief that the facts of recorded history reveal themselves clearly in certain classes of objects (architecture, weapons, luxury goods) found in the archaeological record.

[200] The science here was the careful examination of artifacts, such as pottery, in order to develop relative topologies for dating. See for instance, Petrie's mid-19th century publications of early Dynastic pottery and stone tools.

[201] Binford outlined the program of the New Archaeology in two papers, "Archaeology as Anthropology" *American Antiquity*, 28 (1962)

theoretical framework, archaeological context was used to interpret specific groups of artifacts (weapons, tools) as reflective of conventional processes of ecological adaptation or socio-political organization.

New or processual archaeology was followed by the post-processual critique, lead by Ian Hodder in the mid 1980's. One of the primary criticisms that post-processualists had with the New Archaeology, was that only certain kinds of artifacts were scrutinized and thus, certain components of activity (military, technology) were privileged in the history of past cultures. Post-processualists furthermore underscored the vulnerability of what is accepted as true at any one time, that it often resembles whatever appears to be most reasonable to each successive generation of archaeologists. Post-processualists introduced the reality of subjectivity in archaeological research designs and interpretation and, as a result, destabilized existing interpretive structures. In the ensuing vacuum of hyper-relativism, archaeological theorists struggled to gain stable ground. Hodder eventually proposed a renewed interest in archaeological context which radically altered approaches to artifactual study. Hodder introduced Contextual Archaeology at the heart of which was the ethnographically well-documented claim that material culture is not merely a reflection of cultural processes but also an active element in group interactions that can be used to disguise as well as to reflect social relations.[202] Hodder's view that material culture is used as an active element in social interaction positions the archaeologists to examine all possible aspects of archaeological remains in order to understand the complex significance of each artifact. Archaeological field work changed in at least two significant ways as the result of the post processualists. First, a far wider range of information began to be recovered from excavated levels (such as microbotanical remains, use-ware data, artifact distribution, maps, etc.) and, second, archaeological deposits no longer bore interpretive labels (such as the "throne room," or the "warrior tomb") but instead were assigned alpha-numeric identifications, thus leaving interpretation to a time when all remains could be pondered in concert.

The most compelling critique of Hodder's Contextual Archaeology comes from the relativists and again bears on the issue of context. In short, relativists, most notoriously Michael Shanks and Christopher Tilley,[203] take the view that preferences within archaeological interpretation for one hypothesis over another depend entirely on factors arising from the social background of the practitioners, rather than from the objects and sites that they study. Questions as to why people prefer one hypothesis over another become a matter not of external standards but of personal interest and background. As there is no compulsion to value one interest or background over another, all versions of history are equally valid and the past becomes at once attainable through every interpretation and completely unknowable. The vehicle? Plastic and plural context. Within this configuration, context no longer acts as a guide to a conclusive knowledge but rather a confederate in the construction of relative realities.

The concept of qualified or mitigated objectivism was posed in response to this interpretive dead-end. Practically, qualified or mitigated objectivism works as an external check on the nature and meaning of evidence brought to bear on a hypothesis. Alison Wylie remains the most coherent proponent of this theoretical scheme, which, in short, accepts certain data as particularly useful (acknowledging that other data are less useful) and watches for the correlation of these data groups across a site. Wylie and other mitigated objectivists recognize that certain information (for example a detailed knowledge of the individual) from artifacts and their archaeological context cannot be gained.[204] A difficult but potentially fruitful path is thus directed through hyper-relativist positions: case by case analysis mindful of the pitfalls of simplistic processual conclusions and contemporary social bias.

Issues of context are important to the study of performance in antiquity because, like all behavior in the past, much of what is left *is* its context. If any knowledge about dancing, procession or bull games in the remote past is to be gained, it must come in large part from their sets, props, accouterments and imprints. These materials can survive in the archaeological record and, once recognized as data groups related to such activities, can be correlated across sites. Evidence which is equally important to the recreation and ultimate understanding of the signification of these events is their illustration or representation. As it is posed here, that each representation of a performed act is a reference to actual performance or social drama, the fixed or intentional contexts for these images are important. Therefore, by association, the interpretation of the context for images of performance reflects on the contexts and ultimate meanings of the performances themselves.

* * *

The practice of the archaeology of the Bronze Age Aegean, theoretical or otherwise, despite an over century long history, has advanced only moderately from its beginnings. Excavation reports are often little more than

---

217-25 and "Archaeological Systemics and the Study of Culture Process," *American Antiquity,* 31 (1965) 203-210.
[202] Contextual Archaeology is most concretely presented in *Reading the Past: Current Approaches to Interpretation in Archaeology* (New York: Cambridge University Press, 1986).
[203] Michael Shanks and Christopher Tilley, *Re-Constructing Archaeology* (New York: Cambridge University Press, 1987).

[204] See "Matters of Fact and Matters of Interest," in S.J. Shennan ed., *Archaeological Approaches to Cultural Identity* (New York: Rutledge, 1989). Later development of the theory in "The Interplay of Evidential Constraints and Political Interests: Recent Archaeological Research on Gender," *American Antiquity* 57 (1992) 15-35 and contra M. Fotiadis, "What is Archaeology's 'Mitigated Objectivism' Mitigated by? Comments on Wylie," *American Antiquity* 59 (1994) 545-555.

lists of artifacts; methodology is seldom mentioned, and some classes of archaeological data (faunal or botanical remains, for instance) are either ignored or go unstudied. This slow development has much to do with Aegean archaeology's alliance with Classical archaeology, a field which to this day still resembles its 18th century antiquarian origins. The less than rigorous archaeological method practiced in the Aegean has had an unfortunate effect upon studies of objects from the area. Indeed, the quote of Evans at the beginning of the chapter is an example of the worst sort of close-mindedness that can be problematic in much of the synthetic work in Aegean Prehistory. A particularly insightful article on this topic and dealing specifically with seals, by Wolf-Dietrich Niemeier, describes the three most daunting problems with a contextual approach for glyptic studies in the Bronze Age Aegean.[205] First, the radical minority of seals from this time and part of the world come from archaeological excavations (and even some of these lack specific contexts). Second, the seals and sealings which have contexts are extremely difficult to study comparatively because they differ, sometimes dramatically, in methods of publication, dating schemes and formal analysis. Lastly, and most importantly, Niemeier raises the question as to the meaning of archaeological contexts to the seals. What, for example, can be said about a seal found in a destruction deposit along with LMIb Marine style sherds aside from the common circumstance of their disposal? It is unknown whether schemes worked out for the stylistic development for decorated pottery (which mark relative chronological periods) parallel the stylistic development of seal stones or any other artistic media, for that matter. In a suggestion surprisingly similar to the case by case method of Wylie, Niemeier calls for case by case analysis of seals from archaeologically sound contexts (regarding finds spots purely as a *terminis post quem*) combined with stylistic/dating topologies based on excavated materials. An unfortunate fact of the matter is that no stylistic topologies exist base solely on excavated materials from Aegean Bronze Age context.

Niemeier's important analysis of the problems of context in Bronze Age Aegean archaeology necessarily encourages new approaches. I propose a more general view of context and one which scrutinizes not the details of provenance, but centers on the general contexts in which the objects were found. By general context I mean the type of site such as palatial, burial, etc. By drawing on this information, one is able at least to take advantage of the interpretive, albeit general, context of the data. The meanings of these general contexts, in essence, the kinds of sites where archaeological materials were found, suggest their function within Bronze Age Greek society. Joining the seals, wall painting, ivories, etc., through their context with broader functional spheres of Minoan and Mycenaean society (such as burial practice for tomb contexts or political imagery for palatial contexts) may in fact result in a richer interpretation of these objects.[206] It may furthermore enhance our understanding of these kinds of sites.

The eighty-five objects I discuss here come from some twenty-nine different sites and numerous individual contexts. Among these loci, four general context groups are identified: palatial, tomb, storage/administration, and settlement. Although specific find contexts within each of these general contexts are discussed, for the work of interpretation, the general context is used. This is because of the nature of these find-spots. For instance, several sealings discovered in storage/administration contexts are from a context clearly disturbed by a disaster in antiquity, such as a fire. This example illustrates how a general context of storage/administration, defined by architectural and other remains, is a meaningful one to the interpretation of the sealings associated with it. Conversely, a more specific context, for instance, stored in a basket or box, is less so. Similarly, a general burial context for an object is important and as well as the other contents of the interment, however the specific location of the seal in relation to other objects is often irrelevant because the original deposition was disturbed in antiquity. In using the idea of general context when considering Bronze Age seals as opposed to specific, exact context or no context at all, important contextual information is highlighted and the unique depositional circumstance of the objects is taken into consideration.

In the following, I present the images of bull leaping and dancing divided among these general contexts, beginning first with a discussion of the nature of each general context. Exploring these general contexts and the glyptic data within them will afford the opportunity to center on four crucial areas of archaeological research in the Aegean: kingship at the palaces, religion at burial contexts, administration in storage/administrative sites, and settlement at non-palatial residential sites.

* * *

I begin with the general archaeological context of palatial centers on Crete and the mainland of Greece. Given the many important functions of the palaces as they are today understood and given their potential role in the creation of images, it is fruitful to investigate what images of performances were found there. The first Bronze Age palace in Greece to be excavated was Tiryns in 1884 by Schliemann. Within the great circuit wall of the site Schliemann discovered a large structure within which was a great divided room containing at one end a large circular hearth and what appeared to be a throne. This configuration of rooms with hearth and throne, called a megaron and later found at Mycenae and Pylos, became

---

[205] W-D. Niemeier, "Probleme der Datierung von Siegeln nach Kontexten," *CMS* Beiheft 1 (1981).

[206] This approach is not to be confused with functionalism. Functionalism (Radcliffe-Brown, Malinowski et alia), although offering an integrative system by which so much cultural remains can be understood, is slim on the explanation of external influences or social change.

the defining element for a Mycenaean palace. On Crete in 1901 Evans discovered what he labeled the throne room at Knossos as well as several other defining elements of Minoan palace such as a central court, storage magazines, and "royal apartments," a series of connected rooms decorated with wall paintings. Eventually, structures containing near-identical elements were discovered at Mallia, Phaistos, and Zakros. The formal qualities of the Minoan palace have been studied by Graham;[207] the function of the Minoan palace is the subject of a volume of papers[208] the majority of which center on administration and economy. Mycenaean palaces (and any kind of architecture, for that matter) have only recently enjoyed as much attention at their Minoan counterparts.[209] *The Pylos Regional Archaeological Project*,[210] remains a model study of a Bronze Age palace and its regional interactions and activities.

Although difficult to compare for various reasons, taken together, these studies of Mycenaean and Minoan palaces provide some synthesis as to their function in Bronze Age society. Based purely on the archaeological evidence, a number of different activities are known to have taken place around and within the palace, including the collection and re-allotment of agricultural goods, the trade of various items with both regional and international entities, the production of luxury goods, the maintenance of deities, the storage of a wide range of materials including military equipment, and the performance of various rituals.[211] Lastly, and potentially most interesting, the palaces were focal points in the production of visual images. This is evidenced by the fact that, between Crete and the Mainland, far more art work has been found at palatial sites than at any other kind and, furthermore, images are found in prominent public spaces at these sites. Examples of art which was intended for public view are the two lions flanking a column on the Lion Gate at Mycenae and the charging bull in the main Northwest entrance at Knossos.

The above discussion is based on the assumption that all the palaces on the mainland and Crete were purely political entities. Perhaps in partial resistance to this idea, recently a new interpretation has been offered of the Minoan palace, as a cosmological center.[212] Soles, who puts forth this theory, uses three criteria in his identification of Knossos as a cosmological center: the imitation of the architecture of Knossos at outlying palaces and villas and even the Greek mainland, the widespread imitation and acquisition of artifacts manufactured in the palace at these places and others, and three, the adoption of Minoan costume at these and other places. Soles insists that this influence of Knossos is an ideological phenomenon and one which, via ethnographic analogy, would have had cosmological power.[213]

Thus, given the importance of palaces, whatever their interpretation in Minoan and Mycenaeans society, and especially that they were centers for what might be perceived as state or religious art, let us turn to the specific examples of seals and sealings which bear the representation of bull leaping and dancing which were found at this type of site in order to situate these images within a cultural context.

* * *

A total of twenty-six images of performance come from secure palatial contexts, twelve which represent bull leaping, seven procession and seven dance. Glyptic examples include five impressions and one seal. Three glyptic representations of dancing from palatial contexts were found at Knossos and Pylos and are all sealings. The first (fig. 70) comes from the East Wing of the Palace and the second (fig. 109) from fill on its South East boarder. The first sealing, because of its more secure context can be dated to LMII-IIIa,[214] or the third palace period. The second example, impressed by an oval seal, dates to just prior to the palace's LMIIIb third palace period destruction.[215] The last example, (fig. 82) found at Pylos in room 98 of the northeast wing of the palace, dates to the LHIIIb2-c1 or third palace period.[216] The one glyptic example which illustrates procession (fig. 108) comes from room 105 of the palace of Pylos, and dates to LHIIIb2-c1.[217]

---

[207] Walter Graham, *The Palaces of Crete* (Princeton: Princeton University Press, 1987).
[208] R. Hägg & N. Marinatos eds. *The Function of the Minoan Palaces*. (Athens: Skrifter utgivna av Svenska Institutet I Athen, 1987).
[209] M. L. Galaty and W. A. Parkinson eds. *Rethinking Mycenaean Palaces: New Interpretations of an Old Idea* (Los Angeles: The Cotsen Institute of Archaeology University of California, Monograph 41, 1999). K. Demakopoulou, "Palatial and Domestic Architecture in Mycenaean Thebes" in Pascal Darcque and René Treuil, eds. *L' habitat égéen préhistorique. Actes de la table ronde internationale, Athènes, 23-25 juin 1987. BCH* Suppl. XIX. École française d'Athènes (1990) 307-317.
[210] Davis, Jack L., Susan E. Alcock, John Bennet, Yannos G. Lolos, and Cynthia W. Shelmerdine "The Pylos Regional Archaeological Project. Part I: Overview and the Archaeological Survey," *Hesperia* 66 (1997) 391-494.
[211] See Hägg and Marinatos eds. *The Function of the Minoan Palaces* (Athens: Skrifter utgivna av Svenska Institutet I Athen, 1987) for a variety of papers dealing with Minoan palatial function. No similar collection of papers exists for the Mainland, although a good recent review of research on Mycenaean palaces can be found in C. Shelmerdine, "The Palatial Bronze Age of the Southern and Central Greek Mainland," American Journal of Archaeology 101 (1997) 558-580.

[212] Jeffrey Soles, "The Functions of a Cosmological Center: Knossos in Palatial Crete." *Politeia: Society and State in the Aegean Bronze Age*, Aegaeum 12 (1995) 405-414.
[213] Ibid. 408. Soles interpretation does not preclude the more traditional political interpretation of Knossos and the other palaces. Indeed, I believe that his view is a fascinating fleshing out of the traditional interpretation and brings us closer to what was surely the very rich complex meaning of these buildings.
[214] J. Weingarten argues that this is a sealing on a wine stopper. See J. Weingarten, "Sealing Structures of Minoan Crete, Part I" *Oxford Journal of Archaeology* 7 (1988) 22.
[215] M. Gill, "The Knossos Sealings: Provenance and Identification" *Annual of the British School at Athens* 60 (1965) 58-98.
[216] Carl. W. Blegen, "Pylos, 1957 "*American Journal of Archaeology* 62 (1958)180.
[217] Carl W. Blegen, "Pylos, 1958" *American Journal of Archaeology* 63 (1959) 122ff., plate 30.

Figure 109: Seal impression from Knossos; after CMS II8.267. Catalogue # 51.

There are two glyptic representations of bull leaping from palace contexts. One is an impression (fig.47) found in the Room of the Niche at Knossos and dates to LMIII-IIIa.[218] The other is an agate half cylinder seal (fig. 54) dating to the third palace period, LHIIIb, at Thebes.[219]

Several examples of painting which illustrate bull leaping, dancing and procession are found in palatial contexts. The first two are examples of painted pottery illustrating dancing women, both from the palace of Phaistos, found in a room opening onto the West Court of the Old palace (fig. 77 and fig 78). Dating to the following second or new palace period, there are four examples of performance all if which come from Knossos; three illustrate bull leaping, one dancing. The Sacred Grove and Dance fresco (fig. 16), found fallen on a late basement floor of a small room at the north end of the central court is a representation of dance.[220] The first

of the bull leaping images is found on a crystal plaque (fig. 110) in the Room of the Throne and dating to LMIa.[221] Another, in the form of a miniature ivory sculpture, a leaper in mid leap (fig. 27), was found with a miniature bull in the Temple Treasury and dates to the very early phase of the second palace, MMIIIb/LMIa.[222] The last example from Knossos is an example of relief plaster painting, this one representing the arm of a bull leaper grasping the horn of a bull (fig. 30) found in the East Hall basement level, the East Corridor, near the School Room and Lapidary's Workshop.[223] This plaster relief dates to LMIb.

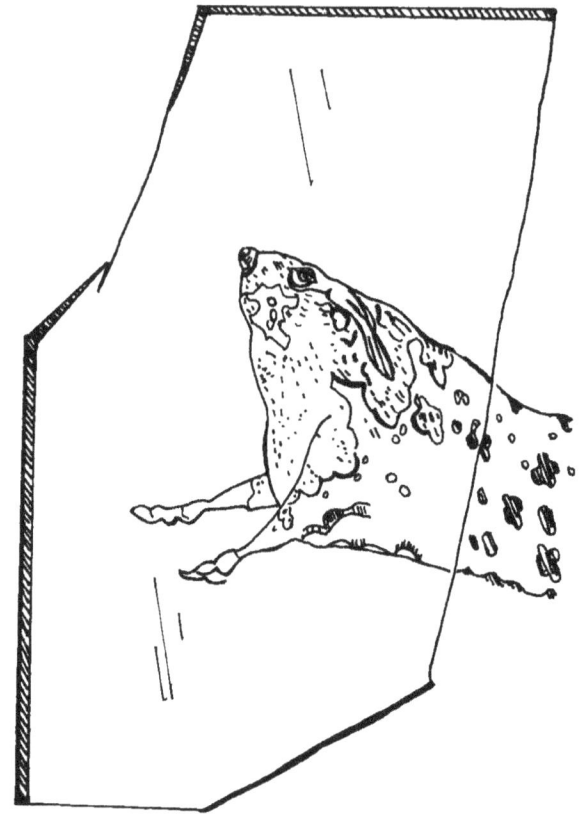

Figure 110: Crystal plaque from Knossos; after PofM III, pl. XIX. Catalogue # 69.

From a general palatial context during the third palace period come another five images of performance, again all from Knossos, all wall painting. The first is the famous cupbearer procession fresco (fig. 5) which was found on the east wall of the Corridor of the Procession and dates to LMII/IIa.[224] A painting which illustrates dancing, the Dancing Lady from the Queen's Megaron (fig. 94), also dates to LMII.[225] The remaining three wall

---

[218] Evans, *Scripta Minoa*, vol. 1, pg. 43, fig. 20a; *PofM*, vol. IV, 617, fig. 604a; Popham, Mervyn R., and Margaret A. V. Gill. *The Latest Sealings from the Palace and Houses at Knossos*. British School at Athens Studies 1 (Oxford: Alden Press, 1995)
[219] *Archaeological Reports*, 1964-65, pg. 15, fig. 17.
[220] A. Evans, "Knossos 1989" *Annual of the British School at Athens* (1899-1900) 47-48; *PofM*, vol III, 66ff, pl. XVIII. See also discussion of this painting in chapter one.

[221] *PofM* vol. III, 108, plate XIX.
[222] *PofM* vol. III, 428ff., fig. 296.
[223] *PofM*, vol. III, 504ff., fig. 350.
[224] Ibid, Evans (1899-1900)12-16; *PofM*, vol II2, 682f, 704ff, 719ff, figs. 428, 450 and suppl. Pls. XXV-XXVII.
[225] A. Evans, "Knossos 1901" *Annual of the British School at Athens* (1901-2)55ff, fig. 28; *PofM* vol. III 70-71, fig. 40; 369-71, pl. XXVb.

paintings illustrate bull leaping, one again discovered in the Queen's Megaron, but in an upper stratum, which illustrates female bull leapers (fig. 44).[226] From the Court of the Stone Spout come the famous Toreador panels[227] (fig. 9) and lastly, in the Northwest Treasure House, were found fragments of a bull leaping scene called the Bull and Tree Grappling Scene (fig.. 43), dating to an LMII/III context.[228]

Of this same general context in the third palace period but from the mainland come no fewer than nine examples of bull leaping and processions; dancing is not included. Beginning with Tiryns, from a small court northeast of the south bathroom of the palace comes the famous bull leaping painting (fig. 48), the first found in the Mediterranean, dating to LHIIIb.[229] From the palace of Pylos come fragments of a wall painting that included bull leaping (fig. 49) found in a drain next to Wine Magazine 105, no doubt fallen from the upper level dating to LHIIIa.[230] The next example, another fragmentary wall painting of a bull leaping scene, was discovered in the Ramp House deposit at Mycenae (fig. 50). These fragments came from beneath the Ramp House which contained pottery dating to LHIIIa1.[231] The last example of an illustration of bull leaping from a palatial context comes from the 19th century excavations of the Athenian Acropolis, around the area of the Mycenaean citadel, and is a fragment of a steatite stone vase (fig. 51) which illustrates the full torso of a bull leaper arching over the head of a bull.[232]

The remaining five illustrations of performance are of procession and are all wall paintings. The first comes from Pylos, from the plaster dump on the northwest slope of the palace and illustrates a number of women in a procession carrying various objects (fig. 76).[233] Another example, from the same plaster dump at Pylos shows a male procession, also carrying various objects and wearing elaborate dresses (fig. 101).[234] From Mycenae comes another wall painting illustrating at least one man engaged in a procession (fig. 102), the fragments of this painting found beneath the floor of the main corridor of the House of the Oil Merchant and dating to LHIIIa. This figure carries a palanquin although it is unclear what he carries on it. At nearby Tiryns, a wall painting which illustrates a group of life-sized women carrying objects in a procession (fig 100) was uncovered in the west slope rubbish deposit which dates to the LHIIIb period.[235] Lastly, from Thebes, in room north of the Kadmeia, come fragments of another life-sized frieze of women carrying objects in a procession (fig. 99), dating to the LHII period.[236]

* * *

The second general archaeological context group is burial. Burials which have been found to contain seals and rings are chamber tombs, beehive or tholos tombs and shaft graves. On the mainland, beginning in the MH period and spanning to LHIIIc, chamber tombs, stone-built tombs, and tholoi were the norm. All had an open dromos and interior roofed chamber, often linked by a narrow roofed-over stomion. On Crete, burials from MMII-III on were mostly chamber tombs, although a few Mycenaean tholoi dating to the LM period are known. Often found in these mainland and Cretan burial structures were cist graves dug into the floor. Most Minoan and Mycenaean burials of the late Bronze Age were used repeatedly with little care given to the integrity of each burial. The result of this practice is several interments and grave goods from a long period of time found mixed together in these structures with little or no indication of what belonged to whom during what period. In response to this situation archaeologists when publishing tombs will often give a mean date for the objects found within it, or alternatively a *terminus ante quem* date for the whole deposit. This dating problem involved with objects found in burials has a direct impact upon glyptic studies as so many seal stones and rings are found in this sort of archaeological context.

Despite a great number of Bronze Age burials published, there have been few synthetic or analytical works on the topic.[237] This is unfortunate because interesting

---

[226] *PofM*, vol III, 208ff, fig. 143.
[227] Ibid, Evans (1901-2), 94ff, *PofM* vol. III, 209 ff.
[228] A. Evans, *PofM*, vol. II2, pg. 619-622, fig. 389.
[229] H. Schliemann *Tiryns* (New York: Arno, reprint of 1896 ed.) 303-7, pl. XIII; A. Reichel, " Die Stierspiele in der Kretisch Mykenischen Cultur," *Mitteilungen des Deutschen Archäologischen Instituts* 34 (1909) 85ff.
[230] K. Blegen, *Pylos II* (Princeton: Princeton Univeristy Press, 1966) 49-50, 77, plts. 24, 116.
[231] A. Rodenwaldt "Fragmente mykenischer Wandgemälde," *Mitteilungen des Deutschen Archäologischen Institut* 36 (1911) 230ff, pl. 9, 1; W. Lamb "Frescoes from the Ramp House," Annals of the British School at Athens 24 (1919-21) 192-4, Pl. VII, 406, S. Immerwahr *Aegean Painting in the Bronze Age* (College Park: Pennsylvania State Univeristy Press, 1990) My No. 1; M. Shaw, "Bull-Leaping Fresco from Below the Ramp House at Mycenae: A Study in Iconography and Artistic Transmission," *Annals of the British School at Athens* 91 (1996).
[232] I. Sakellerakis, "Mycenaean Stone Vases,: *Studi micenei ed egeo-anatolici* 17 (1976) pl, XII-32; M. Mayer, "Mykenische Beitrage I, *Jahrbuch des Deutschen Archäologischen Instituts* 7 (1892) 80-81.
[233] Ibid, Blegen (1966) 52ff, (51 H NWS) pls. 34-38. The remains of this fresco are very fragmentary and it is unclear how many people process. At least two women are clear, however.

[234] Ibid. (54-9 H NWS) 60-62, 91-95, pls, 41-44, 117, 129-130.
[235] G. Rodenwaldt, *Tiryns II. Die Fresken des Palastes*, (Athens: Deutschen Archäologischen Instituts, 1912) 69ff. no. 71-111, figs. 27-34, 37, pls. VII-X.
[236] Keramopoulos, *Archaeologike Ephemeris* (1909) 90ff., pl. I-III, 2-3.
[237] Important exceptions to this rule are I Pini, *Beiträge zur minoischen Gräberkunde* (Wiesbaden: Steiner, 1968), and R. Laffineur ed. *Thanatos: Les Coutumes Funeraires en Egee a l'Age du Bronze*, Aegeaum 1, 1987, and M. Dabney and J. Wright "Mortuary Customs, Palatial Society and State Formation in the Aegean Area: J Comparative Study, in R. Hägg and C. Nodquist eds. *Celebrations of Death and Divinity in the Bronze Age Argolid* (Stockholm: Swedish Institute of Archaeology, 1990); C. Mee and W. Cavanagh, "Mycenaean Tombs as evidence for Social and Political Organization", *Oxford Journal of Archaeology* 3 (1985)45-61; J. Soles *The Prepalatial Cemeteries at Mochlos and Gournia and the House Tombs of Bronze Age Crete*, Hesperia Supplement 24, 1992, stands alone in its concern for the

information about social organization and rank could be derived from the study of these deposits. This seems clear from the many important studies have been made of burial remains from other cultures. Ian Morris' important work *Burial and Ancient Society* (Cambridge 1987) for the first time associated burial custom and state development in the ancient Mediterranean by looking at burial and other cultural information (texts, settlement data) together. Morris' thesis was made possible by the important work of Binford and Brown, who were among the first to explore the "social dimensions" of burial remains.[238] The critical assumption in these studies is that mortuary practice bears a direct relationship to and helps to build and maintain social relationships and positions in society. In other words, the nature, situation and wealth of burials are relative to social rank.

Twenty-three glyptic images come from tombs that feature performances of dancing, procession and bull-games, eleven seals and twelve rings. Representations of dancing number twelve. Beginning with those found on the mainland, three examples come from the Mycenae vicinity, one (fig.75) dating to the LHII-III period from Panajia chamber tomb #103 which was disturbed but yielded several whole vases an well as fragments of gold.[239] The other two examples also dating to LHII-III come from chamber tombs in the Unknown Necropolis in the Lower Town. The first (fig. 105) was discovered in chamber tomb number five[240] and the second (fig. 98) from chamber tomb number seven.[241] Although both tombs were plundered, fragments of what at one time furnished them remain such as painted pottery, fragments of bronze and bits of faience. From the site of Dendra, in grave ten, dating to LHII-LHIII a gold ring was discovered (fig. 104) which illustrates two women dancing and facing architecture. This ring was found along with several large delicately painted palace-style jars as well as a good bit of bronze and a gold cup.[242] The next example, showing two women dancing, is a chalcedony lentoid, (fig. 58) and was found in the very wealthy Vaphio tholos and dates to LHIIa.[243] Another example is a gold ring in excellent shape (fig. 97) which was found in grave and dates to LHIIIa2-b at Mega Monasitri. Along with this ring several other pieces of gold jewelry were discovered in the tomb as well as bronze and painted pottery.[244]

Three more examples of women dancing (figs. 103, fig, 11, fig, 72), all represented on exquisite gold rings, were discovered in the same small chamber cut in the wall of chamber tomb seven in the necropolis at Aidonia. The tomb itself had been pillaged and these were the only (quite valuable) objects extracted from it, apparently missed by past grave robbers. The remaining pottery, yields a date of LHII-IIIa-b.[245] The last example of a representation of women dancing in glyptic art from the Mainland in a burial context is not a seal or ring but rather a steatite mold which was, likely used to create metal rings. The object was found in a family graven number 9, in the West Necropolis at Eleusis and dates to the LHII-III period.[246] The image (fig. 106) is carved into the small block of steatite, above a scene depicting a bird.

The only glyptic example of procession from a burial context from the mainland dates to the third palace period, LHII, and comes from the tomb south of the Agora at the Treasury Acropolis, South of the Grave Circles, within the ruins of the Rampin Houses at Mycenae. The ring was found along with great treasure such as a gold cup, other gold jewelry and elaborate painted pottery.[247] It is a gold ring and it illustrates two women in procession towards another seated at the base of a tree (fig. 19).

Seals and rings from burial contexts from Crete number only two. First, (fig. 95), an electrum ring, comes from chamber tomb 6 at the Isopata cemetery near Knossos. The scene on the ring shows two women holding hands facing each other with their legs spread wide apart; plants frame the scene on either side. The grave in which this ring was discovered was a rich one, with finds including faience and gold beads, the remains of an elaborate bronze dagger and an ivory pyxis, as well as several inhumations. It also included an interesting architectural element, an engaged pier similar to the one found in the Tomb of the Double Axes in the same cemetery. The other example (fig.6; cat.#24) found in tomb 1 at the Isopata cemetery is a gold ring which illustrates four women dancing, two together and two separately, very similar in composition to the women who dance in the Sacred Grove and Dance fresco at Knossos. Two seals were also found in the tomb as well as palace style pottery and a charcoal lamp. The chamber tombs at Isopata date to the third palace period, LMIIIa1 and LHII

---

reflection of social groupings in burial. However, this is outside of the chronological limit of the book.
[238] J. Brown ed. *Approaches to the Social Dimensions of Mortuary Practices*, Society for American Archaeology, Memoire 25. his introduction and L. Binford "Mortuary Practices: Their Study and Their Potential" 6ff.
[239] Schliemann, *Mycenae*, fig. 530; Tsountas, *Revue Archeologique*, 37 (1900) p. 12, fig. 2.
[240] Tsountas, "Mycenae," *Ephemeris Arhaiologiki*, 1888 119ff., fig. 5.3.
[241] Tsoutnas, *Revue Archeologique*, 37, 1900, pg. 9ff.
[242] A.W. Persson, *New Tombs at Dendra Near Midea*, Oxford University Press, London, 1942., pg. 59ff.
[243] C. Tsountas, "Mycenae," *Ephemeris Arhaiologiki* (1889) 130 ff plate 10.33.

[244] D Theocharis, D."Arheotites ke mnimia Thessalias" *Archaiologikon Deltion* 19 (1964) 241-249, 255-267..
[245] C.W. Blegen, "Pylos" *American Journal of Archaeology* 31 (1927) 439.
[246] G. Mylonas, "Eleusis" *Ephemeris Arhaiologiki* (1956) 77-86, fig. 6 and 7.
[247] H. Schliemann, *Mycenae: A Narrative of Researches and Discoveries at Mycenae and Tiryns* (Concord: Ayer, 1880, pg. 354f, fig 530.

respectively.[248]

Moving on to representations of bull leaping found in burial contexts from the Mainland, there are eight, six seals and two rings. Interestingly, the two rings are very similar. The first (fig. 107) comes from a very large and rich chamber tomb, tomb 1, at Asine. Two articulated skeletons were found in this tomb both lying on stone benches accompanied by much pottery, another gold ring, ivory inlays (likely part of a piece of wooden furniture), gold leaf and a number of seal stones.[249] The objects in the tomb date to the LHIIIa1 period. The ring itself is made of bronze with an oval bezel of thin sheet gold, the lower half of which has disintegrated. The upper portion, however, shows a leaper over the back of a bull which is in mid-stride with head down and horns forward. Similar to this ring is a complete gold example (fig. 7) from chamber tomb 4 at Anthia. The beautifully preserved scene on the ring shows two leapers sailing over the back of a bull which leaps with its head down, as seen in the other ring, but here over a hatched ground line. The tomb from which the ring comes contained a number of inhumations as well as another gold ring, ivory beads, bronze, and a kylix. The objects found in chamber tomb 4 at Anthia date to LHIIb-IIc, stretching into the post-palatial period. Four of the six examples of seals in this group come from chamber tombs located in the lower town at Mycenae. The first (fig. 57) a carnelian amygdaloid, found in chamber tomb #44 at Kato Fourni, was accompanied in the tomb by a number of burials, glass paste beads, jewelry and shells. The execution of this seal is simple, with little detail given to the musculature of the bull or the costume of the leaper. The next example (fig. 11), an onyx lentoid from Panajia chamber tomb #47, was found with a burial in the dromos of the tomb along with gold foil, jewelry, pottery and bronze.[250] The representation on this seal is a delicate one in which the leaper looks as if he were gently leaning over the slim bull, steadying himself with his hand on its neck, than leaping over its back. Beneath the bull an elegant tulip-like flower grows. The last seal (fig. 56) a carnelian amygdaloid, comes from the small chamber tomb 504 in the Lower Town which contained several terra-cotta figurines and little else.[251] This seal, like the one (fig. 55) discussed above, illustrates the bull moving from right to left. Also unusual is the Linear B sign, for wheat, included on the seal. All three of these seals are dated to LHII-III. Finally (fig. 12), a carnelian amygdaloid with gold finials comes again from the cemetery in the lower town at Mycenae, on the floor of chamber tomb #518, and shows a leaper coming over the hind legs of the bull in mid-leap. The tomb in which this seal was found was quite rich and included finds such as silver cord, ivory pyxides, a bronze dagger, and boars' tusks.[252]

The two remaining glyptic representations of bull leaping found in burial contexts on the mainland are both seal stones and come from the most elaborate kind of grave of the period, a tholos tomb. The first of these (fig. 53), an agate lentoid, comes from tomb 1 at Dimini which contained several burials and yielded extraordinarily rich finds such as gold vessels, bronze weapons and pieces of ivory.[253] Here the leaper has one hand on the back of the bull as he leaps over it while the animal throws its head up and opens its mouth. The next example (fig. 55), a chalcedony lentoid, from tholos grave 1 at Koukounara, was also among very rich burial remains such as bronze vessels, other seal stones and the horn of a great dear.[254] The illustration of bull leaping on this seal is somewhat unusual in that the bull moves from right to left; also, there is a ground line from which a small plant sprouts beneath its feet. Both of these seals from tholoi date to LHIII, the third palace period.

Turning to Crete, there are only two examples of bull leaping scenes found in burial contexts. The first example (fig. 46), a lapis lentoid, was found in a larnax burial in the dromos of a chamber tomb at Gournes along with other jewelry, other seal stones, a scarab and stirrup jars.[255] The leaper is shown floating over the back of the bull which turns, in mid-stride, toward the viewer. The other example from Crete (fig. 45) an agate lentoid, comes from a cist tomb from the first acropolis at Praissos. This tomb was completely empty (and in fact reused in the Hellenistic period) but yielded the seal when a powerful rain occurred after its excavation.[256] This stone illustrates a man grasping the horns of a majestic bull seated on a strong ground line as he leaps over its back. Both of these stones date to LMIIIb, the third palace period.

Images of performance in media other than glyptic are less numerous in burial contexts and, interestingly, only includes a representation of bull leaping. There are two examples from the mainland and three from Crete. The earliest of these, two clay rhyta, come from the Mesara plain on Crete and date to the prepalatial period. The first, from Koumasa and dating to EMIII shows a bull with leapers holding on to its horns (fig. 25).[257] The vase was found among several vases and other clay figures. The other example from the Mesara, from Tholos II at

---

[248] A. Evans, "The Tomb of the Double Axes and Associated Groups at Knossos," *Archaeologia* 65 (1914) 8ff, 31ff., C.Tsountas, "Trois Chatons de Bagues Mycéniennes" *Revue Archéologique* 37 (1900) 12-15.
[249] O. Frödin and A. Person *Asine: Results of the Swedish Excavations 1922-1930* (Stockhold: GLAF, 1938) 356-77.
[250] Tsountas, "Mycenae," *Ephemeris Archaiologiki*, 1888, 178ff.
[251] A. Wace, *Chamber Tombs at Mycenae*, Archaeologia 82 (1932) 10-15.
[252] A. Wace, *Chamber Tombs at Mycenae*, Archaeologia 82 (1932) 202.
[253] H. Lolling and P. Wolters, "Das Kuppelbrab bei Dimini" *Mitteilungen des Deutschen Archäologischen Institutes* 11 (1886) 435-443.
[254] *Ergon* (1963) 84, 82ff.
[255] Chatzidakis, *Ephemeris Archaiologiki* (1918) p. 66ff.
[256] Bosanquet "Praissos" *Annals of the British School at Athens* 8 (1901/2) 252-67
[257] S. Xanthoudides, *The Vaulted Tombs of the Mesara* (Liverpool: University Press, 1924) 40ff, plate XXVIII.

Porti, is a very similar object, a bull shaped rhyton with bull leapers attached to its horns (fig. 26). This was found among EM and MM vases, stone vases, a copper dagger and gold and silver jewelry.[258] Also from Crete but dating to the third palace period is an ivory pyxis (fig. 28) from Tomb H at Katsambas. The pyxis illustrates, among other images, bull leaping and was found in one of the wealthiest tombs at the site, along with two larnakes, fine ceramics, other ivory objects, including a carved comb, and gold foil.[259]

From mainland burial contexts come two more examples of illustrations of bull leaping. The first, dating to the second palace period is a fragment of ivory (fig. 39) from the area of Grave Circle B at Mycenae[260] on which is carved a bull leaping scene; only the foot of the bull and human survive. Lastly, dating to the very end of the third palace period/post palatial period, there is a larnax from Tanagra. Found in tomb 22 at the site,[261] on one side is the illustration of no fewer than three men jumping on the backs of three bulls (fig. 52). In and around the larnax was found fine pottery, figurines and glass-paste beads.

* * *

The third general archaeological context in which glyptic representations of performances are found is storage/administration. The designation storage/administration refers to spaces which are designed for storage and areas in which large numbers of sealings have been found together, believed to have an archive or administrative function. The reason I have lumped these two seemingly different kinds of provenance together is because of the way seals are thought to have been used in the storage, collection and redistribution of materials during the Bronze Age. Based upon the translation of Linear B texts and archaeological finds, it is understood that goods were brought from outlying areas into collection and redistribution centers where they would be handled, stored and eventually sent out again. Seals were important at almost every stage of this process as materials coming in would bear a sealing of origin, would be stored in a container closed with a different seal and then be sent out again stamped with yet a different seal. The doors and containers which held goods were also believed to have been "locked" with seals. The method by which sealing was accomplished changed throughout the middle to late Bronze Age. Put briefly, clay nodules were pressed directly onto objects (primarily matting, wooden pommels or pegs, judging from the backs of the preserved sealings) from the period of the establishment of the palaces in MMIb and continued through to the MMIIb destructions of the first palaces. During the second palace period, clay nodules were no longer impressed on objects but were instead clamped around strings which were in turn attached to things, and these were stamped. This system, as quite simply described here, remained in place until the destructions at the end of the second palace period, and it was replaced by a reintroduction of direct object sealing and a hybrid combination of direct objects sealing and hanging nodules in the third palace period.[262] Thus, examples from this general provenance can come from either archive deposits or storage areas but refer to the same function, the administration of goods.

The details of the function of seals and their articulation to administration, however, are more complicated and only sketchily known. The general understanding is as follows. During the time of the first palaces, when sealings were placed directly on objects, it is believed that this was for local control of materials, dependant upon the recognition of the seals and symbols marked on them. Then in the second palace period, when hanging nodules were used, it is believed that commodities were accompanied by documents (made of some perishable materials) which, in theory, would describe, in Linear A language, the nature of the materials, their origin, ownership and destination. Then, in the third palace period, when direct object sealing was revived, seals were again used as identification.[263] As this description of seal function implies, during at least two periods, the images found on seals had great importance in administration. Here I review the seals and sealings which have been found in such contexts.

There are eleven representations of the performance of dancing, procession and bull leaping found on sealings from storage/administration deposits. Dancing is found on only one impression (fig. 73) from the House of the Oil Merchant in the lower town at Mycenae and dating to the LHIIIb, third palace period. The House of the Oil Merchant featured a basement with eight storerooms opening off a long straight corridor where large pithoi of oil were stored. The sealing comes from one of thirty large stirrup jars which were waiting in the corridor,

---

[258] Ibid, 54-69, plate 62.
[259] S. Alexiou, "Ysterominoikoi tafoi limenos knosou. Axaiologikhs etaireias, 56 (1985) 26-40, plate 30-33.
[260] S. Mylonas. Tafikos kuklos B ton mykynon (Athens, 1973) 23, pl 11. This piece was found in between tombs alpha, delta and rho, and is thought to be from rho.
[261] T. Spyropoulos, "Excavations at the Mycenaean Nekorpolis at Tanagra" Athens Annals of Archaeology, 2 (1970)195-197, fig. 16.

[262] J. Weingarten, "Three Upheavals in Minoan Sealing Administration: Evidence for Radical Change," Aegaeum 5 (1990) 105-114. V. Aravantinos, "The Use of Sealings in the Administration of Mycenaean Palaces," in T. Palaima ed. Pylos Comes Alive: Industry and Administration in a Mycenaean Palace, (New York: Forham University Press,1984) 41-48
[263] There are a number of key articles and books which describe all this in much better and interesting detail: J. Weingarten, "The sealing structures of Minoan Crete: MMII Phaistos to the Destruction of the Palace of Knossos Parts I and II" Oxford Journal of Art 5 (1986 379-98., Oxford Journal of Art 7 (1988) 1-18); J. Bennett, "Knossos in Context: Comparative Perspectives on the Linear B Administration of LMII-III Crete" American Journal of Archaeology 94 (1990) 193-212., E. Hallager, The Minoan Roundel and Other Sealed Documents in the Neopalatial Linear A Administration, Aegaeum 14 (1996), V. Aravantinos, "The Mycenaean Inscribed Sealings from Thebes: Problems of Content and Function," Aegean Seals, Sealings and Administration, Aegaeum 5 (1990), 149ff.

presumably to be sent away.²⁶⁴ The sealing illustrates three women standing in a row striking identical poses, each with their arms raised and looking to the right. Judging by the shape of the impression, a ring made it. The remaining six sealings from a storage/administration context illustrate bull games. This group can be divided into three examples from Crete, all from Zakros, and one from the Mainland. The examples from Zakros come from the "custom's house" which was found to contain over 500 sealings all of which date to the final destruction of the town in LMIb, or at the end of the second palace period.²⁶⁵ One of these three (figs.36) represents a leaper almost vertical above the back of a great charging bull about to land with his arms outstretched. One other very similar impression (figs. 31) shows a bull charging but here on a strong ground line and with the leaper coming down more on the animal's hind quarters than its back. The last example is a sealing from archive room 8 at the palace of Pylos (fig. 59) and dates to LHIIIb2, or the third palace period.²⁶⁶ It illustrates a man standing before a charging bull either just having dismounted, assisting someone about to dismount or just having mounted or about to leap onto the bull himself. Only the front portion of this sealing remains and thus it is unclear whether there was another jumper, etc. The remaining seven sealings all come from the site of Zakros, House A, room 8, date to LMIb, and all illustrate processions (fig. 84, fig, 84, fig 88, fig 89, fig 90, fig 92, fig 71).

* * *

The final general archaeological context for glyptic representations of performance discussed here is settlement. Under this general label I collapse together settlement types such as villas, farmsteads, and towns. A sophisticated comparative examination of settlement types has been made by Gerald Cadogan for Crete²⁶⁷ however, no such study has been made for the mainland. Cadogan's typology is based upon not only careful architectural analysis but the interpretation of the uses for various buildings within the social life of settlements. Such a functional approach to architectural studies is the norm in Aegean Prehistory (as opposed to the purely tectonic architectural studies typical of classical buildings) and was employed by those in the mid to late 1980s who were interested in the connections between different kinds of sites and political organization.²⁶⁸ Such studies, concentrating on the larger picture of relationships between sites, are important to understanding the role seals and sealings may have played at them. The primary questions for glyptic studies within settlement contexts have focused on the sphragistic fingerprint of the large palatial centers upon the periphery. Few have looked at this evidence set apart from the larger palatial scene.

Like Soles on the topic of the function of the Minoan palaces,²⁶⁹ Hood has proposed that villas, the primary component of the settlement identification, existed to serve as cultic centers in areas remote from the palace.²⁷⁰ He argues this based on the discovery of the same sorts of architectural details (pier and door partitions, sunken rooms) and even cultic finds (such as rhyta) at these kinds of sites. However, the bulk of Hood's argument is based on the negative evidence for any sort of cult outposts outside of palatial centers with the exception of the Peak Sanctuaries. The villas, he believes, must have met the religious need for the rural populace of Crete. Although, as with Soles' argument about the function of the Minoan palace, this configuration of the function of the Minoan villas cannot be confirmed, I believe it is an important addition to the interpretation of these buildings which, like the palaces, no doubt served multiple functions.

Sixteen glyptic images of bull leaping, procession and dancing, four seals, one ring and twelve impressions, come from settlement contexts. Beginning with representations of dancing, from Chania (fig. 74) comes an impression with two dancers of the type already seen (fig. 95) which illustrates two women facing each other holding hands. Framing the scene are architectural elements and from between their hands sprouts a plant. This impression was found at Katre street, 10 and dates to the MMIII-LMI, or the second palace period.²⁷¹ Excavations at Chania have unearthed a number of large typical Minoan structures as well as several seals and linear A inscriptions.²⁷² The remaining five representations of dancing are of the more common type which illustrates women standing together striking the same pose, one hand up and one down. The first of these (fig. 111) is found on a lead ring from the settlement houses at Mallia, house alpha, space 8, and accompanied pottery dating to the MMIII-LMI period.²⁷³ From a similar context, the settlement surrounding Knossos, specifically the House of the Frescos, comes a serpentine cushion seal (fig. 79) on which is carved two women in the same pose. The House of the Frescos, excavated by Evans, is located along the south side of the Royal Road,

---

²⁶⁴ A. Wace, "Mycenae 1950," *Journal of Hellenic Studies* 61 (1951) 254-72.
²⁶⁵ J. Weingarten *The Zakros Master and His Place in Prehistory*. Studies in Mediterranean Archaeology, Pocket Book 26 (Astrom 1981).
²⁶⁶ C. Blegen and M. Rawson, *The Palace of Nestor at Pylos in Western Messenia*, vol 1, 1966, 95ff.
²⁶⁷ G. Cadogan. *Palaces of Minoan Crete*. (New York: Routledge, 1991).
²⁶⁸ See J. Cherry "Polities and Palaces: Some Problems in Minoan State Formation," in J. Cherry and C. Renfrew eds. *Peer-Polity Interaction and Socio-Political Change*. (New York: Cambridge University Press, 1986).

---

²⁶⁹ Ibid., J. Soles (1993).
²⁷⁰ S. Hood, "The Magico-Religious Background of the Minoan Villa" in R. Hägg ed, *The Function of the "Minoan Villa"* (Athens: Swedish Institute of Archaeology, 1997) 105-115.
²⁷¹ C. Tzedakis. Chania, *Archaiologikon Deltion* (1977) 69-70.
²⁷² Y. Tzedakis and E. Hallager, "The Greek-Swedish Excavations at Kastelli Chania 1976 and 1977." *Athens Annals of Archaeology* 11 (1976) 24-28, pl. 4 and 5.
²⁷³ C. Kpaka, "Une Bague Minoenne de Malia" Bulletin de Correspondance Hellénique 106 (1984) 679-80, fig. 5.

and is where the famous second palace period Blue Monkey and Blue Bird frescoes were found.

Figure 111: Onyx lentoid from Mycenae; after CMS I.82. Catalogue # 52.

A strikingly similar seal, a lentoid also made of serpentine, was found at the large settlement of Gournia (fig. 80) in what is referred to as the Old Town.[274] Gournia is the most completely excavated Minoan settlement of any description and contains large buildings, paved streets and a platea.[275] Yet, a particularly elegant example of dancing is found on a sealing from Aghia Triada (fig. 81), one of some 700 sealings found at the site on an upper floor of the northwest portion of building, in a room called the "stanza dei sigilli."[276] Aghia Triada is most frequently referred to as a villa and sometimes as a royal villa because of the very high quality of its artistic remains (wall painting, stone vessels) and the fact that it has administrative connections with the closely adjacent palace of Phaistos.[277] The sealing in question illustrates two slender women wearing long hats, holding one hand up and one back. A second sealing (fig. 83) which illustrates dancing is found in the same context. Three women, a large one flanked by two smaller ones, stand before architecture out from which springs plants. This impression clearly comes from a small gold ring, given its shape and the softness of its carving.

The remaining three sealings (figs. 86, fig.85 and fig. 93) all illustrate processions and all come from Aghia Triada, in the "stanza dei sigilli" and all date to the LMIb destruction of the site. Lastly, there is a seal from the wealthy second palace period villa of Nerokourou in western Crete. Found in the northern portion of the villa, the serpentine lentoid illustrates several women in a row in procession (fig. 91), arms out.[278]

Turning to glyptic representations of bull games from settlement contexts, there are seven examples comprised of six impressions and one seal stone. The seal stone (fig. 13) is an agate lentoid from the third palace period House of the Idols at Mycenae.[279] This seal illustrates a man who poses in a backwards flip over the back of two bulls who stand next to one another, one looking back at him. Beneath the feet of the bulls, there is a strong ground line and before the face of the animal in front, a plant grows. The examples of bull leaping impressed on the sealings are of a more standard type, the first discussed here coming from Chania (fig. 34), also from the Kastelli, Katre St. 10, and dating to the second palace period.[280] This impression illustrates a man who either leaps off or onto the very hind portion of a bull who is in vigorous stride, all four hooves off the ground line and head thrown back.

The remaining impressions which feature representations of bull leaping are all from the "stanza dei sigilli" at Aghia Triada. The first one (fig. 35) is formally very similar to the example just discussed from Chania, featuring the leaper over the hind quarters of the bull, except in this representation the bull moves in the opposite direction, right to left, across the impression. Illustrating bull leaping operations at the other end of the bull are two impressions (figs. 33 and fig. 38) which detail leapers suspended over the head of the animal. Both impressions are somewhat incomplete and thus the details of a ground line and stance of the bull do not survive. Another impression which is somewhat incomplete (fig. 32), also lacking the ground line, illustrates a leaper sailing over the torso of a charging bull, only his arms visible extending towards the neck of the animal which he is either using as a spring board or upon which he is about to alight. Last among this group from Aghia Triada (fig. 37; cat.#39) comes an impression in excellent condition which illustrates a powerful charging bull in open stride, hooves just hovering above a paved surface. Delicately arching over the neck and back of the animal is a bull leaper whose musculature is described in swelling curves and tight tendons, as remarkable as that of the animal beneath.

There are only four examples of illustrations of

---

[274] H. Hawes and B. Williams, Gournia, Vasiliki, and other Prehistoric Sites on the Isthmus of Hierapetra, Crete (Philadelphia: University Museum, 1908) 54.
[275] J. Soles, "The Gournia Palace" American Journal of Archaeology 95 (1991) 17-35. He argues that Gournia is more than just a settlement. Few have followed his palatial identification, primarily because the site lacks the crucial palatial characteristics such as a central court, storage, grand wealth, etc
[276] Doro Levi, "Le cretule de Haghia Triada," Annuario della Sculoa archeologica di Atene e delle Missioni italiane in Oriente VIII-IX (1925-26) 157-201.
[277] For example, identical linear A inscriptions have been found at both.

[278] Y. Txedakis, "Archaiotites kai mnimeia dytikis Dritis," Archaiologikon Deltion 32, pt. 2, 329-30, plate 201.
[279] W. Taylour. "Mycenae, 1968" Antiquity 63 (1969) 91-97.
[280] Ibid, Tzedakis (1977) 33ff

performances which are of media other than glyptic and that come from settlement contexts, two from the second palace period and two from the third; all are from Crete. The first, from the second palace period, is the infamous Boxer Rhyton (fig. 29). Found fallen into a doorway at Aghia Triada , the steatite vase includes among its registers one of the best known illustrations of bull leaping.[281] From the same period at Aghia Triada comes another performance, this time a wall painting of a woman (fig. 112) outside dancing among several plants.[282] From the third palace period, again from Aghia Triada, there is another painting, on the famous Aghia Triada sarcophagus, this time of a procession, dating to LMIIIa (fig. 96).[283] In the scene painted on one side of the sarcophagus three women and three men carry objects in a procession including baskets and small animals Lastly, from Palaikastro, block Delta, dating to the third palace period comes a clay sculpture of four women dancing in a ring holding hands, engaged in a circle dance (fig. 66).[284]

Figure 112: Fresco of dancing woman from Aghia Triada; after Immerwahr (1990), plate 18. Catalogue # 67.

---

[281] F. Halbherr, Enrico Stafani and Luisa Banti, "Haghia Triada nel Periodo Tardo Palaziale," *Annuario della Sculoa archeologica di Atene e delle Missioni italiane in Oriente* 55, (1980) 82-84, pl. 51-52.
[282] Ibid. 86ff, fig. 54-55.
[283] C. R. Long. *The Agia Triadha Sarcophagus: A Study of Late Minoan and Mycenaean Funerary Practices and Beliefs*. Studies in Mediterranean Archaeology 41 (1974) 21, 36, fig. 43.
[284] R. Dawkins, "Excavations at Palaikastro," *Annals of the British School at Athens* 10 (1903-4) 192-231.

* * *

At this point, after the formal presentation of the archaeological provenance of the representations of bull leaping and dancing and before beginning a discussion of their significations (in the following chapter), it is useful to make assessments of similarities and differences among them. Looking across the four general provenance groups in which I have organized the material, a number of generalizations become clear and potentially important to mention. First, representations of bull leaping and dancing are found most frequently in burial contexts, and among the other locations, generally equally distributed (burial 28, palace 25, settlement 21, admin/storage 11). However, from all contexts, bull leaping was the most common of the two performances with thirty-eight representations, compared to twenty-seven of dancing and two of procession.

Looking at the dates of the representations of performances, one finds that more (47) come from third palace period contexts than from second palace period (34); two each come from the first and pre-palatial periods. Within the second palace period, interestingly, all but two examples of the representation of bull leaping and dancing come from Crete, and most examples of performances were found in settlement contexts (18) with fewer coming from palatial (4) and storage/administrative (9), and only one from a tomb context. As mentioned above, most performances were of bull leaping (13), only a few of dancing (8), and of procession (11).

During the third palace period the majority of examples come from the Mainland (34) and fewer from Crete (13). Of the images from Crete, four came from burial, seven from palatial contexts, and two from a settlement context. Interestingly, among these there is almost an equal number of bull leaping and dancing scenes. From the mainland, the majority of representations of bull leaping and dancing came from burial contexts (19) and most of the remaining (12) were from palatial contexts. Of the burial finds, nine examples were of bull leaping and ten were of dancing, equally nine rings and nine seals and one example of painting. The twelve examples from palatial contexts yielded five images of bull leaping and one of dancing, and six procession. The one example from a settlement context on the mainland is a seal which illustrates bull leaping. Lastly, the two examples from a storage/administration context, both impressions, include one representation of bull leaping and one of dancing.

What deductions can we begin to make about how the provenience of these seals and sealings might impact on their interpretation as objects which contribute to the construction and maintenance of social categories? The first and potentially most interesting observation is that during the second palace period, Crete produces by far the most images of bull leaping and dancing, and bull leaping is in the great majority. Furthermore, much of this material comes from settlement and storage/administration contexts. Given the way in which it is understood these sorts of sites functioned, as central storage facilities for the produce of the surrounding land, this fact is not surprising. Therefore, during the second palace period on Crete images of bull leaping and dancing were useful in settlement and central regional storage areas and seemingly less important in burial and palatial areas.

It is important to note here that the paucity of images found in burial contexts in the second palace period is not only due to what we might conclude is conscious choice but also it is due to the fact that there are simply very few second palace period burials. Indeed, burial practice, especially on Crete in the second palace period is one of the great mysteries of Aegean prehistory. It is important to keep this circumstance in mind when considering the small number of images in this context.

During the third palace period, we find on Crete that the situation has changed. There are fewer examples of representations of bull leaping and dancing, and they are found in different places. These images are found divided almost equally between burial and palatial contexts and there is an almost equal amount of representations of bull leaping and dancing. However, these numbers are much smaller compared to representations on the Mainland. This seems to indicate a reduced need for images like bull leaping and dancing at settlement areas and a rise in need for these in burial and in palatial contexts. This rise in the number of images of performance in burial contexts at this time is also in part due to the rise in burial practices during this period.

At the same time during the third palace period on the mainland, where in the previous period there had been no examples of glyptic representations of bull leaping and dancing, there are several, three times the number found on Crete. Predictably, the large majority of these new glyptic images were found in wealthy burial contexts, the rest roughly equally distributed between the other three context types. Interestingly, there seem to be roughly equal numbers of representations of bull leaping, dancing and procession, and many are featured on gold rings. Therefore, it would appear that images of bull leaping, dancing and procession were popular in Mycenaean contexts and specifically in graves.

Certain circumstances make sense of the information above. As I have already discussed, the larger number of images coming from burial contexts is due to the fact that the majority of glyptic materials come from burial contexts, especially from the mainland and especially in the third palace period. That no illustrations of performance come from tomb contexts in the second palace period on Crete stems from the fact that burial deposits during that period are largely unknown. Further, the great number of representations of performance found on sealings is a result of the fact that the four or five large burned sealing deposits found on the mainland and Crete also make up a large proportion of glyptic evidence. However, some provenience information about representations of bull leaping and dancing in glyptic cannot be explained by these circumstances. Why were there no representations of bull leaping and dancing on the mainland until the third palace period when this was a popular image on Crete, a place with which there was much contact? Given that these images had their origin on that island, one must conclude that in the third palace period they are borrowed from there. Here I am not interested in the idea that the formal compositions of bull leaping and dancing migrated north but rather that what these images might have symbolized socially was suddenly useful outside of Crete. But, why predominantly in tombs?

In the next chapter I look at these questions against the backdrop of the social history of the late Bronze Age. Refocusing on the relative values of the social categories produced and maintained in the representations of bull leaping and dancing and providing the historical matrix of these social categories, I explain the use and meaning of these images as badges of identity. I argue that such badges came about and were important during the second and third palace periods and in certain contexts because this was a time of political expansion and consolidation in the Aegean.

Chapter Five:
Meanings of Performance: Interpreting the Images

"...it is one thing to observe people performing the stylized gesture and singing the cryptic songs of ritual performances and quite another to reach an adequate understanding of what the movements and words mean to *them*."
    Victor Turner, *The Ritual Process: Structure and Anti-Structure* (New York: Aldine de Gruyter, 1969) 7.

At the end of the first chapter of the dissertation I discussed performative bodies in relation to two performed acts illustrated in glyptic art, bull leaping and dancing, and I proposed three social categories which these acts and bodies invoke: gender, age and social status. The second and third chapters examined representations of the performed acts of bull leaping and dancing and both concluded that various details of the representations served to convey and, in some cases, exaggerate aspects of these three social categories. The fourth chapter examined the archaeological provenience for these images of bull leaping and dancing with the aim of determining their context in material culture. Find spots for the images were reviewed and four general context groups were recognized: burial, storage/administrative, palatial and settlement. Two general conclusions are drawn: first, that images of bull leaping and dancing come from elite contexts and second, that they can all be associated with the prestige of the palaces, palatial administration, or personal wealth. More specifically, it is revealed that images of bull leaping and dancing are found only on Crete during the second palace period and mostly in settlement and storage/administration sites, and there is a relatively equal distribution of images of the two themes. During the third palace period fewer images of bull leaping and dancing are found on Crete, but their numbers dramatically rise on the mainland, found mostly in burial and palatial contexts and equally distributed between the two types. These conclusions pose interesting questions about the function of these images over time and between Crete and the mainland. This, the fifth chapter, returns primary focus to performances and social categories and attempts to answer these questions. I shall argue that the representations of the performances of bull leaping and dancing functioned on seals as signs of identification for the social authority of the palaces, first on Crete and later on the mainland. By this I mean that these images served as an index to larger representations of social dramas at the palaces, in the form of wall paintings, which were themselves representations of actual events, social dramas. I hypothesize that these social dramas, likely rites of passage ceremonies, functioned as a means of reiterating social groupings and as a means of social control during times of political change and upheaval.

This control which the social dramas of bull leaping and dancing brought about, I shall argue, was at first the establishment of new social groupings and identifications in the second palace period which were at odds with the older social groupings of the prepalatial and first palace periods. By establishing new social groupings and hosting the social dramas which reinforced these groupings, the palaces consolidated their power. Further, seals and rings which bore reference to these social dramas were imbued with special authority, as were the individuals who used them. Then, later in the second palace period on Crete, these same social dramas addressed a new problem, a lack of confidence or discontent with the ruling class because of natural disasters associated with the Theran eruption. In the following third palace period, I argue that the Mycenaeans took up the visual symbolic system of social control from their Minoan predecessors on Crete in order to maintain Knossos, which they then occupied, and employed it as well back at Mainland centers.

* * *

Before I explore the ways in which signs of identification worked in the late Aegean Bronze Age, it is important to pause and explore the meaning of the term. Most simply, by signs of identification I mean a short-hand image, small enough to be portable on an object or person, which aids in identification. An example is useful here: Renaissance commemorative medal. Popular since the early 16th century, bronze or lead twp-sided relief medals were a way of circulating a likeness of someone to a chosen few. Renaissance medals, in imitation of Roman coins which were their inspiration, primarily featured portraits which stressed the individual character and personal achievements.[285] The practice of striking portrait medals carried on after the Renaissance in Europe, most especially in France in the eighteenth century. By this time, it was popular to include more than just an emblematic image on the reverse, as had been traditional; historical events were often portrayed as well.[286] A bronze medal by Bertrand Andrieu dating to 1789 commemorates the storming of the Bastille, now in the collection of the British Museum.[287] The scene shows a great crowd equipped with rifles engulfed in smoke moving in toward the Bastille which is at the top left, its distinctive towers already aflame. Although it is unknown for whom this medal was commissioned, its point of reference, the event which touched off the French Revolution, is clear. The intended owners of such a medal is also unknown, however, we might imagine it was not Louis XVI or his supporters. What is known is that an event, no doubt, what Victor Tuner would call a social drama, is the inspiration.

But, how did this medal function as a sign of identification? In an abbreviated fashion, it represents a

---

[285] Mark Jones, *The Art of the Medal* (London: British Museum Press, 1979) 32ff.
[286] Ibid, 90-120.
[287] Mark Jones, *A Catalogue of the French Medals in the British Museum* (London: British Museum Press, 1982) cat # 253.

social/political event with which individuals associate. First, the image itself is important; it is an unambiguous reference to a discrete event, the storming of the Bastille. The event the image represents has political meaning; rejection of arbitrary and secret imprisonment by the crown and, more broadly, rejection of that political body. The event in its full extent and complexity is not represented; merely a snap-shot of the most dramatic moment of the story. Second, the way in which owners of such a medal identified with it is important. Presumably, only supporters of the revolution were those who would own such a medal. When such a person looked at it, held it in his or her hand, the event would be remember, in a way restaged, and the goals of the French revolution (liberty, equality, fraternity) would be reiterated and asociated with the owner. The image helped to "play out" the social drama again in the mid of the owner, an event which defined him or her socially and politically.

Although, obviously, there are significant differences between eighteenth century France and the late Aegean Bronze Age and between objects like commemorative medals and glyptics, I believe these objects worked performatively in largely the same fashion. I propose that the images of bull leaping and dancing on Minoan and Mycenaean seals and sealings reiterated the performances of social dramas at the palaces in the same way this particular medal reiterated the storming of the Bastille. However, in order to more fully understand exactly how and what got "played out," in the mind of a Minoan or Mycenaean when he or she looked at a bull leaper or dance, we need to clarify as well as possible what exactly these images meant to a contemporary audience.

* * *

What did the new performative bodies of the second palace period, the performed acts of bull leaping and dancing, and the social dramas performed and illustrated at palaces mean? In detail, these meanings will likely never be known. However, looking at the articulation of these performances to the social categories of gender, class and age, some meanings are perhaps comprehensible. Beginning with performativity and gender, the visual evidence speaks overwhelmingly for strong gender differentiation. Male and female gender is different in its comportment, body shape and proportion. These gendered bodies also dramatically emphasize, almost exaggerate, secondary sexual characteristics. Women's wide hips and large breasts are prominent as are men's broad chests and narrow waist. Interestingly, performative gender seems to imply reproduction or sex. Visual evidence of performativity and age stresses youth and agility; bodies are youthful and strong, dancing and leaping. Performative age, then, emphasizes youthful physical abilities. Lastly, visual evidence of performativity and social status is primarily found in elaborate costumes worn by leapers and dancers. Intricately woven cloth and the complex construction of costumes differentiate these bodies from others and likely emphasize a special access to the labor and luxury goods which constructed them.[288]

What meanings can be derived from looking at the performed acts of bull leaping and dancing? Let us first review the visual evidence of these performed acts which I discussed in chapters two and three. Representations of dancing include elegant sweeping movement, drawn by the arms and often framed within a built environment such as a pavement or a post and lintel structure. Details in the representation of bull leaping stress movement too but not sweeping, as seen in representations of dancing, but a swift flying or leaping movement.

Setting the visual details of performed acts against the meanings derived from performative bodies, what conclusions about bull leaping and dancing emerge vis-a-vis social categories? In other words, what might these performed acts have meant in terms of gender, class and age? Beginning with dance, the activity itself, the pose of the body further emphasizes the female secondary sexual characteristics which develop in adolescent youth. We might conclude that only women of status performed this act as only those who have access to luxury items are represented doing it. A built environment is another detail found in representation of bull leaping, most often pavement, and in representations of dance, most often a post and lintel structure. These architectural details, I have argued, indicate a special location, likely a palatial association. Such an association alludes to a high social status. Lastly, the physical movement of the dance and the indications of age, such as hair style, reveal that only youthful women performed. So, we can safely conclude that the performed act of dancing was exclusive to youthful elite females.

Bull leaping is a performed act restricted by gender; only males do it or at least only those visually gendered male. Further, as is the case with dancing women, their secondary sexual characteristics are emphasized on the performative bodies which engage in the activity. Also similar to dancing, bull leaping seems most likely to have taken place in an architectural environment and thus too is special. The skill needed to bull leap likely also connotes a status value. Lastly, and again similar to dancing, the act of bull leaping seems only to have been practiced by youthful vigorous males. So, like dancing, bull leaping was an activity exclusive in age and gender and associated with high status.

Having now shed some light on the representations of the performed acts of bull leaping and dancing as illustrated we might turn now to the representations of social drama to which I argue these representations bear an indexical relationship. As described in the first chapter, the Sacred Grove and Dance fresco and the fragments of a miniature bull leaping fresco found at Knossos included the

---

[288] See discussion of the performativity of bodies in Chapter One.

performance of dancing and bull leaping in front of an audience and in a palatial architectural environment. Given what we now understand about these performed acts, how might we reconstruct these social dramas? Again, specifics are very difficult but some details are revealing. The audience in the Sacred Grove and Dance and the miniature bull leaping fresco are separated by gender. Also, the audiences in these frescoes bear all the signs of youth that the performers do; they wear long locks and their bodies are youthful. The audience seems to be wearing the same costumes as the performers. In the Sacred Grove and Dance fresco, both genders' costumes are visible, flounced skirts and jackets for women and a short skirt or loin cloth for the men. Only the upper torso of the male audience remains from the miniature bull leaping fresco, but this shows that the men are nude from the waist up. Lastly, the details of the architecture in these paintings, as I have discussed in chapter three, indicate a palatial location for these dramas. What emerges are two social dramas which were performed and witnesses by those of the same age group which take place in or around the palatial centers. Both performed acts are the centerpiece of the drama which emphasizes skilled action. Performative bodies which engage in these performed acts emphasize secondary sexual characteristics.

Although the specifics cannot be known, I offer the following general reconstruction of these two social dramas. These dramas, although different in the act performed, are similar in that they unite a large number of people under the same broad social categories, age, gender and class. Could such an event which unites so many people who share similar aspects of social identity take place in part to reinforce this identity and form a bond among these people? I think this is highly likely. Unlike in the scene from Xeste 3 at Thera, where different age groups are depicted among men and women, or in the miniature frieze from the West House at the same site where some differentiation in class is indicated through dress, these two scenes stress the homogenization of individuals, and I believe this was very much the point of the social drama. It is important also to remember that these social dramas are represented as being performed at a palatial center; the connection between these ceremonies and the palaces, I believe, was an important component in the representation. This is potentially how the palace created a connection between their authority and social dramas.

I have posed that the glyptic representations of bull leaping and dancing functioned as badges of identification of palatial authority. If so, those who held or used these seal stones or rings would be identified with this power or authority. But, how exactly did this identification work? And why would a palatial authority choose a social drama which grouped individuals by broad social categories as a means of identification? Before the ways in which signs of identity worked, let us first explore just how close the connection was between the palaces and the manufacture and use of these visual identifiers.

* * *

In the previous chapter I connected glyptic art with high order centers. Yet, the presence of seals at these sites does not necessarily mean that their production was controlled there. Logically, one assumes that where production is controlled, so is design. As it is the decoration of the seals which is in question, the issue of where they were produced is important. If indeed the meanings of the images carved on seals are to be associated with high order centers, a direct relationship between these places and the design and manufacture of the stones must be drawn.

In fact, evidence for the manufacture of seal stones at palatial centers is well documented. From the Old Palace levels at Mallia in *Qartier Mu* there is evidence of a sizable workshop including tools for seal carving and raw materials.[289] In the second palace period evidence of seal manufacture is much more plentiful but again, almost exclusively limited to elite centers on Crete.[290] For instance, at Knossos in the "south-west basements" there is evidence for various kinds of manufacture including an area thought to be for the carving of stone, called the lapidary's workshop.[291] Even more extensive are the workshops in the harbor town of Knossos, Poros-Katsambas. A recent study of the area describes ateliers of seal and jewel making and metalsmiths installations including tools, partially finished pieces and raw materials.[292] At the palace of Phaistos, Levi's excavations on the ground floor of the first palace uncovered a workshop which, judging from the debitage and tools, was engaged in the manufacture of seal stones.[293] Lastly, at Zakros evidence of stone working was found in the workshop unit of the south wing including raw quartz, chlorite and another unnamed variegated stone as well as bronze tools.[294] On the mainland during the third palatial period, evidence of

---

[289] Jean-Claud Poursat, "Fouilles de Mallia," *Bulletin Correspondence Hellenique*, 102 (1978) 831-834; Jean-Claud Poursat, "Ateliers et sanctuaries à Mallia: nouvelles données sur l'organisation sociale à l'époque des premiers palais," in Krzyszkowska and Nixon eds. *Minoan Society*, (Bristol: Bristol Classics Press,1983) 277-81.
[290] There is some evidence of seal manufacture at Gournia and Palaikastro during the second palace period, yet it is at a much smaller scale than found at palatial centers, likely indicating incidental manufacture as opposed to an organized workshop. See Keith Branigan's discussion of this (especially pgs. 27-8) in Krzyszkowska and Nixon eds. *Minoan Society*, 23-32.
[291] *PofM*, vol. IV, 594-5,;vol. 1 p. 453. See J. Younger's discussion of the date of the workshop - which he desires to push back to LMIb, although more conventionally believed to be LMIIIb, "Lapidary's Workshop at Knossos" *Annual of the British School at Athens* 74 (1979)259-270.
[292] Nota Dimopoulou, "Workshops and Craftsmen in the Harbour-Town of Knossos at Poros-Katsambas" in *TEXNH: Craftsmen, Craftswomen and Cratfsmanship in the Aegean Bronze Age*. Aegaeum 16 (1997) 433-437.
[293] D. Levi, *Festòs e la Civiltà Minoica* I, (Rome, Incunabula Graeca 60.Edizioni dell'Ateneo, 1976) 205-22.
[294] N. Platon, *Zakros*, (New York: Scribners, 1971) 218ff.

large scale seal manufacture is similarly limited to palatial centers, among them, Mycenae, near the House of the Columns, otherwise known as the East Palace wing[295] and at Thebes,[296] both dating to the LH IIIb period. Contemporary Linear B records found at Pylos and other Mycenaean centers also mention large groups of specialized workgroups, which include those who worked with stone.[297]

Thus, the premise that there existed palatial control over what was carved on seals seems likely. Ideally, one would desire some evidence for the direction of artisans in these workshops to specific themes carved on seals stones; this evidence is lacking and it is unlikely it will ever surface given what is known about the nature of information documented by the palaces. However, along these lines, there exists a fascinating fragment of evidence, again from the Linear B archives. Among the tablets found in the archives at Pylos are lists of inventories of furniture in which each piece is described. Instead of, as one might expect, the shape or design of the furniture serving as the distinguishing characteristics by which the scribe has noted each entry in his list, each piece of furniture is instead described by its material and, significantly, the details of its decoration.[298] These descriptions are extraordinarily detailed, including even the notation of abstract designs such as the running spiral. Could this be evidence of the importance and possible control of even the decoration of the palatial artistic product?

I argue here that it is highly likely. From the meticulous study of seal usage during the second and third palatial period,[299] it is clear that seals used for stamping documents, both by those disbursing and those receiving commodities, played an important role in palatial accounting and administration. The connection between seals and palatial interests is clear. If, as I argue above, the palaces controlled the creation of the devices, rings and seals, which were instrumental in the operation of administrative systems, it is logical that the distinguishing mark on such devices be determined by the palace as well. So, what emerges is a system by which the palatial elites, involved in administration, used images such as bull leaping and dancing to identify themselves as associated with the palatial authority. I believe that images such as bull leaping and dancing were potent choices not only because of the socially charged images of performative bodies but as references to social drama held at the palaces. Bull leaping and dancing were emblematic of the kinds of social structures maintained by palatial authority.

What evidence exists which connects palatial elites to these images? If representations of bull leaping and dancing were to have functioned as identifiers of palatial elites, this connection must be reflected in the archaeological record. Striking evidence for this can be found in the phenomenon of "look alike" or replica rings or gems. "Look alike" or replica rings and gems look identical to one another, presumably having been made all from the same mold or by the same artist or workshop. These rings and stones are typically known only from the sealings made by their impression. The clearest example of the "look alike" or replica phenomenon are the Knossos replica rings, all presumably manufactured at Knossos during the LMIb period.[300] The primary reason why it is believed that these rings came from Knossos is that they are of an extraordinarily high quality. During the second palace period only Knossos and other palatial sites can be associated with such high quality workmanship as we have seen above.[301] The decorations on these rings include a scene with two horses and a chariot, two running lions in front of a palm tree, two combat scenes and six different bull leaping scenes. Fifty-three impressions found at six different sites on Crete have been identified as having been made from these ten rings, 36 of which illustrate bull leaping. The

---

[295] H. Schliemann, *Mycenae: A Narrative of Researches and Discoveries at Mycenae and Tiryns* (Concord: Ayer, 1880) 121, n.1.

[296] Sarantis Symeonoglou, *Kadmeia I. Mycenaean Finds from Thebes, Greece, Excavation at 14 Oedipus St*. Studies in Mediterranean Archaeology 35 (1973) chapter V.

[297] See Chadwick, *The Mycenaean World*, (New York: Cambridge University Press, 1976) 135-158, and Ventris and Chadwick, *Documents in Mycenaean Greek*, (New York, Cambridge University Press, 1956) 179-83. It is unclear whether these stone workers are masons or lapidaries.

[298] Ibid Ventris and Chadwick, 332-348 for a selected listing of such furniture inventory tablets from Pylos, specially tables such as Ta707 and Ta708, which include descriptions of animals and people. See J.T. Hooker, *Linear B, An Introduction* (Bristol: Bristol Classics Press, 1980) 127 for bibliography.

[299] Best, most comprehensive and synthetic works are the following. For 2nd palace period Crete, Erik Hallager, *The Minoan Roundel and Other Sealed Documents in the Neopalatial Linear A Administration*, Aegaeum 14, vols I and II, 1996., supplemented by Judith Weingarten "The Sealing Structures of Minoan Crete: MMII Phaistos to the Destruction of the Palace of Knossos, Part I: The Evidence until the LMIB Destructions," *Oxford Journal of Archaeology* 5.3 (1986)379-98. For 3rd palace period Crete, see Judith Weingarten, "The Sealing Structures of Minoan Crete: MMII Phaistos to the Destruction of the Palace of Knossos, Part II The Evidence from Knossos Until the Destruction of the Palace," *Oxford Journal of Archaeology*, 7(1988) 1-34. For the mainland in the 3rd palace period, see Tom Palaima, "Mycenaean Seals and Sealings in Their Economic and Administrative Contexts." Peter Ilievski and Ljiljana Crepajac, eds. *Tractata Mycenaea. Proceedings of the Eighth International Colloquium on Mycenaean Studies, Held in Ohrid* (15-20 September 1985) (Macedonian Academy of Sciences and Arts, Skopje, 1987) 249-266, supplemented by Tom Palaima, "Origin, Development, Transition and Transformation: The Purposes and Techniques of Administration in Minoan and Mycenaean Society," in T,. Palaima ed., *Aegean Seals, Sealings and Administration*, Aegaeum 5 (1990) 83-104.

[300] The primary research on the Knossos Replica rings was done by John Betts, New Light on Minoan Bureaucracy," *Kadmos* 6 (1967) 15-40. Some additions to the original sealing count as well as some corrections were made by Hallager (1996) 207-209.

[301] This is point is difficult to dispute on archaeological grounds, despite how counter intuitive it seems. For instance, a recent publication of workshops adjacent to the very wealthy settlement site of Mochlos in east Crete (Jeffrey Soles. "A Community of Craft Specialists at Mochols," in *TEXNH: Craftsmen, Craftswomen and Craftsmanship in the Aegean Bronze Age. Aegaeum* 16 (1997) 425-450) lists the discovery of workshops for the manufacture of stone vases, textiles, bronze implements and pottery but none for the manufacture of seal stones.

Knossian replica rings were used to stamp flat-based nodules which likely sealed written documents, dome noduli, believed to have functioned as tokens used by officials and hanging nodules which were attached to movable objects such as a box. The one sealing system with which the Knossos replica rings cannot be connected is that of the roundel, which is believed to have only been used on the inter-local exchange level, the only sealing use thought not to function in connection with the palaces.[302]

What has been reconstructed from the evidence of the Knossos replica rings is that their owners were Knossian officials who traveled around Crete in an administrative capacity and signed official records of their dealings with rings which indicated their identity. Interestingly, all sealings made from look-alike rings are of local clay.[303] We can see the look alike sealings, then, as a physical example of a palatial image imposed on local activity. Assuming that this reconstruction is true, it is important to my thesis that the image most often chosen in the manufacture of these rings and most often used among them is bull leaping. It is interesting to note that dancing was not among the images chosen for the look-alike rings and gems.

More evidence for a more personal connection between elite individuals and seals comes from tombs. In 1977, detailing the non-sphragistic use of seal stones and rings, John Younger gathered together all known examples of seals which had been found in tombs and used as personal adornment, that is, in direct association with a deceased individual.[304] Among these he lists rings, necklaces, bracelets, and anklets; not surprisingly, all date to the third palace period, a time during which burials are plentiful in the archaeological record. That rings were worn by individuals is not disputed and indeed, in the third chapter I described a number of gold rings found in tombs which illustrate women dancing and bull leaping scenes. The importance of Younger's article is its detail about seal stones either mounted or strung for bodily adornment, several of which were found on articulated skeletons or closely adjacent to secondary burials. Among his evidence for this kind of use for seal stones, Younger brings our attention to the near life-sized Cupbearer fresco (fig. 5), dating to the second palace, found by Sir Arthur Evans at Knossos[305] which illustrates a man in left profile carrying a long conical rhyton. On his left wrist is a sealstone strung on a string which we might assume was his to use in official transactions.

Thus, the look-alike rings, especially the Knossian examples, burial evidence and wall painting support not only the use of seals and rings decorated with illustrations of performed acts for palatial administration but also support a connection between these objects and elite individuals. It is not hard to imagine that in the Bronze Age a personal connection between elite individuals and the objects and images associated with palatial activity was desirable as that connection no doubt imbued that individual with special status and authority, in short, an identification with the palaces and their power. Interestingly, at no village site such as Pseira or Myrtos-Pyrgos has any seal or sealing been found which bears representations of bull leaping or dancing. Similarly, at these sites there is little evidence for palatial administration or involvement.[306] This negative evidence supports the hypothesis that representations of performed acts which invoked social drama taking place at the palaces had a currency only at sites which were directly associated with central palatial administration.

* * *

If from the above evidence we can imagine of images of bull leaping and dancing on seals and rings as bearing some sort of meaning vis-a-vis the palatial administrative authority, we might begin to look for some evidence of the currency of these images in other media at the palaces themselves. Some of this evidence has already been discussed, for instance, the wall paintings of the Sacred Grove and Dance and miniature bull leaping frescoes at Knossos (figs. 16, fig 21, fig. 22, fig. 23, fig. 24). These wall paintings were introduced in the first chapter in order to establish the relationship between the representation of the performed act of bull leaping and dancing and their context within social drama. Now, looking back again at this relationship in light of the importance of illustrations of bull leaping and dancing as used in administration, we can understand more fully the significance of these paintings. In other words, the wall paintings were important first and foremost because they associated social drama with the palaces not only because they were painted in them but because included in the paintings were details of palatial architectural. Through this, the location of the social drama at and in strong association with the palaces is reiterated.

What other evidence associates the social drama of bull leaping and dancing to the palaces? As I discussed in the second chapter, the miniature bull leaping scene is not the only wall painting which illustrates bull leaping at Knossos. The famous Toreador fresco (Fig. 9; cat.#87), found in the Court of the Stone Spout in the east wing of the palace, dating to the LMII period, is the image which most people associate with bull leaping in the Aegean Bronze Age.[307] Very similar to the composition of some

---

[302] Ibid, Hallager, (1996) 209.
[303] B and P Hallager, "The Knossian Bull - Political Propaganda in Neo-Palatial Crete?" *Politeia: Society and State in the Aegean Bronze Age*. Aegaeum 12 (1995) 551.
[304] John Younger, "Non-Sphragistic Uses of Minoan-Mycenaean Sealstones and Rings," *Kadmos* 16 (1977) 141-159.
[305] *PofM* II, 2, pl. XII.

[306] Only five non-palatial sites have yielded evidence of second palace period administration. They are Pyrgos, Ayia Triada, Gournia, Kea and Samothrace. See E. Hallager, (1996*)* 121- 134.
[307] A. Evans, "Knossos 1900" *Annual of the British School at Athens* (1900-1901) 94ff; *PofM* III, 209ff.

bull leaping scenes found on sealings,[308] the images consists of one, two or three bull leapers, at the front, rear or over the back of the bull. Another possible toreador scene was discovered in the ante-room of the throne room at the palace. However, all that remains from the painting, is the hoof of the bull.[309] Were this indeed a painting of bull leapers, it would place the scene significantly close to what is assumed to be the seat of authority in the palace, whether religious or political, at least in its later phases.[310] Regardless, the toreador painting is one of ten image of bull leaping which survive on Crete in media other than glyptic. As outlined in chapter five, there are no fewer than eight examples of dancing from Crete in media other than the glyptic.

As I discussed in the second and third chapter, on the Greek mainland there are a number of examples of both motifs, all dating to the third palace period. At Mycenae, a fragment of a larger scene, found under the Ramp House[311] shows just the back of a spotted bull (fig. 50). From near-by Tiryns, there is the largely preserved bull leaping scene (fig. 48), found by Schliemann, in a small court northeast of a washroom.[312] These are only two of the five images of bull leaping found on the mainland other than in the glyptic medium. This coverage is similar with images of dancing. In the Peloponnese, at the palace of Pylos, fragments of dancing women have been found (fig. 76) as well as at the site of Thebes (fig. 99). These are two of five images of dancing which survive from the mainland in media other than the glyptic.

Therefore, we find that at palatial sites on Crete and the mainland, wall paintings of bull leaping and dancing in media other than glyptic are not uncommon. Based upon this, I believe that the performances of the social dramas of bull leaping and dancing can be safely associated with the palaces on both the Mainland and Crete. If then we have identified two common decorative motifs from the palaces which are used in relationship to palatial administration and bear social meaning, are these, in their glyptic application, signs of palatial identification?

Precisely this sort of conclusion has been reached from the examination of the glyptic art from ancient Ur in Mesopotamia. During the Ur III period, dating to the last two centuries of the third millennium BC, political organization (under a central kingly rule), economy, literature and the visual arts flourished as never before. The glyptic arts in this period (cylinder seals in the Near East as opposed to stamp seals in the Mediterranean) were highly regularized in decoration, primarily in presentation scenes. These scenes consisted of a man, the owner of the seal (this known by his identification inscribed on the seal), often escorted by an intercessor, standing before a king. In two important articles,[313] Irene Winter has argued that this standardized scene legitimated not only the power of the king but the relationship of the owner of the seal pictured therein to that authority. Crucial to the strength of Winter's argument is the knowledge of the ways in which these cylinder seals were used during the period, namely, to seal or witness economic, legal and social transactions and how the images on them reiterated royal sponsored art. Could illustration of bull leaping and dancing found on seals and sealings from the Aegean also be a means of association with the ruling authority?

I believe that the Ur III model opens an interesting avenue of thought. If seals which featured bull leaping and dancing associated their user with the ruling authority and legitimized transactions used with them, then wouldn't these objects only be present in the archaeological record when such legitimization was required? In other words, certain circumstances would have been necessary to support, or lead to, the sort of conscious creation of visual ideology such as the Ur III model describes. What sort of circumstances might these be and why choose to reference in this visual ideology social dramas which stress large social groupings? In the interest of answering these questions, our attention now turns to an overview of what is known about the politcal developmenet in the second and third palace periods on Crete and the mainland. In this overview I emphasize social/political organization and processes, as these are the most useful lines of development given the nature of our questions.

* * *

Before the construction of the palaces on Crete people lived in small village communities where kinship ties were the backbone of social interaction. These communities have yielded little evidence of social stratification.[314] Much of the evidence for these kinship

---

[308] See especially CMS II6.39, II8.221 and V Sup.IB.135, all examples with two leapers at different positions of mount and dismount.
[309] *PofM* IV.2, 893, fig. 872.
[310] W-D. Niemeier, "On the Function of the 'Throne Room' in the Palace of Knossos," in R. Hägg and N. Marinatos eds, *Function of the Minoan Palaces* (Athens: Swedish Institute of Archaeology, 1987) 163-8. The examples of paintings of bull leaping found at other locations at Knossos, such as in the Queen's Megaron, do not take away from the power of the example in the throne room. Indeed, this painting, whether bull leapers or only charging bull, would have been special because of its location so close to the throne.
[311] G. Rodenwaldt, "Fragmente mykenischer Wandgemälde," *Athenische Mitteilungen*, 36 (1911) 221-50, pl 9. See also Maria Shaw, "The Bull-Leaping Fresco from Below the Ramp House at Mycenae: A Study in Iconography and Artistic Transmission, *Annual of the British School at Athens* 91 (1996) 167-190, color plates A-D, plates 36-37.
[312] H. Schliemann, *Tiryns*, (Leipzig, 1886) 303-307, pl. 13.

[313] Irene Winter, "Legitimation of Authority Through Image and Legend: Seals Belonging to Officials in the Administrative Bureaucracy of the Ur III State," in *The Organization of Power: Aspects of Bureaucracy in the Ancient Near East*. McGuire Gibson and Robert Biggs eds., *Studies in Ancient Oriental Civilization*, 46 (1987); Irene Winter, "The King and the Cup: Iconography of the Royal Presentation Scene on Ur III Seals," in M. Kelley-Buccellati, ed., *Insight Through Images: Studies in Honor of Edith Porada*, Bibliotheca Mesopotamica, 21 (1986).
[314] An important exception to this generalization are the very wealthy EM tombs found at Mochlos. For an interpretation of this evidence of social stratification see J. Soles, *Prepalatial Cemeteries at Mochlos And*

ties and lack of social rank come from the burial evidence found in family tombs.[315] Further, these tombs are believed to be the focal point for ceremonies which reiterated kinship ties.[316] The first palaces were constructed at Knossos, Phaistos and Mallia. The size and full extent of these palaces are not perfectly known because succeeding constructions either destroyed or obscured their plans. It was during this period that sealing practices start in earnest and seem in structure to be largely imitative of large-scale storeroom administration found in the contemporary Near East. Evidenced clearly at Phaistos, where over 6500 nodules have been recovered, this system was one in which direct sealing, that is, sealing directly on objects, was primarily used in addition to inscribed nodules and clay documents.[317] This complex and variate system reflects the growth of economic activities endemic to the first palaces. Scale here, however, is not to be exaggerated. The sorts of transactions in evidence and recorded are simple ones (receive, dispense), in relatively small quantities (individual or family size) and involving basic food stuffs (olives, barley, grapes).[318] This economic profile has lead a number of archaeologists to conclude that the early palaces functioned primarily as regional storage facilities, especially in the event of failed crops.[319] Sealing systems, we then understand, were developed to simply keep track of who gave and who got what at the central storage facility. Despite this redistributive roll of the early palaces, there is little evidence for the breakdown of the prepalatial kinship social units, again based on burial evidence.[320]

Art during the first palace period, as I discussed in chapter one, was almost totally aniconic, limited to abstract designs and illustrations of nature such as animals and plants. This in general describes the decorations found on the seals used in the Old Palace system. To the modern viewer, these first palace period seals seem crude due to their non-human subjects and free-wheeling abstract composition. However, these images got the job done, in the administrative sense, being used to uniquely mark foodstuffs moving in and out of the palaces.

After a destruction of unknown source necessitated the reconstruction of the palaces across Crete, the era of the second palaces began. A book by Driessen and MacDonald proposes that this next period was divided into two distinct parts, LMIa and LMIb. The earlier, LMIa phase is regarded as the height of Minoan civilization.

> The new face of Crete can be interpreted in at least two different ways. Either new independent centers emerge basing themselves more or less on the palatial model, or one or more palaces establish new centers as a means of controlling large areas of land...[321]

The latter view is generally held and is described specifically as one of economic and administrative development.[322] This was achieved when the central regional power, the palace, converted the system of administration more and more to its own advantage in terms of the use and consumption of raw materials, manpower and manufactured goods. This is indeed reflected in palatial administration habits which seem to have, for the first time, accommodated much intra and inter site activities throughout the island. For instance, villa sites become hubs of extra palatial administrative activity and then important places in association with palatial centers.[323] These sites function as small scale redistributive centers, taking part of this responsibility from the palaces, which included more limited storage space in their reconstructions. Administrative mechanisms changed too. Direct sealing is finished,[324] but in its place emerge a greater variety of types and patterns of applications of sealing. Among these types of sealing system is the multiple sealing system which was used to authenticate economic activities. Other mechanisms used in new types of sealing practices are roundels and flat-based nodules (used to seal ephemeral written documents) and hanging nodules.[325] With all of these new sealing systems, the Linear A script was used extensively. Most of the information about the second palace period of Cretan administration comes from deposits at villas, primarily Aghia Triada. Weingarten has proposed four interconnected administrative areas for the island, divided geographically on roughly the same lines as the modern nomes of Crete, each approximately a quarter of the island.[326] These areas, Weingarten says, were overseen by a central authority, Knossos, as evidenced by, for instance, the Knossian look-alike rings.

Gournia and the House Tombs of Bronze Age Crete. Hesperia, Supplement 24 (1992).
[315] John Cherry, "The Emergence of the State in the Prehistoric Aegean," *Proceedings of the Cambridge Philological Society* 210 (1984) 18-48.
[316] K. Branigan. *Dancing With Death: Life and Death in Southern Crete c.300-2000 BC.* (London: Haakert, 1993) 137-141.
[317] J. Weingarten, "Three Upheavals in Minoan Sealing Administration: Evidence for Radical Change," in *Aegaeum* 5 (1990) 106ff.
[318] Ibid, Palaima (1990) 86f.
[319] K. Branigan, "Social Security and the State in Middle Bronze Age Crete," *Aegeaeum* 2 (1988) 11-16. P. Halstead, "From Determinism to Uncertainty: Social Storage and the Rise of the Minoan Palace," in A. Sheridan and G. Bailey eds., *Economic Archaeology* (Oxford, Oxford University Press, 1981).
[320] K. Branigan. "Some Observations on State Formation in Crete," in E. French and K. Wardle eds. *Problems in Greek Prehistory* (Bristol: Bristol Classical Press, 1988) 68.

[321] Jan Driessen and Colin MacDonald *The Troubled Island: Minoan Crete Before and After the Santorini Eruption.* Aegaeum 17 (1997) 12.
[322] Ibid, Cherry (1984) pg. 23ff.
[323] Villas I have discussed under the general provenience category of settlement in chapter three. Driessen and MacDonald see these as Knossos colonies. Ibid, Driessen and MacDonald, (1997) 37-40.
[324] Ibid, Weingarten (1990).
[325] Hallager 1996, 236ff.
[326] Ibid. Weingarten 1990. Seal evidence for contacts between Zakros and Sklavokamos, Zakros and the Messara and vice versa.

This first half of the second palace period on Crete is clearly one of greater social stratification evidenced at least by the rapid reconstruction of the first palaces and the ability to organize and maintain centralized control of materials and labor resources. This is likely the most profound indication of social stratification.[327] Where kinship relations were what unified people in the pre palatial and first palace periods, now, we must conclude, extra-familial social authority had central control.

This sort of centralization of control can also be seen in other areas of Minoan culture, for example, at the peak sanctuaries. Peak sanctuaries are religious sites situated, as their name implies, high atop mountains and hills. These sorts of sites become common at the beginning of the middle Minoan period, and regional studies have indicated that during the first palace period there is almost a one-to-one correlation between larrg sites and sanctuaries. In the second palace period, however, the number of peak sanctuaries dramatically declines and the only remaining ones are located directly adjacent to the palaces, such as Juktas by Knossos and Petsophas by Palaikastro. Peatfield has suggested that this radical reduction in the number of peak sanctuaries during the second palace period is the result of the consolidation of religious activities and, in turn, of political power around the palaces.[328] Another example of consolidation of control around the palaces comes from the study of cult practice. Whereas in the first palace period there was an abundance of cult sites outside of the palaces, in the second palace period, cult is brought inside the palaces and access controlled.[329] Jennifer Moody has interpreted these and other aspects of the centralization of control of the palaces in the symbolic sphere. Specifically, she suggests that the palaces, as they increased the control of cult activity and the production of luxury goods (as for instance in production of seal stones), took on more of a symbolic prestige identity, typified, she argues, by ceremonies and feasting.[330] I shall return to this idea later.

During the contemporary Late Helladic I-IIa period on the mainland, no centralized authority of any variety can be recognized. There is little evidence of any complex social organization or large-scale commodity storage of any kind, agricultural or otherwise. The only noticeable evidence of social stratification at the end of this period is the frequency of burials of wealthy individuals. It is believed that this conspicuous consumption at burial is indicative of competing wealth among individuals.[331] Dating to this same period, the shaft graves, found in grave circles A and B at Mycenae, contain the richest finds ever unearthed in the Aegean including much gold and silver, bronze, glyptic art, and ivory carving. Because of their high value and fine quality, these objects and others from contemporary burials have been attributed to Cretan palatial workshops, a view which I share.[332] For the present investigation a precise determination of the origin of the impressive finds from the Shaft Graves is unimportant. What is important is that ruling elite individuals at Mycenae chose contemporary Minoan objects and styles for the visual expression of their wealth and status.

The second half of the second palace period on Crete, LMIb, as Driessen and MacDonald see it, was a time of great turmoil. This was, in their view triggered by the infamous Santorini eruption at the end of LMIa. The aftermath of this geographical event the authors describe as a time of continuing geological and atmosphiric crisis including other smaller eruptions, tsunamis, poisonous gasses, acid rain, and scorching winds, pumice showers, climatic anomalies, ash fall, and, possibly most importantly, social effects.[333] Specific results of these conditions that can be observed archaeologically are the reduction in the number and extent of settlements, public spaces in settlements converted to private, possible population decrease, food and industrial production increasingly centered around settlements, bronze hoarding and possibly the construction of defensive structures.[334] As the authors explain, the elite during this

---

[327] M. Dabney. "The Later Stages of State Formation in Palatial Crete," *Politeia: Society and State in the Aegean Bronze Age*, Aegeaum 12, 1995, 47. See also J. Cherry, "Generalization and the Archaeology of the State. In D. Green et al. eds, *Social Organization and Settlement* (New York: Cambridge University Press, 1978) 411-437. Cherry argues for generalized "energy trends" in state evolution such that as long as it is to the advantage of the elite, structures of energy flows are progressively heightened.
[328] Alan Peatfield, "Palace and Peak: The Political and Religious Relationship Between Palaces and Peak Sanctuaries," in Hägg and Marinatos eds, *The Function of the Minoan Palaces* (Athens: Swedish Institute of Archaeology, 1987) 89-93.
[329] G. Gesell. "The Minoan Palace and Public Cult," in R Hägg and N. Marinatos eds. *The Function of the Minoan Palaces*, (Athens: Swedish Institute of Archaeology, 1987) 123-128.
[330] J. Moody "The Minoan Palace as a Prestige Artefact" in R Hägg and N. Marinatos eds. *The Function of the Minoan Palaces*, (Athens: Swedish Institute of Archaeology, 1987) 235-241. See also Yannis Hamilakis, "Wine, Oil and the Dialectics of Power in Bronze Age Crete: A Review of the Evidence," *Oxford Journal of Art* 15 (1996) 1-32, where it is presented that in the second palace period wine production reached it's height, possibly need for such feasting.

[331] C. Mee and W. Cavanaugh, "Mycenaean Tombs as Evidence for Social and Political Organization," *Oxford Journal of Archaeology* 3.3 (1984) 48-57.
[332] For a full catalog of the contents of the Shaft Graves, Emily Townsend. *The Art of the Shaft Graves of Mycenae*. Lectures in Memory of Louise Taft Semple; Series 3.(Cincinnati: University of Cincinnati, 1975).. For the more important points of the Minoan vs. Mycenaean manufacture of these contents see: E. Davis, *The Vaphio Cups and Aegean Gold and Silver Ware* (New York: Garland, 1977); J. Crouwel, "Pictorial Pottery from Mycenae at the Time of the Shaft Graves, " in R. Laffineur, ed. *Transition, Le mond égéen du Bronze moyen au Bronze récent*. Aegeaum 3 (1989) 37-48; OTKP Dickinson, *The Origins of Mycenaean Civilization* (Göteborg Åstrom, 1977), ibid "Cretan Contacts with the Mainland During the Period of the Shaft Graves," in Hägg and Marinatos eds, *Minoan Thallasocracy* (Athens, Swedish Institute of Archaeology, 1984) 115-8. S. Hill, "On the Origins of the Shaft Graves," in R. Laffineur, ed. *Transition, Le mond égéen du Bronze moyen au Bronze récent*. Aegeaum 3 (1989) 91-99; G. Karo, *Die Schachtgräber von Mykenai* (Munich, 1930), G.E. Mylonas, *Mycenae and the Mycenaean Age* (Princeton: Princeton University Press, 1966).
[333] Ibid Driessen and MacDonald, pgs. 89-95.
[334] Ibid, 82-3.

period,

> tried with, amongst other things, new religious propaganda, to maintain the status quo and keep a more elitist system going. This attempt failed. Because of problems with food production and distribution, the network which had existed, disintegrated, resulting in decentralization which went hand in hand with an increase of elitist power. The latter then incrementally led to inner Cretan conflict and a massive wave of fire destructions implying anarchy by the end of the period. That Mycenaeans from Mainland Greece arrived at some state on the island during the late Bronze Age is clear....the 'crisis years' of LMIb-II appear to be the most opportune moments.[335]

Although what Driessen and MacDonald describe might be dramatic conjecture certainly during the following third palace period on Crete, radical change occurs. Very few sites were reinhabited after the destructions at the end of the prior period, Knossos being the only one with an extensive rebuilding. The new Mycenaean ruling class at Knossos and the other sites exhibited a preference for Mycenaean pottery styles, methods of burial, and the proto-Greek Linear B language. As a result, this phase at Knossos is called Mycenaean, and there is little reason to believe that the remainder of the island could not also be described this way. At the rebuilt Knossos a new three tiered administrative sealing system was practiced. Sealings, if inscribed, could function as primary documents. Leaf-shaped tablets functioned as primary or secondary documents, and page shaped tablets, which were generally stored in central archives, represent the third tier and were used to compile and summarize the information stored on the leaf-shaped tablets for further administrative purposes.[336] Although clearly based on the earlier Linear A bureaucratic system, this one is a Mycenaean invention.

The same system is found in an almost identical form on the mainland of Greece, most clearly described at the palace site of Pylos. Clear social hierarchy exists in the Linear B documents, the head of which was a character called the Wanax.[337] Interestingly, the seals and rings used in this system bear illustrations of performed acts, reviewed in chapter one, most frequently among them, bull leaping and dancing, clearly another imitation of Minoan practices. Pylos is just one of a number of palaces which rapidly grows during the third palace period on the mainland where a strict social hierarchy develops in which the palatial authority and wealth grows increasingly at the expenses of the lower classes. This social hierarchy can be observed on the one hand by the impressive Mycenaean architectural evidence such as throne rooms and eleborate decoration and on the other hand the rapid reduction of wealthy burials outside of palatial areas during the period. It is believed that the overall decline in wealth and elaboration of tombs outside palatial centers is the result of the full concentration of conspicuous display on palatial elites, both in their burial and in the decoration of the palaces.[338] Painted within the walls of these new palaces and preserved at the Palace of Knossos are illustrations both of bull leaping and dancing, as we have seen above. In a period of Mycenaean influence in the Aegean, the visual record of these powerful people continues to draw on earlier Minoan visual themes.

In sum, on Crete during the first half of the second palace period, all signs seem to point to a greater concentration of centralized authority at Knossos. This is typified by the consolidation at the palaces of control of cult, administrative activity based in Linear A script (in conjunction with the villas) and luxury craft production. Dating to the second palace period, the first illustration of social dramas is found painted on the walls of Knossos and related representations of performed acts are seen on seal stones and rings. It is almost impossible to know when during the second palace period, LMIa or LMIb, these illustrations of social drama were painted on the walls of the palace. In actuality, it is unimportant. What is important is that by the end of the period these images were in place and functioning in tandem with similar images on seals and other media, perhaps, as Driessen and MacDonald have posited, as religious propaganda.

The mainland during this period seems to exhibit no single centralized authority but instead a concentration of wealth around individuals. Some of the wealth of these "chiefs" bear the mark of influence from Crete including Cretan imagery, although, interestingly, no images of bull leaping and dancing. In the following third palace period, Knossos is, for all intents and purposes, under Mycenaean authority and a new and more complex Linear B administration is installed. Palaces arise on the mainland, and all of them use this same Linear B system. Both on Crete at Mycenaean Knossos and at the Mainland Palaces, images of the social dramas, bull leaping and dancing can be found.

---

[335] Ibid 117-8.
[336] Ibid, Palaima (1990) 102; Weingarten 1988: 13-14.
[337] K. Killiam "The Emergence of *Wanax* Ideology in the Myceaean Palaces," *Oxford Journal of Archaeology* 7 (1988) 293ff and fig. 1.

[338] S. Voutsaki, "Social and Political Processes in the Mycenaean Argolid: The evidence from the Mortuary Practices," in *Politeia: Society and State in the Aegean Bronze Age*, Aegaeum 12 (1995) 62. Ibid Mee and Cavanaugh pg. 59-61. M. Dabney and J. Wright, "Mortuary Customs, Palatial Society and State Formation in the Aegean Area: A Comparative Study, in R. Hägg and G. Nordquist eds. *Celebrations of Death and Divinity in the Bronze Age Argolid. Proceedings of the Sixth International Symposium at the Swedish Institute at Athens, 11-13 June, 1988.* (Athens: Swedish Institute of Archaeology, 1990) 52; J. Wright, "Death and Power at Mycenae: Changing Symbols in Mortuary Practice," *Thanatos. Les coutumes funéraires en Egée à l'âge du Bronze.* Aegaeum 1 (1987) 171-184.

Conclusion

Given the historical back ground reviewed in the previous chapter, we can now investigate the impetus for social drama in the second palace period on Crete and its adoption in the next period by the Mycenaeans. To begin, we might turn briefly back to Victor Turner and his explanation of the function of social drama. As mentioned in chapter one, Turner argued that social dramas are, among other things, reactions to crisis.

> They confront problems and contradictions of the social process, difficulties arising in the course of social life in communities, corporate groups, or other types of social fields. They are concerned with the breaches of regular norm-governed relationships, involving action of the sort we would call in our culture crime, sin, deviance, offense, misdemeanor, injury, tort, damage, and so forth....[339]

Thus, social drama seeks to address tension in society. In the above brief description of the history of the second and third palace period on Crete and the mainland, there is ample evidence for social pressure, both the kind emanating from growth, for instance evident in the political consolidation in second palace period Crete, or the kind resulting from conflict, which no doubt occurred around the Santorini eruption and in the Mycenaean acquisition of Knossos. Could representations of bull leaping and dancing found on seals and rings and the social dramas at the palaces they reference have a relationship to social pressure or consolidation?

I believe they do. The social pressure to which they are an answer is the result of political control around palatial centers, that is, the imposition of a new hierarchical social construct on an old kinship based system. What I propose is the following. In the second palace period human representation suddenly occurs and is coincidental with the growth of a palatial administrative system. This system, which, by definition, imposes a hierarchy, would have worked against previously existing kinship systems which, although dating to the EM period, were still a part of social practice during the period proceeding the first palaces. The social dramas of dancing and bull leaping themselves, as we understand them from wall painting and the examination of the social categories which they invoke, emphasized extra-familial social groupings such as gender, age and class and represented groups of people alike in affiliation with them. In other words, the ideological view which these social dramas, and the wall paintings which represent them, communicated identified with broad social groupings such as age, gender and class. This identification was at the expense of old kinship systems. In kinship systems, individuals are connected to one another primarily through familial ties and not through social or political associations.[340] This sort of transition must have been a source of profound upheaval; individuals and families who had enjoyed prestige and authority in the past would have been forced to give this up and instead identify equally with other members of society. The social dramas not only served to break down old systems of social identification but created new ones, around social categories and specific values within them. Let us look more closely at these specific values.

As discussed at the beginning of the chapter, certain aspects of these social categories were emphasized in the performative bodies engaging in the acts of bull leaping and dancing. These were vigorous youths, within the social category of age and gender differentiation and possibly sex or reproduction, in the social category of gender. How can we understand these values as being important for promotion by the palaces? This is hard to say. Possibly youths served a ceremonial or religious function in the palaces. Indeed, perhaps the performances of bull leaping and dancing by youths were themselves critical ceremonies for this age group in relation to the palaces. Gender differentiation and an emphasis on sex may have had a connection with fertility. Both of these ideas may indicate some sort of coupling or marriage ceremonies.

In the conclusions to chapters two and three, the reiterative sense of the three social categories of age, specifically youth, gender, and social status, specifically high, is drawn out from formal details. This evidence, I noted, compels one to think that what is represented in these social dramas is a rite of passage ceremony. What exactly took place at such a ceremony is, however, difficult to know. We can safely conclude that dancing, procession as a subset, and bull leaping were part of the show. Despite this lack of specific knowledge, there is evidence that a part of the rite of passage or perhaps its purpose was a group marriage. This idea, proposed by Ellen Davis,[341] finds some support in the myth of Theseus and Ariadne and the Athenian youths who accompanied Theseus to Crete. Willetts has suggested that the myth can be seen as a metaphor for an ancient right of passage which results in marriage. As he points out, when Theseus sails away from Crete he lands on Delos and danced a dance with the other young men who had survived the labyrinth. After this dance, after the ordeal of surviving the Minotaur, he marries Ariadne.[342] The performance of bull leaping might also bear a relationship

---

[339] V. Turner, *The Anthropology of Performance* (New York, Performing Arts Journal, 1988) 94-95.

[340] R. Keesing. *Kin Groups and Social Structure*. (New York: Holt, 1975) 45-8.

[341] Ellen Davis, "The Knossos Miniature Frescoes and the Function of the Central Courts," in Robin Hägg and Nanno Marinatos eds., *The Function of the Minoan Palaces*. (Athens: The Swedish Institute of Archaeology, 1987) 157-161.

[342] R. F. Willetts, *Cretan Cults and Festivals*. (London: Routledge, 1962) 124.

to this story, as a metaphor for the mastering of the Minotaur, or at least as a dangerous feat accomplished. As I noted in chapter two, Koehl and others have offered strong evidence for male rites of passage ceremonies, the Algeda, which might have included bull leaping.[343] Marriage could have followed such a performance as well. There is no evidence for marriage specifically, a problem stemming from the fact that the existence and/or nature of Aegean Bronze Age marriage is unknown.

Yet, using just these hypotheses we can tentatively reconstruct a visual ideology of the palaces that promotes identification with extra-familial social groupings of youth and fertility. Returning to Moody's proposition that ceremonies were an element in the configuration of the palaces as prestige objects, we might now be able to hypothesize that bull leaping and dancing occurred at these events. Although the details of such events are impossible to know, we can say that they took place somewhere around the palaces and they involved large groups of same-gender, same-age people. These people were both audience and participants, both enjoying and taking part in the activities. Interestingly, there is no evidence for an individual authority, either historically, archaeologically, or visually. Although this negative evidence is strong, it is difficult to believe an event which involved large groups of people occurred without some sort of organization and/or authority. We might imagine this entity was associated with the palaces, however it is impossible to know lacking evidence.

Finally, how did signs of identity, as I have called them, the glyptic representations of bull leaping and dancing work vis-à-vis this reconstruction? As the social dramas which were staged at the palaces were important to the palatial authority as a means of control, no doubt, images which referred to these performances would be meaningful and important. In chapter one, I argued that the seals bore an indexical relationship to the representations of the social dramas of bull leaping and dancing at the palaces. Through this indexical relationship, those who saw glyptic representations of bull leaping and dancing would think of the social dramas at the palaces and, implicitly, their message of power consolidation: the new social organization. The user of a seal or ring with such images would then be identified with the power that the control of this new social organization implied. For instance, we might imagine a mature person of the second palace period who lives in a settlement near a palace. He or she has participated in a rite of passage ceremony at the palace and is a member of the new social grouping. This person may bear a ring with a reminder of this event, an image of dancing. When that individual uses that ring, they associate themselves with not only the ceremony in which thy have participated but in the power of the palace which hosted it. Like the medal which bears the image of the storming of the Bastille, we might image the owner of the ring remembering their participation in a dancing ceremony and with it, membership in a new grouping. The values of that group, the performative bodies and performed acts tell us value youth, high social status and procreation. Anyone who sees this person's ring or a stamp from it know that the owner is a member of this group, the entry into which the palaces controls.

Given the suggestions of Driessen and MacDonald, if we set our hypothetical character in the later part of the second palace period, after natural disasters occurred in connection to the eruption of the Theran Volcano, what might be different? This is even more difficult to say. If these scholars' conclusions are correct, the use of signs of identity might have become more contentious. If, indeed, the palaces were more and more anxious about loosing the social control they had gained during the period at the hands of those who were loosing faith in them (perhaps people interested in reestablishing the old kinship system?) perhaps, to combat this, social dramas occurred more and more often and of differing sorts. Concomitantly, there would be a rise in their representation. This might explain the somewhat greater variety of representations of performed acts found on seals in this period (see appendix A). In order to prove this, however, we would need to be able to date the glyptic materials to pre and post the Santorini explosion, LMIa or b. This is, as Driessen and MacDonald admit,[344] at the moment impossible.

Chapter four showed that the distribution of images of bull leaping and dancing was different between the second and third palace periods. Specifically, in the conclusion of the fourth chapter, I present the following from my study of the temporal and spatial distribution of glyptic examples of bull leaping and dancing. From the second palace period, Crete is the only source for these objects, they come mostly from settlement and storage/administration contexts and with roughly equal proportions of images of bull leaping and dancing. In the third palace period the majority of representations of bull leaping and dancing are found on seals and sealings from the mainland, primarily in burial contexts and with roughly equal representations of each performed act. On Crete during the period, there are also equal numbers of representations of bull leaping and dancing, but they come mostly from palatial and burial contexts. How can we make sense of this pattern now that we have a better idea how these images functioned?

As I noted in chapter four, that the whole of glyptic representations of bull leaping and dancing come from Crete in the second palace period can be readily explained by the fact that there were no palaces on the mainland at that time. If, indeed, these images were used to reference the consolidation of power around palaces,

---

[343] R. Koehl, "The Chieftain Cup and a Minoan Rite of Passage," *Journal of Hellenic Studies*. 106 (1986) 99-110.

[344] Ibid Driessen and MacDonald, 61ff.

especially in the LMIb period, there would have been no use for them on the mainland of Greece. During that time not only were there no palatial centers but, according to burial evidence, regional chiefs were competing for prestige with luxury goods, ironically, Minoan in origin. That the majority of images of bull leaping and dancing should come from settlement and storage/administration contexts on Crete in the second palace period makes good sense when we recall that this general provenience category is constituted mainly of villas. These complexes, with their strong administrative connection with the palaces, would naturally bear witness to much reiteration of the power of paramount locations.

Given what we have discussed about the changes between the second and third palace periods, the sudden appearance of glyptic representations of bull leaping and dancing on the mainland comes as no surprise. The Mycenaeans, who had used other Minoan images in their conspicuously wealthy burial display in the previous period and who had used the Minoan Linear A administration system as a basis for their Linear B system, seem to have also appropriated the visual ideology of power consolidation of the Minoan palaces as well. Interestingly, at this time, paintings of bull leaping and dancing are also found at Mycenaean palaces along with glyptic examples. It is again predictable that the majority of these glyptic examples come from burials as it was at burials and at the palaces where power consolidation was aimed. In addition to a new parity of representations of bull leaping and dancing among glyptic examples in third palace period Crete, we find these objects equally divided between palatial and burial contexts. This may indeed reflect the dual consolidation of power in new Mycenaean burials and a continuation of the central role of the palaces as ideological focal points.

* * *

As the proceeding chapters have hopefully made clear, I propose that images of bull leaping and dancing worked on the island of Crete during the second palace period as identifiers of palatial authority through their indexical relationship to larger representations of social drama found at the palaces. These social dramas emerged at the palaces at first to mitigate the social pressure of a change from kinship-based to greater social identity based systems and later the social pressures created by the aftermath of the Santorini explosion. The Mycenaeans, when they controlled Knossos in the third palace period, adopted this means of visual identification as their own, even practicing it in palatial centers back on the Greek mainland.

Bibliography

Akademie der Wissenscheften (1964-2003) *Corpus der minoischen und mykenischen Siegel*. Berlin, Gebr. Mann Verlag.

Alexandri, Alexandra (1994) *Gender Symbolism in Late Bronze Age Aegean Glyptic Art*. Unpublished Ph.D. dissertation, University of Cambridge University.

Alexiou, S. (1967) *Isterominoikou Tafoi Limenos Knosou (Katsama)*. Athens, University of Athens.

Alexiou, S. (1985) Ysterominoikoi tafoi limenos knosou.. *Axaiologikhs etaireias*, 56, 26-40.

Anigbo, O.A.C. (1996) Commensality as Cultural Performance: the Struggle for Leadership in an Igbo Village. *In*: D. Parkin *et al.* (eds) *The Politics of Cultural Performance*. London: Berghahn Books. p. 26-47.

Aravantinos, V. (1984) The Use of Sealings in the Administration of Mycenaean Palaces. *In*: T. Palaima (ed) *Pylos Comes Alive: Industry and Administration in a Mycenaean Palace*. New York: Forham University Press.

Aravantinos, V. (1990) The Mycenaean Inscribed Sealings from Thebes: Problems of Content and Function. *Aegeaum*, 5, 149-155.

Archer, L. *et al.* (eds) (1994) *Women in Ancient Societies*. New York: Routledge.

Arnott, W. Geoffrey. (1993) Bull Leaping as Initiation Ritual. *Liverpool Classical Monthly*, 18, 114-116.

Aruz, Joan. (1995) Syrian Seals and the Evidence of Cultural Interaction. *Sceaux Minoens et Mycéniens, Ive symposium international 10-12 septembre 1992, Clermont-Ferrand, Corpus der Minoischen und Mykenischen Siegel*, Beiheft 5. p.13-28.

Bal, Mieke and Bryson, Norman (1991) Semiotics and Art History *Art Bulletin*, 75, 174-208.

Bennett, J. (1990) Knossos in Context: Comparative Perspectives on the Linear B Administration of LMII-III Crete. *American Journal of Archaeology* 94, 193-212.

Barber, Elizabeth (1991) *Prehistoric Textiles: The Development of Cloth in the Neolithic and Bronze Ages with Special Reference to the Aegean*. Princeton, Princeton University Press.

Betancourt, Philip (1985) *The History of Minoan Pottery*. Princeton, Princeton University Press.

Betts, John (1967) New Light on Minoan Bureaucracy. *Kadmos*, 6, 15-40.

Billigmeier, Jon-Christian and Turner, Judy (1981) The Socio-Economic Roles of Women in Mycenaean Greece: A Brief Survey from evidence of the Linear B Tablets. *In*: Helene Foley (ed) *Reflections of Women in Antiquity*. New York, Gordon and Breach Science Publisher. p. 196-218

Binford, Lewis (1962) Archaeology as Anthropology *American Antiquity*, 28, 217-25.

Binford, Lewis (1965) Archaeological Systemics and the Study of Culture Process. *American Antiquity*, 31, 203-210.

Blegen, Carl W. (1958) Pylos, 1957. *American Journal of Archaeology*, 62, 162-85.

Blegen, Carl W. (1959) Pylos, 1958. *American Journal of Archaeology*, 63, 122-142.

Blegen, Carl W. (1966) *The Palace of Nestor at Pylos in Western Messenia*, vol. I. Princeton, Princeton Univeristy Press.

Blegen, Carl W. (1966) *The Palace of Nestor at Pylos in Western Messenia*, vol II. Princeton: Princeton Univeristy Press.

Bosanquet, C. (1901/2) Praissos. *Annual of the British School at Athens*, 8, 252-67.

Boulotis, Christos (1987) Nochmals zum Prozessionsfresko von Kossos: Palast und Darbringung von Prestige-Objekten. *In:* R. Hägg and N. Marinatos (eds) *Function of the Mionan Palaces*. Stockholm, Swidish Institute in Athens. p. 145-155.

Bourdieu, Pierre (1977) *Outline of a Theory of Practice*. New York, Cambridge University Press.

Branigan, Kieth (1988) Social Security and the State in Middle Bronze Age Crete. *Aegeaeum*, 2, 11-16.

Branigan, Kieth (1988) Some Observations on State Formation in Crete. *In:* E. French and K. Wardle (eds) *Problems in Greek Prehistory*. Bristol, Bristol Classical Press.

Branigan, Kieth (1993) *Dancing With Death: Life and Death in Southern Crete c.300-2000 BC*. London: Haakert.

Broodbank, Cyrpian and Strasser, T. (1991) Migrant Farmers and the Neolithic Colonization of Crete. *Antiquity*, 65, 233-45.

Brown, J. (ed) (1975) *Approaches to the Social Dimensions of Mortuary Practices*. New York: Society for American Archaeology.

Bryson, Norman (1997) Cultural Studies and Dance History. *In:* Jane C. Desmond (ed) *Meaning in Motion: New Cultural Studies of Dance.* Durham, Duke University Press. p. 61-79.

Burkert, Walter (1985) *Greek Religion* (trans. John Raffan). Cambridge, Harvard University Press.

Butler, Judith (1990) *Gender Trouble: Feminist and the Subversion of Identity.* New York, Routledge.

Butler, Judith (1993) *Bodies That Matter: On the Discursive Limits of "Sex".* New York Routledge.

Bynum, Caroline (1995) Why All the Fuss About the Body? A Medievalist's Perspective. *Critical Inquiry,* 22, 1-33.

Cadogan, G. (1991) *Palaces of Minoan Crete.* New York, Routledge.

Carter, Jane and Morris, Sarah (eds) (1995) *The Ages of Homer: A Tribute to Emily Townsend Vermeule.* Austin, University of Texas Press.

Case, Sue-Ellen (ed) (1990) *Performing Feminisms: Feminist Critical Theory and Theatre.* Baltimore, Johns Hopkins University Press.

Cass, Joan (1993) *Dancing Through History.* Englewood Cliffs, Prentice Hall.

Catling H.W. (1972-3) Central Crete. *Archaeological Reports,* 24, 27-30.

Chadwick, J. (1967) *The Mycenaean World,* New York, Cambridge University Press.

Cherry, J. (1978) Generalization and the Archaeology of the State. *In:* D. Green *et al.* (eds) *Social Organization and Settlement,* New York, Cambridge University Press. p. 411-437.

Cherry, J. (1984) The Emergence of the State in the Prehistoric Aegean. *Proceedings of the Cambridge Philological Society,* 210, 18-48.

Cherry, J. (1986) Polities and Palaces: Some Problems in Minoan State Formation. *In:* J. Cherry and C. Renfrew (eds) *Peer-Polity Interaction and Socio-Political Change.* New York, Cambridge University Press.

Cherry, J and C. Renfrew (eds) (1986) *Peer-Polity Interaction and Socio-Political Change.* New York, Cambridge University Press.

Cleland, E. (ed) (1977) *For the Director: Research Essays in Honor of James B. Groffin.* Ann Arbor, University of Michigan Press.

Collon, Domonique (1975) The Seal Impressions from Tell Atchana/Alalakh. *Alter Orient und Altes Testament,* 27, 456-473.

Collon, Domonique (1994) Bull-Leaping in Syria. *Äypten und Levante,* 4, 81-2.

Cook, Arthur Bernard (1965) *Zeus: A Study in Ancient Religion.* Vol. I. New York, Biblo and Tannen.

Crouwel, J. (1989) Pictorial Pottery from Mycenae at the Time of the Shaft Graves. *Aegaeum,* 3, 37-48.

Dabney, M. and Wright, J. (1990) Mortuary Customs, Palatial Society and State Formation in the Aegean Area: J Comparative Study. *In:* R. Hägg and C. Nodquist (eds) *Celebrations of Death and Divinity in the Bronze Age Argolid.* Stockholm, Swedish Institute of Archaeology.

Dabney, M. (1885) The Later Stages of State Formation in Palatial Crete. *Aegeaum,* 12 (1995).

Davis, Jack *et al.* (1997) The Pylos Regional Archaeological Project. Part I: Overview and the Archaeological Survey *Hesperia,* 66, 391-494.

Davies, Morpurgo and Duhoux, Y. (eds) (1985) *Linear B: a 1984 Survey.* Louvian-la-Neuve, Institute de Linguistique de Louvain.

Davis, Ellen (1977) *The Vaphio Cups and Aegean Gold and Silver Ware.* New York, Garland.

Davis, Ellen (1986) Youth and Age in the Thera Frescoes. *American Journal of Archaeology,* 90, 399-406.

Davis, Ellen (1987) The Knossos Miniature Frescoes and the Function of the Central Courts. *In:* Robin Hägg and Nanno Marinatos (eds) *The Function of the Minoan Palaces.* Stockholm, The Swedish Institute of Archaeology. p.157-161.

Davis, Ellen (1990) The Cycladic Style of the Thera Frescoes. *In:* L. Hardy and C. Renfrew (eds) *Thera and the Aegean World III.* Athens: Mellisa, 214-227.

Dawkins, R. (1903-4) Excavations at Palaikastro. *Annual of the British School at Athens,* 10, 192-231.

Demakopoulou, K. (1990) Palatial and Domestic Architecture in Mycenaean Thebes. *In:* Pascal Darcque and René Treuil (eds) *L' habitat égéen préhistorique. Actes de la table ronde internationale, Athènes, 23-25 juin 1987. BCH Suppl. XIX.* Paris, École française d'Athènes. p. 307-317.

Deonna, W. (1953) *Symbolisme de L'acrobatie Antique.* Paris, Boccard, 1953.

Desmond, Jane C. (ed) (1997) *Meaning in Motion: New Cultural Studies of Dance.* Durham, Duke University Press..

Dickinson, O.T.K.P. (1977) *The Origins of Mycenaean Civilization.* Göteborg, Åstrom.

Dickinson, O.T.K.P. (1984) Cretan Contacts with the Mainland During the Period of the Shaft Graves. *In:* Hägg and Marinatos (eds) *Minoan Thallasocracy.* Stockholm, Swedish Institute of Archaeology. p.115-8.

Dimopoulou, Nota (1997) Workshops and Craftsmen in the Harbour-Town of Knossos at Poros-Katsambas. *Aegaeum,* 16, 433-437.

Douglass, Carrie B. (1997) *Bulls, Bullfighting, and Spanish Identities.* Tucson, University of Arizona Press.

Doumas, Christos (1992) *The Wall-Paintings of Thera.* Athens, The Thera Foundation.

Driessen, Jan and MacDonald, Colin (1995) *The Troubled Isle: Minoan Crete Before and After the Santorini Eruption, Aegaeum,* 17.

Eisenstadt, S.N. (1956) *From Generation to Generation: Age Groups and Social Structure.* Glencoe, Free Press.

Elsner, J. and Cardinal, R. (eds) (1994) *The Cultures of Collecting.* New York, Cambridge University Press.

Errington, Frederick (1990) The Rock Creek Rodeo: Excess and Constraint in Men's Lives. *American Ethnologist,* 17, 628-645.

Evans, Arthur, J. (1899-1900) Knossos 1899. *Annual of the British School at Athens,* 7, 12-56.

Evans, Arthur, J. (1900-1901) Knossos 1900, *Annual of the British School at Athens,* 8, 15-65.

Evans, Arthur, J. (1902-1903) Knossos 1901. *Annual of the British School of Athens,* 9, 38-94.

Evans, Arthur, J. (1903-1904) Knossos 1902. *Annual of the British School at Athens,* 10, 42-98.

Evans, Arthur, J. (1914) The Tomb of the Double Axes and Associated Groups at Knossos. *Archaeologia,* 65, 78-90.

Evans, Arthur, J. (1921) On a Minoan Bronze Group of a Galloping Bull and Acrobatic Figure from Crete. *Journal of Hellenic Studies,* 41, 247-259.

Evans, Arthur, J. (1921-36) *The Palace of Minos; a Comparative Account of the Successive Stages of the Early Cretan Civilization as Illustrated by the Discoveries at Knossos.* Vol I-IV. London, MacMillan and Co.

Foley, Helene (ed) (1981) *Reflections of Women in Antiquity.* New York: Gordon and Breach Science Publisher.

Foster, Susan Leigh (ed) (1996) *Representation Corporealities: Dancing, Knowledge, Culture and Power.* New York, Routledge.

Fotiadis, M. (1994) What is Archaeology's 'Mitigated Objectivism' Mitigated by? Comments on Wylie. *American Antiquity,* 59, 545-555.

French, E.B. and Wardle, K. (eds) (1988) *Problems in Greek Prehistory.* Bristol, Bristol Classical Press.

Frödin, O. and Person, A. (1938) *Asine: Results of the Swedish Excavations 1922-1930.* Stockhold: GLAF.

Galaty, M. and Parkinson, W. (eds) (1999) *Rethinking Mycenaean Palaces: New Interpretations of an Old Idea.* Los Angeles, The Cotsen Institute of Archaeology, University of California.

van Gennep, E. (1960) *The Rites of Passage* (trans. Monika B. Vizedom and Gabrielle Caffee). Chicago, University of Chicago Press.

Gesell, G. (1987) The Minoan Palace and Public Cult. *In:* R Hägg and N. Marinatos (eds) *The Function of the Minoan Palaces.* Stockholm, Swedish Institute of Archaeology,123-128.

Gill, M. (1965) The Knossos Sealings: Provenance and Identification. *Annual of the British School at Athens,* 60, 58-98.

Grahm, J. (1987) *The Palaces of Crete.* Princeton, Princeton University Press.

Green, D. *et al.* (eds) (1978) *Social Organization and Settlement.* New York, Cambridge University Press.

Groenewegen-Frankfort, H.A. (1978) *Arrest and Movement: An Essay on Space and Time in the Representational rt of the Ancient Near East.* New York, Hackert Art Books.

Hägg. R and Marinatos, N. (eds) (1987) *The Function of the Minoan Palaces.* Stockholm, Swedish Institute in Athens.

Hägg. R and Nodquist, C. (eds) (1990) *Celebrations of Death and Divinity in the Bronze Age Argolid.* Stockholm, Swedish Institute of Archaeology.

Halbherr, Federico et al. (1977) Hagia Triada nel Perido Tardo Palaziale. *Annualrio della Sculola Archaeologica di Atene e delle Missioni Italiane in Oriente*, 55, 147-178.

Hall, E.H. (1906-1907) The Decorative Art of Crete in the Bronze Age. *University of Pennsylvania Transactions of the Department of Archaeology, Free Museum of Science and Art*, 2, 45-68..

Hallager, E. (1996) *The Minoan Roundel and Other Sealed Documents in the Neopalatial Linear A Administration, Aegaeum* 14.

Hallager, Birgitta and Erik (1995) The Knossian Bull: Political Propaganda in Neo-Palatial Crete? *Aegaeum*, 12, 547-556.

Halstead, Paul (1981) From Determinism to Uncertainty: Social Storage and the Rise of the Minoan Palace. *In:* A. Sheridan and G. Bailey (eds) *Economic Archaeology*. Oxford, Oxford University Press. p. 112-125.

Hamilakis, Yannis (1996) Wine, Oil and the Dialectics of Power in Bronze Age Crete: A Review of the Evidence, *Oxford Journal of Art*, 15, 1-32.

Hanna, Judith Lynne (1988) *Dance, Sex and Gender: Signs of Identity, Dominance, Defiance, and Desire*. Chicago, University of Chicago Press.

Hardy, L. and C. Renfrew (eds) (1990) *Thera and the Aegean World III*. Athens, Mellisa.

Hartshorne, C. and Weiss, P. (eds) (1931-1935) *Collected Papers of Charles Sanders Peirce*, vols. 1-6. Cambridge, Harvard University Press.

Hauser, Arnold (1985) *The Social History of Art*. New York, Vintage.

Hawes, H. and Williams, B. *(1908) Gournia, Vasiliki, and other Prehistoric Sites on the Isthmus of Hierapetra, Crete*. Philadelphia, University Museum.

Hazzidakis, Joseph (1921) *Tylossos a l'Époque Minoenne*. Paris, Libraire Paul Geuthner, 1921.

Hill, S. (1989) On the Origins of the Shaft Graves. *Aegeaum*, 3, 91-99.

Hitchcock, L. (2000) Engendering Ambiguity in Minoan Crete: It's a Drag to be a King. *In:* M. Donald and Hurcombe, L. (eds) *Representations of Gender from Prehistory to the Present*. New York, Palgrav Macmillan. p. 69-86.

Hood, S. (1997) "The Magico-Religious Background of the Minoan Villa" in R. Hägg (ed) *The Function of the "Minoan Villa"* .Stockholm, Swedish Institute of Archaeology. p.105-115.

Hooker, J.T. (1980) *Linear B, An Introduction*. Bristol, Bristol Classics Press.

Immerwahr, Sara (1990) *Aegean Painting in the Bronze Age*. College Park: Pennsylvania State University Press.

Immerwahr, Sara (1981) The People of the Frescoes. *In:* O. Krzyszkowska and L. Nixon (eds) *Minoan Society*. Bristol, Bristol University Press. p. 26-47.

Impey, Oliver (1997) *The Art of the Japanese Folding Screne: The Collections of the Victoria and Albert Museum and the Ashmolean Museum*. Oxford, Ashmolean Museum.

Indelicato, Silvia Damiani (1988) Were Cretan Girls Playing at Bull-Leaping? *Cretan Studies*, 1, 39-47.

Jones, Bernice (1995) *Women's Costume in the Aegean Bronze Age*. Unpublished Ph.D. dissertation, New York University.

Jones, Mark (1979) *The Art of the Medal*. London, British Museum Press.

Jones, Mark (1982) *A Catalogue of the French Medals in the British Museum*. London, British Museum Press.

Karo, G. (1930) *Die Schachtgräber von Mykenai*. Munich, Von Zabern.

Keesing, R. (1975) *Kin Groups and Social Structure*. New York, Holt.

Kenna, V.E.G. (1960) *Cretan Seals. With a Catalogue of the Minoan Gems in the Ashmolean Museum*. Oxford, The Ashmolean Museum.

Kilian-Dirlmeier, I (1986) Beobachtungen zu den Schachtgräbern von Mykenai und zu den Schmuchbeigaben mykenischer Männergräber. Untersuchungen zur Sozialstruktur in späthelladischer Zeit. *Jahrbuch des Römisch-germanischen Zentralmuseums Mainz*, 33, 159-168.

Killian, K. (1985) The Linear B Tablets and Mycenaean Economy. *In:* Morpurgo Davies and Y.Duhoux (eds) *Linear B: a 1984 Survey*. Louvian-la-Neuve, Institute de Linguistique de Louvain. P. 45-52.

Killian, K. (1988) The Emergence of *Wana*x Ideology in the Myceaean Palaces. *Oxford Journal of Archaeology*, 7, 293-311.

Koehl, Robert (1986) The Chieftain Cup and a Minoan Rite of Passage. *Journal of Hellenic Studies* 106, 99-110.

Kokkinidou, Dimitra and Niklolaïdou, Marianna (1993) *Archaeologia kai H Koinonike Tetoteta tou Felou: Prosegises sthn aigaike Prestoria.* Thessaloniki, Banias.

Kpaka, C. (1984) Une Bague Minoenne de Malia. *Bulletin de Correspondance Hellénique,* 106, 660-679.

Krzyszkowska, O. and Nixon, L. (eds) (1981) *Minoan Society.* Bristol, Bristol University Press.

Laffineur, Robert (1992) Iconography as Evidence of Social and Political Status in Mycenaean Greece. *Aegaeum,* 8, 105-111.

Laffineur, Robert (1990) The Iconography of Mycenaean Seals and their Status of Their Owners. *Aegaeum,* 6, 117-160.

Laffineur, Robert (ed) (1985) *Iconographie Minoenne.* Athens: Ecole francaise d'Athens.

Laffineur, Robert (1987) *Thanatos: Les Coutumes Funeraires en Egee a l'Age du Bronze, Aegeaum,* 1.

Lamb, W. (1919-1921) Frescoes from the Ramp House. *Annual of the British School at Athens,* 24, 192-4.

Lang, Mable (1966) *The Palace of Nestor at Pylos in Western Messenia, Vol. II, The Frescoes.* Princeton, Princeton University Press.

Lawler, Lillian (1951) The Dance in Ancient Crete. *In:* G. Mylonas (ed) *Studies Presented to David Moore Robinson.* St. Louis, Washington University Press. p. 14-28.

Lawler, Lillian (1964) *The Dance in Ancient Greece.* Middletown, Wesleyan University Press.

Leiris, Michel (1993) The Bullfight as Mirror. *October,* 63, 21-40.

Lendle, Otto (1965) Das kretische Stiersprunspiel. *Marburger Winckelmann-Programm,* 51, 30-37.

Leonardo, Micaela de (ed) (1991) *Gender at the Crossroads of Knowledge: Feminist Anthropology in the Postmodern Era.* Berkeley, University of California Press.

Levi, Doro (1925-1926) Le cretule de Haghia Triada. *Annuario della Sculoa archeologica di Atene e delle Missioni italiane in Oriente,* VIII-IX, 157-201.

Levi, Doro (1976) *Festòs e la Civiltà Minoica* I. Rome, Incunabula Graeca 60, Edizioni dell'Ateneo.

Levine, L and Young, T. Cyler (eds) (1977) *Mountains and Lowlands.* Malibu, University of Hawaii Press.

Lolling, H. and Wolters, P. (1886) Das Kuppelbrab bei Dimini. *Mitteilungen des Deutschen Archäologischen Institutes,* 11, 435-443.

Long, C. R. (1977) *The Ayia Triadha Sarcophagus: A Study of Late Minoan and Mycenaean Funerary Practices and Beliefs. Studies in Mediterranean Archaeology* 41.

Lonsdale, Steven H. (1993) *Dance and Ritual Play in Greek Religion.* Baltimore, Johns Hopkins University Press.

Lonsdale, Steven H. (1995) A Dancing Floor for Ariadne (*Iliad* 18.590-592): Aspects of Ritual Movement in Homer and Minoan Religion. *In:* J. Carter and S. Morris (eds) *The Ages of Homer: A Tribute to Emily Townsend Vermeule.* Austin, University of Texas Press. p.156-64.

Loughlin, Eleanor (2004) Grasping the Bull by the Horns: Minoan Bull Sports. *In:* S. Bell and G. Davies (eds) *Games and Festivals in Classical Antiquity.* BAR International Series 1220. Oxford, BAR Publishing. p. 1-8.

Mackenzie, Duncan (1903) The Pottery of Knossos. *Journal of Hellenic Studies,* 23, 190-212.

Manning, Stuart (1995) *The Absolute Chronology of the Aegean Bronze Age: Archaeology, Radiocarbon and History. Monographs in Mediterranean Archaeology* 1.

Marcus, Michelle (1996) Sex and the Politics of Female Adornment in Pre-Achaemenid Iran (1000-800 BCE). *In:* N. Kampen (ed) *Sexuality in Ancient Art.* New York, Cambridge University Press. p. 128-144.

Marinatos, Nanno (1994) The 'Export' Significance of Minoan Bull Hunting and Bull Leaping Scenes. *Egypten und Levante,* 4, 263-271.

Marinatos, Nanno (1987) Public Festivals in the West Courts of the Palaces. *In:* R. Hägg and N. Marinatos (eds) *Function of the Minoan Palaces.* Athens: Skrifter utgivna av Svenska Institutet Athen. p. 138-41.

Marinatos, Nanno (1993) *Minoan Religion: Ritual, Image and Symbol* (Columbia, University Of North Carolina Press.

Mayer, M. (1892) Mykenische Beitrage I. *Jahrbuch des deutschen archäologischen Instituts,* 7, 72-96.

McFee, Graham (1992) *Understanding Dance.* New York, Routledge.

Mee, C. and Cavanagh, W. (1985) Mycenaean Tombs as Evidence for Social and Political Organization. *Oxford Journal of Archaeology,* 3, 45-61.

Mellaart, James (1967) *Çatal Hüyük*. New York, MacGraw-Hill.

Meyers, J. *et al.* (eds) (1992) *The Aerial Atlas of Ancient Crete*. Berkeley, University of California Press.

Moody, Jennifer (1987) The Minoan Palace as a Prestige Artefact. *In:* R Hägg and N. Marinatos (eds) *The Function of the Minoan Palaces*. Stockholm, Swedish Institute of Archaeology. p. 235-241.

Muscarella, Oscar White (1977) Unexcavated Objects and Ancient Near Eastern Art. *In:* L. Levine and T. Cyler Young, Jr. (eds) *Mountains and Lowlands*. Malibu, University of Hawaii Press. p.153-207.

Mylonas, G. (ed) (1951) *Studies Presented to David Moore Robinson*. St. Louis, Washington University Press.

Mylonas, G. (1966) *Mycenae and the Mycenaeans Age*. Princeton, Princeton University Press.

Niemeier, Wolf-Dietrich (1988) The 'Priest King' Fresco from Knossos. A New Reconstruction, *In:* E.B. French and K. Wardle (eds) *Problems in Greek Prehistory*. Bristol, Bristol Classical Press. p. 34-51.

Niemeier, Wolf-Dietrich (1981) Probleme der Datierung von Siegeln nach Kontexten. *Corpus der minoischen und mykenischen Siegel*. Beiheft 1.

Niemeier, Wolf-Dietrich (1987) On the Function of the 'Throne Room' in the Palace of Knossos. *In:* R. Hägg and N. Marinatos (eds) *Function of the Minoan Palaces*. Stockholm, Swedish Institute of Archaeology. p.163-8.

Nilsson, Martin, P. (1968) *The Minoan-Mycenaean Religion and its Survival in Greek Religion*. Lund: Gleerup.

Nixon, Lucia (1994) Gender Bias in Archaeology. *In:* L. Archer *et al.* (eds) *Women in Ancient Societies*. New York, Routledge. P. 1-23.

Okrant, Mark J. and Starrs, Paul F. (1995) Rodeo. *In:* Karl B. Raitz (ed) *The Theater of Sports*. Baltimore, Johns Hopkins University Press. p. 69-88.

Ortner, Sherry and Whitehead, Harriet (eds) (1981) *Sexual Meanings: The Cultural Construction of Gender*. New York: Cambridge University Press.

Palaima, T. (ed) (1984) *Pylos Comes Alive: Industry and Administration in a Mycenaean Palace*. New York, Forham University Press.

Palaima, T. (1987) Mycenaean Seals and Sealings in Their Economic and Administrative Contexts. *In:* Peter Ilievski and Ljiljana Crepajac (eds) *Tractata Mycenaea. Proceedings of the Eighth International Colloquium on Mycenaean Studies, Held in Ohrid (15-20 September 1985)*. Skopje, Macedonian Academy of Sciences and Arts. p. 249-266.

Palaima, T. (1990) Origin, Development, Transition and Transformation: The Purposes and Techniques of Administration in Minoan and Mycenaean Society. *Aegaeum*, 5, 83-104.

Parkin, D. *et al.* (eds) (1996) *The Politics of Cultural Performance*. London, Berghahn Books.

Percy, James (1912) *Bulls, Ancient and Modern*. Dublin: Mecredy, Percy & Co.

Peatfield, Alan (1987) Palace and Peak: The Political and Religious Relationship Between Palaces and Peak Sanctuaries. *In:* R. Hägg and N. Marinatos (eds) *The Function of the Minoan Palaces*. Stockholm, Swedish Institute of Archaeology. p. 89-93.

Pelon, O. (1985) L'acrobate de Malia et L'art de l'epoque Protopalatial en Crete. *In:* R. Laffineur (ed) *Iconographie Minoenne*. Athens, Ecole francaise d'Athens.

Perodotto, J and Sullivan, J. (eds) (1984) *Women in the Ancient Word: The Arethusa Papers*. Albany, State University of New York Press.

Persson. A.W. (1942) *New Tombs at Dendra Near Midea*. London, Oxford University Press.

Pini, Ingo (1990) The Hieroglyphic Deposit and the Temple Repositories at Knossos. *Aegaeum*, 5, 52-69.

Pini, Ingo (1968) *Beiträge zur minoischen Gräberkunde*. Wiesbaden, Steiner.

Platon, N. (1971) *Zakros: the Discovery of a Lost Palace of Ancient Crete*. New York: Scribners.

Pomeroy, Sarah B. (1984) Selected Bibliography on Women in Classical Antiquity: The Bronze Age. *In:* J. Perodotto and J. Sullivan (eds) *Women in the Ancient Word: The Arethusa Papers*. Albany, State University of New York Press. p. 221-224.

Popham, Mervyn R. *et al.* (1995) *The Latest Sealings from the Palace and Houses at Knossos*. British School at Athens Studies 1. Oxford, Alden Press.

Poursat, Jean-Claude (1977) *Catalogue des Ivories Mycéniens du Musée National d'Athénes*. Athénes, École Française d'Athénes.

Poursat, Jean-Claude (1978) Fouilles de Mallia. *Bulletin Correspondence Hellenique*, 102, 831-834.

Poursat, Jean-Claude (1983) Ateliers et sanctuaries à Mallia: nouvelles données sur l'organisation sociale à l'époque des premiers palais. *In:* O. Krzyszkowska and L. Nixon (eds) *Minoan Society*. Bristol, Bristol Classics Press. p. 277-81.

Preston, Suzanne Elaine (1981) *Wall Painting in the Aegean Bronze Age: The Procession Frescoes.* Unpublished Ph.D. dissertation, University of Minnesota.

Rehak, Paul (1996) Aegean Breechcloths, Kilts, and the Keftiu Paintings. *American Journal of Archaeology*, 100, 35-51.

Reichel, A. (1909) Die Stierspiele in der kretisch-mykenischen Cultur. *Mitteilungen des Kaiserlich Deutschen Archäologischen Instituts*, 34, 85-99.

Reusch, H. (1948-1949) Der Franenfries von Theben. *Archaeologische Anzeiger*, 63-64 240-253.

Rice, Michael (1998) *The Power of the Bull*. New York, Routledge.

Robins, Gay (1996) Dress, Undress, and the Representation of Fertility and Potency in New Kingdom Egyptian Art. *In:* N. Kampen (ed) *Sexuality in Ancient Art*. New York Cambridge University Press. p.127-139.

Rodenwaldt, G. (1911) Fragmente mykenischer Wangemälde. *Mitteilungen des deutschen Archäologischen Instituts*, 36, 230-242.

Royce, Anya Peterson (1977) *The Anthropology of Dance*. Bloomington, Indiana University Press.

Sakellerakis, I. (1976) Mycenaean Stone Vases. *Studi Micenei ed Egeo-Anatolici*, 17, 780-195.

Schapiro, Meyer (1969) On Some Problems in the Semiotics of Visual Art: Field and Vehicle in Image-Signs. *Semiotica*, 1, 3-35.

Schechner, Richard (1988) *Performance Theory*. New York, Routledge.

Shelmerdine, C. (1997) The Palatial Bronze Age of the Southern and Central Greek Mainland. *American Journal of Archaeology*, 101, 558-580.

Sheridan, A and G. Bailey (eds) (1981) *Economic Archaeology*. Oxford, Oxford University Press.

Schliemann, H. (1885) *Tiryns: The Prehistoric Palace of the Kings of Tiryns.* New York: Scribners Sons.

Scott, Joan (1986) Gender: A Useful Category of Historical Analysis. *American Historical Review*, 91, 1053-1075.

Shanks, Michael (1999) *Art and the Early Greek State: An Interpretive Archaeology*. New York: Cambridge University Press.

Shanks, Michael and Christopher Tilley (1987) *Re-Constructing Archaeology*. New York, Cambridge University Press.

Shaw, Maria (1996) Bull-Leaping Fresco from Below the Ramp House at Mycenae: A Study in Iconography and Artistic Transmission. *Annual of the British School at Athens*, 91,167-90.

Sherwood, Lauralee (1997) *Human Physiology: From Cells to Systems*. Belmont, Wadsworth Publishing Company.

Smith, Tyler Jo (2004) Festival? What Festival? Reading Dance Imagry as Evidence. *In:* S. Bell and G. Davies (eds) *Games and Festivals in Classical Antiquity*. BAR International Series 1220. Oxford, BAR Publishing. p. 9-23.

Soles, J. (1995) The Functions of a Cosmological Center: Knossos in Palatial Crete. *Aegaeum*, 12, 405-414.

Soles, J. (1992) *The Prepalatial Cemeteries at Mochlos and Gournia and the House Tombs of Bronze Age Crete*. Princeton: American School of Classical Studies.

Soles, J. (1997) A Community of Craft Specialists at Mochols. *Aegaeum*, 16, 425-450.

Sparshott, Francis (1988) *Off the Ground: First Steps to a Philosophical Consideration of the Dance*. Princeton, Princeton University Press.

Spencer, Paul (ed) (1985) *Society and the Dance: The Social Anthropology of Process and Performance*. New York, Cambridge University Press.

Spyropoulos, Theodore (1970) Excavation at the Mycenaean Nekropolis of Tanagra. *Athens Annals of Archaeology*, 2, 184-197.

Stalheim-Smith, Ann and Fitch, Greg (1993) *Understanding Human Anatomy and Physiology*. Mineapolis/St. Paul: West Publishing.

Symeonoglou, Sarantis (1973) *Kadmeia I. Mycenaean Finds from Thebes, Greece, Excavation at 14 Oedipus St.. Studies in Mediterranean Archaeology 35.*

Talalay, L. (1994) A Feminist Boomerang: The Great Goddess of Greek Prehistory. *Gender and History*, 6, 165-83.

Taylour, W. (1969) Mycenae, 1968. *Antiquity*, 63, 91-97.

Theocharis, D. (1964) Arheotites ke mnimia Thessalias. *Archaiologikon Deltion*, 19, 241-249 & 255-267.

Thompson, James G. (1985) The Bull-Jumping Exhibition at Mallia. *Archaeology News*, 14, 1-8.

Tsountas, N. (1888) Mycenae. *Ephemeris Archaiologiki*, 7, 119-126.

Tsountas, N. (1900) Trois Chatons de Bagues Mycéniennes. *Revue Archéologique* 37, 12-15.

Turner, Victor (1974) *Dramas, Fields, and Metaphores: Symbolic Action in Human Society*. Ithaca, Cornell University Press.

Turner, Victor (1982) *From Ritual to Theatre: the Human Seriousness of Play*. New York, Performing Arts Journal Publication.

Turner, Victor (1988) *The Anthropology of Performance*. New York, Performing Arts Journal Publication.

Tzedakis, Y. (1941) Archaiotites kai mnimeia dytikis Dritis. *Archaiologikon Deltion*, 32, pt. 2, 329-34.

Tzedakis, Y. and E. Hallager (1976) The Greek-Swedish Excavations at Kastelli Chania 1976 and 1977. *Athens Annals of Archaeology*, 11, 24-28.

Ventris, Michael and John Chadwick (1956) *Documents in Mycenaean Greek*. New York, Cambridge University Press.

Vermule, Emily Townsend (1975) *The Art of the Shaft Graves of Mycenae*. Lectures in Memory of Louise Taft Semple; Series 3. Cincinnati, University of Cincinnati.

Voutsaki, S. (1995) Social and Political Processes in the Mycenaean Argolid: The evidence from the Mortuary Practices. *Aegaeum*, 12, 62-78.

Wace, A. (1932) Chamber Tombs at Mycenae. *Archaeologia*, 82, 10-15.

Wace, A. (1951) Mycenae 1950. *Journal of Hellenic Studies*, 61, 254-72.

Walber, G. (1978) *The Kamares Style: Overall Effects*. Uppsala, University of Uppsal.

Walber, G. (1976) *Kamares: A Study of the Character of Palatial Middle Minoan Pottery*. Uppsala, Univeristy of Uppsala.

Wallen, L. Ager and Acocella, J. (eds) (1987) *A Spectrum of World Dance: Tradition, Transition and Innovation*. Boston, Cord Press.

Ward, Anne (1968) The Cretan Bull Sports. *Antiquity*, 42, 117-122.

Warren, Peter (1984) Circular Platforms at Minoan Knossos. *Annual of the British School at Athens,* 79, 307-323.

Warren, Peter (1988) *Minoan Religion as Ritual Action*. London, Cambridge University Press.

Weingarten, Judith (1981) *The Zakros Master and His Place in Prehistory*. Studies in Mediterranean Archaeology, Pocket Book 26. Göteborg: Paul Åströms Förlag,

Weingarten, Judith (1990) Three Upheavals in Minoan Sealing Administration: Evidence for Radical Change. *Aegaeum*, 5, 105-114.

Weingarten, Judith (1986) The sealing structures of Minoan Crete: MMII Phaistos to the Destruction of the Palace of Knossos Part I. *Oxford Journal of Art*, 5, 379-98.

Weingarten, Judith (1988) The sealing structures of Minoan Crete: MMII Phaistos to the Destruction of the Palace of Knossos Part II. *Oxford Journal of Art*, 7, 1-18.

Willetts, D. (1962) *Cretan Cults and Festivals*. London, Routledge.

Winter, Irene (1987) Legitimation of Authority Through Image and Legend: Seals Belonging to Officials in the Administrative Bureaucracy of the Ur III State. *In:* M. Gibson and R. Biggs (eds) *The Organization of Power: Aspects of Bureaucracy in the Ancient Near East. Studies in Ancient Oriental Civilization*, 46. p. 57-69.

Winter, Irene (1986) The King and the Cup: Iconography of the Royal Presentation Scene on Ur III Seals. *In:* M. Kelley-Buccellati (ed) *Insight Through Images: Studies in Honor of Edith Porada*. Bibliotheca Mesopotamica, 21, p. 141-161.

Wobst, Martin (1977) Stylistic Behavior and Information Exchange. *In:* E. Cleland (ed) *For the Director: Research Essays in Honor of James B. Groffin*. Ann Arbor, University of Michigan Press, 211-227.

Wright, James (1987) Death and Power at Mycenae: Changing Symbols in Mortuary Practice. *Aegaeum,* 1, 171-184.

Wylie, Alison (1989) Matters of Fact and Matters of Interest. *In:* S.J. Shennan (ed) *Archaeological Approaches to Cultural Identity*. New York, Rutledge.

Wylie, Alison (1992) The Interplay of Evidential Constraints and Political Interests: Recent Archaeological Research on Gender. *American Antiquity* 57, 15-35.

Xanthoudides, S. (1921) *The Vaulted Tombs of the Mesara*. Liverpool, Liverpool University Press.

Younger, John (1976) Bronze Age Representations of Aegean Bull-Leaping. *American Journal of Archaeology*, 80, 120-142.

Younger, John (1977) Non-Sphragistic Uses of Minoan-Mycenaean Sealstones and Rings. *Kadmos*, 16, 141-159.

Younger, John (1982) Aegean Seals of the Late Bronze Age: Masters and Workshops I-VII" *Kadmos*, 21, 13-29.

Younger, John (1983) A New Look at Aegean Bull-Leaping. *Muse*, 17, 72-80.

Younger, John (1992) *The Iconography of Late Bronze Age Glyptic*. Bristol, Bristol University Press.

Younger, John (1995) Bronze Age Representations of Aegean Bull-Games, III. *Aegaeum*, 12, 507-545.

Younger, John (1979) Lapidary's Workshop at Knossos. *Annual of the British School at Athens* 74, 259-270.

Appendix One

List of Performed Acts

CMS#	Provenence	Locus	Date	Form	Material	Shape	Performance
II8.202	Knossos	Queen's Megaron	LMII-IIIa	impression	clay	round	acrobatic
I.131	Mycenae	Lower Town (Panajia), Chamber Tomb #91	LHII-III	seal	chalcedony	lentoid	acrobatic
II3.067	Knossos	Sellopoulo field, Grave I	LMIIIa2-IIIb	seal	agate	lentoid	acrobatic
II3.010	Knossos	Palace	LMII	seal	carnelion	lentoid	acrobatic
I.216	Prosymna	Chamber Tomb, grave 41	LHIII	seal	agate	lentoid	acrobatic
II3.066	Knossos	Sellopoulo, grave I	LMIIIa2-LMIIIb	seal	sardonyx	lentoid	animal combat
II3.009	Knossos	Over the Wall of the 9th Magazine	LMII-IIIa	seal	sardonyx	lentoid	animal combat
V1.264	Armeni	Chamber Tomb 39	LMIIIa2-b1	seal	serpentine	lentoid	animal combat
I.331	Pylos	Palace, Room 99	LHIIIb2-c1	impression	clay	ring?	animal combat
I.112	Mycenae	Lower Town, Around Kalkani Nekropolis, ChamberTomb #79	LHII-III	seal	floruit	amygdaloid	animal combat
II7.033	Zakros	House A, room 8	LMIb	impression	clay	square cushin	animal combat
II7.032	Zakros	House A, room 8	LMIb	impression	clay	round?	animal combat
V2.656	Jalysos, Makri Vounara	Grave 21	LHIIIc	seal	agate	lentoid	animal combat
I.199	Asine	Chamber Tomb 1	LHIIb-IIIa, IIIc	seal	agate	cushin	animal combat
II3.105	Phaistos, Kalyvia	Tombe dei Nobili, grave 7	LMIIIa1-2	seal	carnelion	cushin	animal combat
I.227	Vaphio	Beehive Tomb	LHII	seal	chalcedony	lentoid	animal combat
V2.595	Mycenae	Citidel House/House of the Idols	LHIIIb2	impression	clay	unclear	animal combat
I.274	Pylos, Rutsi, Mirsinochori	Tholos Tomb, Shaft 2	LHI-IIa	seal	gold	amygdaloid+	animal combat
II8.235	Knossos		?	impression	clay	unclear	animal combat
I.290	Pylos	Beehive Tomb Delta, Grave IV	MH/LHI-III	seal	amythist	amygdaliod	animal combat
I.224	Vaphio	Beehive Tomb	LHII	seal	jasper	lentoid+	animal combat
I.165	Mycenae	Lower Town, House of the Shield	LHIIIb	impression	clay	unclear	animal combat
I.228	Vaphio	Beehive Tomb	LHII	seal	hematite	lentoid	animal combat
I.009	Mycenae	Grave Circle A, Grave III	LHI	seal	gold	cushin	animal combat
I.294	Pylos	Beehive Tomb, Vagena, V, grave circle, trench M	MHIII/LHI-LHIIIa	seal	jasper	lentoid	animal combat
V.sup.1A.174	Chania, Kastelli	Katre st. 10	MMIII-LMI	impression	clay	round?	animal husbandry
V.sup.1B.341	Palaikastro	Building 5, room 9	LMI	impression	clay	oval, ring?	animal husbandry
V.sup.1A.137	Chania, Kastelli, Agia Akaterini square	House I, room D	LMIb	impression	clay	oval?	animal husbandry
I.340	Pylos	Palace, Room 104	LHIIIb2-c1	impression	clay	illiptical	battle
I.sup.173	Pylos	Palace, Archive Room 8	TAQ LHIIIb/c	impression	clay	unclear	battle
I.307	Pylos	Palace, Archive Room 8	LHIIIb2-c1	impression	clay	unclear	battle
I.306	Pylos	Palace, Archive Room 8	LHIIIb2-c1	impression	clay	illiptical	battle
II6.017	Agia Triada	NW upper floor, "stanza dei sigilli"	LMIb	impression	clay	oval, ring?	battle
II6.015	Agia Triada	NW upper floor, "stanza	LMIb	impression	clay	round?	battle

List of Performed Acts

CMS#	Provenence	Locus	Date	Form	Material	Shape	Performance
		dei sigilli"				unclear	
I.324	Pylos	Palace, Room 98	LHIIIb2-c1	impression	clay	round	battle
II7.020	Zakros	House A, room 8	LMIb	impression	clay	oval	battle
II6.021	Agia Triada	NW upper floor, "stanza dei sigilli"	LMIb	impression	clay	round	battle
I.011	Mycenae	Grave Circle A, Grave III	LHI	seal	gold	cushin	battle
I.012	Mycenae	Grave Circle A, Grave III	LHI	seal	carnelian	cushin	battle
I.016	Mycenae	Grave Circle A, Grave IV	LHI	ring	gold	ring	battle
II7.019	Zakros	House A, room 8	LMIb	impression	clay	unclear	battle
V2.643	Koukounara, Gouvalari	Tholos I	LHIII	seal	amythist	cushin	battle
I.263	Pylos, Tagana, Viglitia	Tholos Tomb, Grave 1	LHIII	seal	chalcedony	lentoid	battle
V.sup.1A.138	Chania, Kastelli, Agia Akaterini square	House I, room D	LMIb	impression	clay	oval?	boat
V.sup.1A.055	Makrijalos	Villa	LMIb	seal	serpentine	amygdaloid	boat
II8.282	Knossos	E. Temple Repository	TAQ LMI	impression	clay	unclear	boxer
II8.223	Knossos	Landing on Grand Staircase	LMII-IIIa	impression	clay	oval?	bull leaping
II8.228	Knossos	East Wing	LMII-IIIa	impression	clay	unclear	bull leaping
V.sup.1B.135	Anthia, Field of Ellinika	Floor of Shaft Grave in Chamber Tomb 4	LHIIIa1	ring	gold	ring	bull leaping
II4.157	Gournes	Grave I, Dromos	LMIIIb	seal	lapis	lentoid	bull leaping
V2.638	Koukounara, Akona	Tholos Grave I	LHIII	seal	chalcedony	lentoid	bull leaping
V.sup.1A.171	Chania, Kastelli	Katre st. 10	MMIII-LMI	impression	clay	oval?	bull leaping
I.408	Dimini	Beehive Tomb 1	LHIIIa	seal	agate?	lentoid	bull leaping
II8.231	Knossos		?	impression	clay	round?	bull leaping
V2.674	Thebes	Corner of Epaminondas & Antigone sts.	LHIIIb	seal	agate	half cylinder	bull leaping
II8.226	Knossos		?	impression	clay	unclear, oval?	bull leaping
II7.036	Zakros	House A, room 8	LMIb	impression	clay	oval	bull leaping
II8.222	Knossos	Room of the Niche	LMII-IIIa	impression	clay	oval	bull leaping
II8.221	Knossos	E. Temple Repository	TAQ LMI	impression	clay	unclear	bull leaping
I.342	Pylos	Palace, Room 105	LHIIIb2-c1	impression	clay	unclear	bull leaping
II3.271	Praissos	1st Acropolis, grave D	LMIIIb	seal	agate	lentoid	bull leaping
II7.038	Zakros	House A, room 8	LMIb	impression	clay	oval?	bull leaping
II7.037	Zakros	House A, room 8	LMIb	impression	clay	oval?	bull leaping
I.305	Pylos	Palace, Archive Room 8	LHIIIb2-c1	impression	clay	round?	bull leaping
II7.034	Zakros	House A, room 8	LMIb	impression	clay	unclear	bull leaping
II6.039	Agia Triada	NW upper floor, "stanza dei sigilli"	LMIb	impression	clay	oval?	bull leaping
I.200	Asine	Chamber Tomb 1	LHIIb-IIIa, IIIc	ring	gold on bronze	ring	bull leaping
II8.225	Knossos	unknown	LMII	impression	clay	unclear	bull leaping
I.152	Mycenae	Lower Town, Chamber Tomb #518, found on floor	LHII-III	seal	carnelion	amygdaloid	bull leaping
II6.041	Agia Triada	NW upper floor, "stanza dei sigilli"	LMIb	impression	clay	unclear	bull leaping
II6.042	Agia Triada	NW upper floor, "stanza dei sigilli"	LMIb	impression	clay	unclear	bull leaping
II6.043	Agia Triada	NW upper floor, "stanza	LMIb	impression	clay	round?	bull leaping

List of Performed Acts

CMS#	Provenence	Locus	Date	Form	Material	Shape	Performance
		dei sigilli"					
II6.044	Agia Triada	NW upper floor, "stanza dei sigilli"	LMIb	impression	clay	oval	bull leaping
I.137	Mycenae	Lower Town, Chamber Tomb #504	LHIII	seal	carnelion	amygdaloid	bull leaping
I.082	Mycenae	Lower Town (Panajia), Chamber Tomb #47, Panajia	LHII-III	seal	onyx	lentoid	bull leaping
I.079	Mycenae	Lower Town (Kato Phourou), Chamber Tomb #44	LHII-III	seal	carnelion	amygdaloid	bull leaping
II7.039	Zakros	House A, room 8	LMIb	impression	clay	oval	bull leaping
V2.597	Mycenae	House of the Idols	LHIIIb2	seal	agate	lentoid	bull leaping
II8.224	Knossos		?	impression	clay	unclear	bull leaping
II8.229	Knossos	Magazine4, Gallery 5	LMII-IIIa	impression	clay	round?	bull wrestling
I.095	Mycenae	Lower Town, Unknown Nekropolis, Chamber Tomb #58	LHII-III	seal	amazonite	lentoid	bull wrestling
V.sup.1B.137	Anthia, Field of Ellinika	Tholos South of Chamber Tomb 4	LHIIa-b	ring	gold	ring	chariot
II6.019	Agia Triada	NW upper floor, "stanza dei sigilli"	LMIb	impression	clay	oval, ring?	chariot
I.229	Vaphio	Beehive Tomb, Floor	LHII	seal	carnelion	seal	chariot
I.230	Vaphio	Beehive Tomb	LHII	seal	carnelion	amygdaloid	chariot
I.015	Mycenae	Grave Circle A, Grave IV	LHI	ring	gold	ring	chariot hunt
II6.004	Agia Triada	NW upper floor, "stanza dei sigilli"	LMIb	impression	clay	unclear, oval?	cultic
II6.005	Agia Triada	NW upper floor, "stanza dei sigilli"	LMIb	impression	clay	oval, ring?	cultic
II6.006	Agia Triada	NW upper floor, "stanza dei sigilli"	LMIb	impression	clay	oval?	cultic
I.127	Mycenae	Lower Town (Panajia), Chamber Tomb #91	LHII-III	ring	gold	ring	cultic
II6.003	Agia Triada	NW upper floor, "stanza dei sigilli"	LMIb	impression	clay	unclear, oval?	cultic
I.410	Phylakopi	Settlement	LMIa/LHI	seal	ivory	stamp	cultic
II3.114	Phaistos, Kalyvia	Tombe dei Nobili, grave 11	LMIIa1-2	ring	gold	ring	cultic
I.126	Mycenae	Lower Town (Panajia), Chamber Tomb #91	LHII-III	ring	gold	ring	cultic
II8.256	Knossos	Central Shrine	LMII-IIIa	impression	clay	oval, ring?	cultic
II8.275	Knossos	Little Palace	LMII-IIIa	impression	clay	round	cultic
I.219	Vaphio	Beehive Tomb	LHII	ring	gold	ring	cultic
II6.002	Agia Triada	NW upper floor, "stanza dei sigilli"	LMIb	impression	clay	unclear, oral?	cultic
I.080	Mycenae	Lower Town (Panajia), Chamber Tomb #47	LHII-III	seal	agate	lentoid	cultic/sacrifice
V2.422	Eleusis, Necropolis NW of Classical site	Family Grave Hpie3	LHII-III	seal	steatite	round	dancing
II6.013	Agia Triada	NW upper floor, "stanza dei sigilli"	LMIb	impression	clay	oval?	dancing
V.sup.1A.058	Mallia	House alpha, room 8	MMIII-LMI	ring	lead	oval	dancing
II3.236	Gournia	Old Town	Early MMI	seal	serpentine	lentoid	dancing
V.sup.1A.178	Chania, Kastelli	Katre st. 10	MMIII-LMI	impression	clay	oval	dancing
V.sup.1B.115	Aidonia, Field of Gournospilia	Small Shaft parallel to S. wall of Chamber Tomb 7	LHII-IIIa-b	ring	gold	ring	dancing

List of Performed Acts

CMS#	Provenence	Locus	Date	Form	Material	Shape	Performance
I.132	Mycenae	Lower Town (Panajia), Chamber Tomb #103	LHII-III	seal	quartz	lentoid	dancing
II3.056	Knossos	Isopata, grave 6	LMIIIa1	ring	electrum	ring	dancing
V.sup.1B.113	Aidonia, Field of Gournospilia	Small Shaft parallel to S. wall of Chamber Tomb 7	LHII-IIIa-b	ring	gold	ring	dancing
V.sup.1B.114	Aidonia, Field of Gournospilia	Small Shaft parallel to S. wall of Chamber Tomb 7	LHII-IIIa-b	ring	gold	ring	dancing
V2.728	Mega Monastiri	Grave gamma	LHIIIa2-b	ring	gold	ring	dancing
I.086	Mycenae	Lower Town, Unknown Nekropolis, Chamber Tomb #55	LHII-III	ring	gold	ring	dancing
II8.266	Knossos	East Wing	LMII-IIIa	impression	clay	square, cushin?	dancing
II3.017	Knossos	Settlement, House of the Frescoes	LMIa-b	seal	serpentine	cushin	dancing
I.313	Pylos	Palace, Room 98	LHIIIb2-c1	impression	clay	illiptical	dancing
II3.051	Knossos	Isopata, grave I	LMIIIa1	ring	gold	ring	dancing
I.191	Dendra (Midea)	Chamber Tomb, Grave 10	LHIIb-LHIII	ring	gold	ring	dancing
I.220	Vaphio	Beehive Tomb	LHIIa	seal	chalcedony	lentoid	dancing
I.162	Mycenae	Lower Town, House of the Oil Handlers	LHIIIb	impression	clay	ring?	dancing
II8.267	Knossos	Kapheneion - Rubbish heap on SE boarder of palace	?	impression	clay	oval?	dancing
II6.001	Agia Triada	NW upper floor, "stanza dei sigilli"	LMIb	impression	clay	oval, ring?	dancing
I.108	Mycenae	Lower Town, Unknown Nekropolis, Chamber Tomb #71	LHII-III	ring	gold/silver	ring	dancing?
V.sup.1A.180	Chania, Kastelli	Katre st. 10	MMIII-LMI	impression	clay	oval, ring?	interaction
II8.269	Knossos	k2=Room of the Jewel Fresco; k11=Room of the Warrior Seal	LMII-IIIa	impression	clay	oval, ring?	interaction
V.sup.1B.062	Asine, Barbounas necropolis	grave 5, field of Niotis	LHIII	seal	carnelion	lentoid	master of the animals
I.089	Mycenae	Lower Town, Unknown Nekropolis, Chamber Tomb #58	LHII-III	seal	jasper	cylinder seal	master of the animals
II8.248	Knossos	East Wing	LMII-IIIa	impression	clay	unclear, ring?	master of the animals
II8.249	Knossos	Little Palace?	LMII-IIIa	impression	clay	unclear	master of the animals
V.sup.1B.154	Voundeni, Field of Amygdalia	Chamber Tomb, grave 4	LHIIIa-c	seal	quartz	lentoid	master of the animals
II8.250	Knossos	Lower E-W Corridor	LMII	impression	clay	unclear	master of the animals
V2.669	Thebes	Corner of Epaminondas & Metaxas sts.	LHIIIb2	impression	clay	round	master of the animals
II8.251	Knossos	Lower E-W Corridor	LMII	impression	clay	unclear	master of the animals
II8.253	Knossos	Little Palace	LMII-IIIa	impression	clay	round	master of the animals
II8.238	Knossos	Little Palace?	LMII-IIIa	impression	clay	round	master of the animals
I.163	Mycenae	Lower Town, House of the Sphinx	LHIIIb	impression	clay	round	master of the animals
I.sup.027	Prosymna	Grave 33, Side Chamber	LHIIIa1-b	seal	bandechat	lentoid	master of the animals
I.356	Pylos	Palace, Room 104	LHIIIb2-c1	impression	clay	unclear	master of the animals
I.325	Pylos	Palace, Room 98	LHIIIb2-c1	impression	clay	round	master of the animals
II8.265	Knossos	East Wing	LMII-IIIa	impression	clay	round	mistress of the animals
II3.063	Knossos	Sanitorium Excavations, grave III	LMII-IIIa1	seal	agate	lentoid	mistress of the animals

List of Performed Acts

CMS#	Provenence	Locus	Date	Form	Material	Shape	Performance
II8.254	Knossos	Landing on Grand Staircase	LMII-IIIa	impression	clay	round?	mistress of the animals
I.144	Mycenae	Lower Town, Chamber Tomb #515	LHII-III	seal	carnelion	lentoid	mistress of the animals
I.233b	Vaphio	Beehive Tomb	LHII	seal	amythist	2 sided prism	mistress of the animals
I.145	Mycenae	Lower Town, Chamber Tomb #515	LHII-III	seal	carnelion	lentoid	mistress of the animals
II3.276	Sphakia	Tholos	LMIIIb	seal	jasper	lentoid	mistress of the animals
II8.255	Knossos	Wooden Staircase A	LMII-IIIa	impression	clay	unclear	mistress of the animals
V.sup.1B.116	Aidonia, Field of Gournospilia	Dromos of Chamber Tomb 8	LHII-IIIa-b	seal	carnelion	lentoid	mistress of the animals
V2.654	Jalysos, Makri Vounara	Grave 20	LHIIIc	seal	agate	lentoid	mistress of the animals
I.344	Pylos	Palace, Room 104	LHIIIb2-c1	impression	clay	round	mistress of the animals
V1.173	Athens, less than 1M south of the T. of Ares	Chamber Tomb VIII	LHIIIa1-2	ring	gold	ring	narrative
V.sup.1A.133	Chania, Kastelli, Agia Akaterini square	House I, room D	LMIb	impression	clay	oval	narrative
V2.608	Aplomata	Chamber Tomb 2, Grave B	LHIIIc	seal	agate	cushin	presentation
I.119	Mycenae	Lower Town, Kalkani Nekropolis, Chamber Tomb #84	LHII-III	ring	gold	ring	presentation
II3.015	Knossos	Settlement, near "Hogarth House A"	LMIb	ring	bronze	ring	presentation
I.101	Mycenae	Lower Town, Unknown Nekropolis, Chamber Tomb #66	LHII-III	ring	gold	ring	presentation
II3.145	Mallia	House Delta-alpha	MMIII-LMI	seal	steatite	lentoid	presentation
II3.103	Phaistos, Kalyvia	Tombe dei Nobili, grave 2	LMIIIa1-2	ring	gold	ring	presentation
I.017	Mycenae	Treasury Acropolis, South of the Grave Circles, within the ruins of the Rampen Houses	Early LHII?	ring	gold	ring	presentation
I.292	Pylos	Beehive Tomb Delta, Grave IV	MH/LHI-III	ring	gold	ring	presentation
V.sup.1A.177	Chania, Kastelli	Katre st. 10	MMIII-LMI	impression	clay	unclear	presentation
V.sup.1A.176	Chania, Kastelli	Katre st. 10	MMIII-LMI	impression	clay	round?	presentation
V.sup.1A.175	Chania, Kastelli	Katre st. 10	MMIII-LMI	impression	clay	oval, ring?	presentation
I.302	Pylos	Palace, Archive Room 8	LHIIIb2-c1	impression	clay	illiptical	presentation
V1.253	Armeni	Chamber Tomb 24	LMIIIa-IIIa2-b1	seal	black stone	lentoid	presentation
I.128	Mycenae	Lower Town (Panajia), Chamber Tomb #91	LHII-III	ring	gold	ring	presentation
II7.005	Zakros	House A, room 8	LMIb	impression	clay	unclear	presentation
II6.032	Agia Triada	NW upper floor, "stanza dei sigilli"	LMIb	impression	clay	unclear	presentation
II6.030	Agia Triada	NW upper floor, "stanza dei sigilli"	LMIb	impression	clay	unclear	presentation
II7.008	Zakros	House A, room 8	LMIb	impression	clay	oval?	presentation
II6.008	Agia Triada	NW upper floor, "stanza dei sigilli"	LMIb	impression	clay	round	presentation
II8.268	Knossos	r54=Doorway S. from the	LMII-IIIa	impression	clay	ring	presentation

List of Performed Acts

CMS#	Provenence	Locus	Date	Form	Material	Shape	Performance
		Hall of the Collonnades and Beyond; r51=Lower E-W Corridor; r1=Upper East-West Corridor; q22=Room of the Clay Signet					
II8.243	Knossos	East Wing	LMII-IIIa	impression	clay	round?	presentation
II7.001	Zakros	House A, room 8	LMIb	impression	clay	oval	presentation
II8.239	Knossos	Wooden Staircase B	LMII-IIIa	impression	clay	round	presentation
V.sup.1B.187	Varkisa	Plot of Chatzitheodorou, Chamber Tomb I, shallow grave	LHIIIa2-b	ring	gold and bronze	ring	presentation
I.361	Pylos	Palace, Room 105	LHIIIb2-c1	impression	clay	unclear	presentation/procession
II3.032	Knossos	Mavro Spilia, grave VII, chamber B	LMII/IIIa-late LMIII	seal	steatite	lentoid	presentation/procession
I.309	Pylos	Palace, Near the Archive Rooms	LHIIIb2-c1	impression	clay	lentoid	presentation/procession
II7.002	Zakros	House A, room 8	LMIb	impression	clay	oval	presentation/procession
II8.272	Knossos		?	impression	clay	oval?	presentation/procession
II7.003	Zakros	House A, room 8	LMIb	impression	clay	oval?	presentation/procession
I.sup.179	Pylos	SW House, Outside of SW Wall	TAQ LHIIIb/c	impression	clay	ring?	presentation/procession?
II6.029	Agia Triada	NW upper floor, "stanza dei sigilli"	LMIb	impression	clay	amygdaloid	procession
II7.028	Zakros	House A, room 8	LMIb	impression	clay	oval?	procession
II6.018	Agia Triada	NW upper floor, "stanza dei sigilli"	LMIb	impression	clay	round?	procession
II6.012	Agia Triada	NW upper floor, "stanza dei sigilli"	LMIb	impression	clay	oval	procession
II6.010	Agia Triada	NW upper floor, "stanza dei sigilli"	LMIb	impression	clay	round?	procession
II6.009	Agia Triada	NW upper floor, "stanza dei sigilli"	LMIb	impression	clay	oval, ring?	procession
II8.276	Knossos	Doorway S. from the Hall of the Collonnades and Beyond	LMII	impression	clay	unclear, ring?	procession
II8.259	Knossos		?	impression	clay	unclear	procession
II3.146	Mallia	House Delta-alpha	MMIII-LMI	seal	serpentine	lentoid	procession
II8.278	Knossos	Room of the Seal Impression	LMII - JW, BSA 89	impression	clay	unclear	procession
II7.012	Zakros	House A, room 8	LMIb	impression	clay	unclear	procession
II8.277	Knossos	Room of the Warrior Seal	LMII-IIIa	impression	clay	unclear, ring?	procession
II7.018	Zakros	House A, room 8	LMIb	impression	clay	round	procession
V.sup.1A.186	Nerokourou	Northern portion of Minoan Villa	MMIII-LMI	seal	serpentine	lentoid	procession
II7.007	Zakros	House A, room 8	LMIb	impression	clay	unclear	procession
II7.013	Zakros	House A, room 8	LMIb	impression	clay	unclear	procession
II7.014	Zakros	House A, room 8	LMIb	impression	clay	unclear	procession
II7.015	Zakros	House A, room 8	LMIb	impression	clay	oval?	procession
II7.017	Zakros	House A, room 8	LMIb	impression	clay	oval	procession
II7.016	Zakros	House A, room 8	LMIb	impression	clay	unclear	procession
II6.011	Agia Triada	NW upper floor, "stanza dei sigilli"	LMIb	impression	clay	oval, ring?	procession?
II3.139	Episkopi	Flur Kephala, grave delta	LMIII	seal	jasper	amygdaloid	totemic
II8.233	Knossos	Room of the Egyptian Beans	LMII - JW, BSA 89	impression	clay	unclear	totemic
II7.179	Zakros	House A, room 8	LMIb	impression	clay	round	totemic
II7.171	Zakros	House A, room 8	LMIb	impression	clay	round	totemic

List of Performed Acts

CMS#	Provenence	Locus	Date	Form	Material	Shape	Performance
II7.140	Zakros	House A, room 8	LMIb	impression	clay	round	totemic
II7.141	Zakros	House A, room 8	LMIb	impression	clay	round	totemic
II7.170	Zakros	House A, room 8	LMIb	impression	clay	round	totemic
II3.077	Knossos	Kato Jypsades, sanctuary of Demeter	LMIII	seal	serpentine	lentoid	totemic
II7.169	Zakros	House A, room 8	LMIb	impression	clay	round	totemic
II7.145B	Zakros	House A, room 8	LMIb	impression	clay	round	totemic
II7.147	Zakros	House A, room 8	LMIb	impression	clay	round	totemic
II7.146	Zakros	House A, room 8	LMIb	impression	clay	round	totemic
I.280	Pylos, Rutsi, Mirsinochori	Tholos Tomb, Found with Skeleton	LHIII	seal	carnelion	lentoid	totemic
II7.142	Zakros	House A, room 8	LMIb	impression	clay	round	totemic
II6.108	Agia Triada	NW upper floor, "stanza dei sigilli"	LMIb	impression	clay	amygdaloid	totemic
II7.145A	Zakros	House A, room 8	LMIb	impression	clay	round	totemic
II7.143	Zakros	House A, room 8	LMIb	impression	clay	round	totemic
II7.144	Zakros	House A, room 8	LMIb	impression	clay	round	totemic
V1.274	Armeni Cemetary	Grave 55	LMIII	seal	serpetine	lentoid	totemic
V.sup.1A.123	Chania	Kastelli, Agios Akaterimi-Platz, settlement	LMIIIc	seal	serpentine	lentoid	totemic
II7.148	Zakros	House A, room 8	LMIb	impression	clay	round	totemic
I.222	Vaphio	Beehive Tomb	LHII	seal	onyx	lentoid	totemic
II6.028	Agia Triada	NW upper floor, "stanza dei sigilli"	LMIb	impression	clay	round	totemic
II6.027	Agia Triada	NW upper floor, "stanza dei sigilli"	LMIb	impression	clay	round	totemic
II6.023	Agia Triada	NW upper floor, "stanza dei sigilli"	LMIb	impression	clay	round?	totemic
I.133	Mycenae	Lower Town (Panajia), Chamber Tomb #103	LHII-III	seal	agate	lentoid	totemic
II6.022	Agia Triada	NW upper floor, "stanza dei sigilli"	LMIb	impression	clay	round?	totemic
II6.036	Agia Triada	NW upper floor, "stanza dei sigilli"	LMIb	impression	clay	oval	totemic
II3.008	Knossos	Court of the Stone Spout	MMIII	seal	steatite	lentoid	totemic
II6.107	Agia Triada	NW upper floor, "stanza dei sigilli"	LMIb	impression	clay	round	totemic
I.068	Mycenae	Lower Town (Panajia), Chamber Tomb #27	LHII-III	seal	agate with gold attachments	amygdaloid+	totemic
I.221	Vaphio	Beehive Tomb	LHII	seal	carnelion	lentoid	totemic
I.279	Pylos, Rutsi, Mirsinochori	Tholos Tomb, Found with Sketeton	LHIII	seal	carnelion	lentoid	totemic
I.223	Vaphio	Beehive Tomb	LHII	seal	jasper	lentoid	totemic
II8.264	Knossos	East Wing	LMII-IIIa	impression	clay	amygdaloid	totemic
I.225	Vaphio	Beehive Tomb	LHII	seal	onyx	amygdaloid	totemic
I.226	Vaphio	Beehive Tomb	LHII	seal	sardonyx	amygdaloid	totemic
II8.260	Knossos	Wooden Staricase B	LMII-IIIa	impression	clay	unclear, ring?	totemic
II8.258	Knossos	Threshold between the Room of the Stone Bench and the Room of the Stone Drum	LMII-IIIa	impression	clay	amygdaloid	totemic
I.129	Mycenae	Lower Town, Chamber Tomb, Grave 91	LHII-III	ring	gold	ring	totemic
II8.237	Knossos	E. Temple Repository	TAQ LMI	impression	clay	oval?	totemic
II8.236	Knossos	E. Temple Repository	TAQ LMI	impression	clay	square cushin	totemic

List of Performed Acts

CMS#	Provenence	Locus	Date	Form	Material	Shape	Performance
II6.106	Agia Triada	NW upper floor, "stanza dei sigilli"	LMIb	impression	clay	round	totemic
II7.029	Zakros	House A, room 8	LMIb	impression	clay	round?	totemic
II7.117	Zakros	House A, room 8	LMIb	impression	clay	round	totemic
I.sup.180	Pylos	SW House, Outside of SW Wall	TAQ LHIIIb/c	impression	clay	round	totemic
II4.204	Gournia	Early Cellar East of the Public Court	MMI?	seal	serpentine	lentoid	totemic
II5.323	Phaistos	Old Palace, room 25	MMIb-MMIIb	impression	clay	round?	totemic
II5.324	Phaistos	Old Palace, room 25	MMIb-MMIIb	impression	clay	round	totemic
II7.113	Zakros	House A, room 8	LMIb	impression	clay	round	totemic
V1.239	Kastelli	Trench 4	TAQ LMIIIb	seal	jasper?	lentoid	totemic
II7.112	Zakros	House A, room 8	LMIb	impression	clay	round	totemic
II7.111	Zakros	House A, room 8	LMIb	impression	clay	round	totemic
II7.110B	Zakros	House A, room 8	LMIb	impression	clay	unclear	totemic
II7.110A	Zakros	House A, room 8	LMIb	impression	clay	round	totemic
II7.109B	Zakros	House A, room 8	LMIb	impression	clay	round	totemic
II7.139B	Zakros	House A, room 8	LMIb	impression	clay	round	totemic
II7.083	Zakros	House A, room 8	LMIb	impression	clay	round	totemic
II4.125	Knossos	Mavro Spilia, grave VII, chamber B	LMII/IIIa-LMIII	seal	steatite	lentoid	totemic
II7.023	Zakros	House A, room 8	LMIb	impression	clay	round	totemic
II7.022	Zakros	House A, room 8	LMIb	impression	clay	round?	totemic
V.sup.1A.143	Chania, Kastelli, Agia Akaterini square	between floors of an open courtyard	LMIIIa2/IIIb1	impression	clay	amygdaloid?	totemic
V.sup.1A.142	Chania, Kastelli, Agia Akaterini square	Trench 19, pit V	LMI-II	impression	clay	oval, ring?	totemic
V.sup.1A.173	Chania, Kastelli	Katre st. 10	MMIII-LMI	impression	clay	round	totemic
V.sup.1A.385	Knossos	palace, monolithic pillars	?	seal	florite	lentoid	totemic
V.sup.1A.369	Epidauros	Temple of Apollo Maleteatas, in ashes of alter	?	seal	hematite	lentoid	totemic
V.sup.1A.372	Episkoi Ierapetras	Larnax burial	LMIIIb	seal	unknown	lentoid	totemic
V.sup.1B.058	Asine, Barbounas Necropolis	Chamber Tomb, chamber I delta, grave 1, Notis field	LHIII	seal	carnelion	lentoid	totemic
V.sup.1B.061	Asine, Barbounas necropolis	grave I, NW part of the main chamber, north of Bestattung 2, field of Niotis	LHIII	seal	agate	amygdaloid	totemic
V.sup.1B.077	Mycenae, field of Loupouno	1-5 km NW of Acropolis, chambertomb VIII	LHIIb-IIIa	seal	carnelion + gold	amygdaloid	totemic
V.sup.1B.088	Tiryns vicinity	W. of the Argos-Nauplion road, Grave 12	LHIII	seal	hematite	lentoid	totemic
V.sup.1B.261	Armeni	Chamber Tomb 133, with skelleton gamma-sigma tau	LMIIIa2-b	seal	serpentine	lentoid	totemic
II7.109A	Zakros	House A, room 8	LMIb	impression	clay	round	totemic
II7.127	Zakros	House A, room 8	LMIb	impression	clay	round	totemic
II7.135A	Zakros	House A, room 8	LMIb	impression	clay	round	totemic
V.sup.1B.153	Voundeni, Field of Amygdalia	Chamber Tomb, grave 4	LHIIIa-c	seal	lapis	lentoid	totemic

			List of Performed Acts				
CMS#	Provenence	Locus	Date	Form	Material	Shape	Performance
II7.137	Zakros	House A, room 8	LMIb	impression	clay	round	totemic
II7.134	Zakros	House A, room 8	LMIb	impression	clay	round	totemic
II7.133	Zakros	House A, room 8	LMIb	impression	clay	round	totemic
II3.016	Knossos	Settlement, southwest of the "South House"	LMIa	seal	carnelion	cushin	totemic
II7.132	Zakros	House A, room 8	LMIb	impression	clay	round	totemic
II3.024	Knossos	Settlement, South House	LMIa-b	seal	lapis+ gold	lentoid	totemic
II3.027	Knossos	Mavro Spilia, grave III	LMIII	seal	carnelion	amygdaloid	totemic
II7.131	Zakros	House A, room 8	LMIb	impression	clay	round	totemic
II3.052	Knossos	Isopata, grave I	LMIIIa1	seal	chalcedony	cushin	totemic
II4.165	Mallia	House E, XXIX	LMIIIb	seal	serpentine	lentoid	totemic
II7.138	Zakros	House A, room 8	LMIb	impression	clay	round	totemic
II7.135B	Zakros	House A, room 8	LMIb	impression	clay	round	totemic
II7.121	Zakros	House A, room 8	LMIb	impression	clay	round	totemic
II4.111	Knossos	House of the Frescoes	LMI	seal	steatite	lentoid	totemic
II7.118	Zakros	House A, room 8	LMIb	impression	clay	round	totemic
II7.119	Zakros	House A, room 8	LMIb	impression	clay	round	totemic
II3.239	Sphoungaras	Nekropolis, pithos burial	MMIII-LMI	ring	lead	ring	totemic
II7.120	Zakros	House A, room 8	LMIb	impression	clay	round	totemic
II4.112	Knossos	House of the Frescoes	LMI	seal	serpentine	lentoid	totemic
II7.139A	Zakros	House A, room 8	LMIb	impression	clay	round	totemic
II7.129A	Zakros	House A, room 8	LMIb	impression	clay	round	totemic
II3.124	Tylissos		LMI	seal	steatite	lentoid	totemic
II3.117	Agia Triada	NW upper floor, "stanza dei sigilli"	LMIb-IIIa2	seal	steatite	lentoid	totemic
II7.122	Zakros	House A, room 8	LMIb	impression	clay	round	totemic
II7.124	Zakros	House A, room 8	LMIb	impression	clay	round	totemic
II7.126	Zakros	House A, room 8	LMIb	impression	clay	round	totemic
II7.129B	Zakros	House A, room 8	LMIb	impression	clay	round	totemic
II3.147	Mallia	House Delta-beta	LMIb	seal	sardonyx	amydgaloid	totemic
II6.024	Agia Triada	NW upper floor, "stanza dei sigilli"	LMIb	impression	clay	oval?	totemic/procession
II6.026	Agia Triada	NW upper floor, "stanza dei sigilli"	LMIb	impression	clay	round?	totemic/procession
II6.025	Agia Triada	NW upper floor, "stanza dei sigilli"	LMIb	impression	clay	oval? round?	totemic?
II5.326	Phaistos	Old Palace, room 25	MMIb-MMIIb	impression	clay	round	totemic?

Appendix Two

Cat #	Fig	Provenence	Locus	Date	Object	Material	Shape
001	010	Mycenae	Grave Circle B; grave gamma	early LH	seal	amythist	amygdaloid
002	019	Mycenae	Grave Circle A; grave IV	LHI	ring	gold	ring
003	018	Mycenae	Treasury Acropolis, South of the Grave Circles, within the ruins of the Rampen Houses	Early LHII?	ring	gold	ring
004	002	Mycenae	Lower Town (Panajia), Chamber Tomb #27	LHII-III	seal	agate with gold	amygdaloid
005	057	Mycenae	Lower Town (Kato Phourou), Chamber Tomb #44	LHII-III	seal	carnelion	amygdaloid
007	105	Mycenae	Lower Town, Unknown Nekropolis, Chamber Tomb #55	LHII-III	ring	gold	ring
008	098	Mycenae	Lower Town, Unknown Nekropolis, Chamber Tomb #71	LHII-III	ring	gold/silver	ring
009	075	Mycenae	Lower Town (Panajia), Chamber Tomb #103	LHII-III	seal	quartz	lentoid
010	056	Mycenae	Lower Town, Chamber Tomb #504	LHIII	seal	carnelion	amygdaloid
011	012	Mycenae	Lower Town, Chamber Tomb #518, found on floor	LHII-III	seal	carnelion	amygdaloid
012	073	Mycenae	Lower Town, House of the Oil Handlers	LHIIIb	impression	clay	ring?
013	104	Dendra (Midea)	Chamber Tomb, Grave 10	LHIIb-LHIII	ring	gold	ring
014	058	Asine	Chamber Tomb 1	LHIIb-IIIa, IIIc	ring	gold on bronze	ring
015	107	Vaphio	Beehive Tomb	LHIIa	seal	chalcedony	lentoid
016	003	Vaphio	Beehive Tomb	LHII	seal	onyx	amygdaloid
017	014	Vaphio	Beehive tomb	LHII	seal	sardonyx	amygdaloid
018	059	Pylos	Palace, Archive Room 8	LHIIIb2-c1	impression	clay	round?
019	082	Pylos	Palace, Room 98	LHIIIb2-c1	impression	clay	illiptical
020	108	Pylos	Palace, Room 105	LHIIIb2-c1	impression	clay	unclear
021	053	Dimini	Beehive Tomb 1	LHIIIa	seal	agate?	lentoid
022	001	Knossos	Court of the Stone Spout	MMII	seal	steatite	lentoid
023	079	Knossos	Settlement, House of the Frescoes	LMIa-b	seal	serpentine	cushin
024	006	Knossos	Isopata, grave I	LMIIIa1	ring	gold	ring
025	095	Knossos	Isopata, grave 6	LMIIIa1	ring	electrum	ring
026	080	Gournia	Old Town	Early MMI	seal	serpentine	lentoid
027	045	Praissos	1st Acropolis, grave D	LMIIIb	seal	agate	lentoid
028	046	Gournes	Grave I, Dromos	LMIIIb	seal	lapis	lentoid
029	083	Aghia Triada	NW upper floor, "stanza dei sigilli"	LMIb	impression	clay	oval, ring?
030	086	Aghia Triada	NW upper floor, "stanza dei sigilli"	LMIb	impression	clay	oval, ring?
031	085	Aghia Triada	NW upper floor, "stanza dei sigilli"	LMIb	impression	clay	round?
032	093	Aghia Triada	NW upper floor, "stanza dei sigilli"	LMIb	impression	clay	oval, ring?
033	081	Aghia Triada	NW upper floor, "stanza dei sigilli"	LMIb	impression	clay	oval?
034	015	Aghia Triada	NW upper floor, "stanza dei sigilli"	LMIb	impression	clay	oval
035	038	Aghia Triada	NW upper floor, "stanza dei sigilli"	LMIb	impression	clay	oval?
036	032	Aghia Triada	NW upper floor, "stanza dei sigilli"	LMIb	impression	clay	unclear

Catalogue

Cat #	Fig	Provenence	Locus	Date	Object	Material	Shape
037	033	Aghia Triada	NW upper floor, "stanza dei sigilli"	LMIb	impression	clay	unclear
038	035	Aghia Triada	NW upper floor, "stanza dei sigilli"	LMIb	impression	clay	round?
039	037	Aghia Triada	NW upper floor, "stanza dei sigilli"	LMIb	impression	clay	oval
040	084	Zakros	House A, room 8	LMIb	impression	clay	unclear
041	087	Zakros	House A, room 8	LMIb	impression	clay	oval?
042	089	Zakros	House A, room 8	LMIb	impression	clay	unclear
043	090	Zakros	House A, room 8	LMIb	impression	clay	unclear
044	088	Zakros	House A, room 8	LMIb	impression	clay	oval?
045	092	Zakros	House A, room 8	LMIb	impression	clay	unclear
046	071	Zakros	House A, room 8	LMIb	impression	clay	oval
047	031	Zakros	House A, room 8	LMIb	impression	clay	unclear
048	036	Zakros	House A, room 8	LMIb	impression	clay	oval
049	047	Knossos	Room of the Niche	LMII-IIIa	impression	clay	oval
050	070	Knossos	East Wing	LMII-IIIa	impression	clay	square, cushin?
051	109	Knossos	Kapheneion - Rubbish heap on SE boarder of palace	?	impression	clay	lentoid?
052	111	Mycenae	Lower Town (Panajia), Chamber Tomb #47, Panajia	LHII-III	seal	onyx	lentoid
053	034	Chania, Kastelli	Katre st. 10	MMIII-LMI	impression	clay	oval?
054	074	Chania, Kastelli	Katre st. 10	MMIII-LMI	impression	clay	oval
055	091	Nerokourou	Northern portion of Minoan Villa	MMIII-LMI	seal	serpentine	lentoid
056	103	Aidonia, Field of Gournospilia	Small Shaft parallel to S. wall of Chamber Tomb 7	LHII-IIIa-b	ring	gold	ring
057	011	Aidonia, Field of Gournospilia	Small Shaft parallel to S. wall of Chamber Tomb 7	LHII-IIIa-b	ring	gold	ring
058	072	Aidonia, Field of Gournospilia	Small Shaft parallel to S. wall of Chamber Tomb 7	LHII-IIIa-b	ring	gold	ring
059	007	Anthia, Field of Ellinika	Floor of Shaft Grave in Chamber Tomb 4	LHIIIa1	ring	gold	ring
060	106	Eleusis, Necropolis NW of Classical site	Family Grave Hpie3	LHII-III	seal	steatite	round
061	013	Mycenae	House of the Idols	LHIIIb2	seal	agate	lentoid
062	055	Koukounara, Akona	Tholos Grave I	LHIII	seal	chalcedony	lentoid
063	054	Thebes	Corner of Epaminondas & Antigone sts.	LHIIIb	seal	agate	half cylinder
064	097	Mega Monastiri	Grave gamma	LHIIIa2-b	ring	gold	ring
065	030	Knossos	Great East Hall/basement level of East Corridor near School Room and Lapidary's Workshop	LMIb	relief wall painting of taureador	3D painting	n/a
066	051	Athens	Acropolis	LH?	fragment of stone vase	stone	vase
067	112	Aghia Triada	Room 14 of east wing of villa	LMIB	Wall painting - nature fresco with goddess	wall painting	n/a
068	099	Thebes	Room N of Kadmeia	LHII	Wall painting - women's frieze	wall painting	n/a
069	110	Knossos	Room of the Throne	LMi?	crystal plaque	crystal	plaque
071	008	Knossos	fallen on late basement floor of small room at north end of central court	MMIIIB/LMIA	Wall painting - Grandstand Fresco	wall painting	n/a
072	039	Mycenae	Grave Circle B	LHI	fragmentary plaque	ivory	n/a

Catalogue

Cat #	Fig	Provenence	Locus	Date	Object	Material	Shape
					with bull leaping scene		
073	096	Aghia Triada	Aghia Triada Cemetery	LHIII	Sarcophagus	stone	n/a
074	027	Knossos	Temple Treasury	MMIIIb/LMIa	sculpture of taureador	ivory sculpture	n/a
075	028	Katsamba	Tomb	LMIb	pyxis with representation of bull leaping	ivory	n/a
076	094	Knossos	Queen's Megaron	LMII	Wall painting - Dancing Lady	wall painting	n/a
078	025	Koumasa	Area delta, between tombs Alpha, beta and gamma	EMIII	bull leaping rhyton	ceramic	bull
079	016	Thera	West House	LMI	Wall painting - Miniature Fresco	wall painting	n/a
080	050	Mycenae	Ramp House deposit; From context beneath Ramp House containing LHIIIA1 pottery (cf. Wace [1949] 65)	LHII/IIIA	Wall painting - Toreador scenes	wall painting	n/a
081	102	Mycenae	beneath floor of main corridor of House of the Oil Merchant	LHIIIA?	Wall painting - Man carrying a palanquin	wall painting	n/a
082	077	Phaistos	room opening onto the West Court of the Old Palace	Old Palace	Bowl with Goddess and Dancers	ceramic	open bowl
083	078	Phaistos	room opening onto the West Court of the Old Palace	Old Palace	Fruitstand with Goddess and votaries	ceramic	fruit stand
084	066	Palaikastro	Block Delta	LMIII	sculpture of dancing women	clay sculpture	n/a
085	021-024	Knossos	Thirteenth magazine, lower stratum	LMI	wall painting - miniature bull leaping	wall painting	n/a
086	043	Knossos	North West Treasure House	LMII/III	Wall painting - Tree and Bull grappling scene	wall painting	n/a
087	040-042	Knossos	Court of the Stone Spout	LMII/IIIA	Wall painting - toreador panel	wall painting	n/a
088	044	Knossos	Queen's Megaron, upper stratum	?	Wall painting - female taureadors	wall painting	n/a
089	009	Knossos	Court of the Stone Spout, east wing, found 1.5m above terrace level with LMII pottery	LMII/IIIA; palmer LMIIIB (found above LMIIIB pottery) OKT 180-2, 51-52	Wall painting - Toreador panels	wall painting	n/a
090	026	Porti		MMI	bull leaping rhyton	ceramic	bull
091	004 & 005	Knossos	east wall of Corridor of Procession, fallen backwards from west wall of South Propylaeum	LMII/IIIA	Wall painting - Cupbearer and procession	wall painting	n/a
092	076	Pylos	plaster dump on northwest slope	LHIII	Wall painting - female procession	wall painting	n/a
093	049	Pylos	drain beneath Wine Magazine 105	LHIIIA?	Wall painting - toreador	wall painting	n/a
094	101	Pylos	plaster dump on northwest slope	LHIIIb	Wall painting - male procession	wall painting	n/a
095	020	Knossos	fallen on late basement floor of small room at north end of central court	MMIIIB/LMIA	Wall painting - Sacred Grove and Dance	wall painting	n/a
096	052	Tanagra	Tomb 22	LHIIIc	Tanagra larnax	ceramic	larnax
098	017	Thera	Xeste 3	LMI	wall painting - three adorants	wall painting	n/a
099	048	Tiryns	small court northeast of bathroom	LHIIIB	Wall painting - toreador	wall painting	n/a

Catalogue							
Cat #	Fig	Provenence	Locus	Date	Object	Material	Shape
100	100	Tiryns	west slope rubbish deposit	LHIIIB	Wall painting - lifesized women	wall painting	n/a
102	029	Aghia Triada		LMIb	Boxer Rhyton	serpentine/steatite	conical rhyton

www.ingramcontent.com/pod-product-compliance
Lightning Source LLC
Chambersburg PA
CBHW041706290426
44108CB00027B/2870